Savoring
SAN·DIEGO

COOKBOOK OF AN EVOLVING
REGIONAL CUISINE

A collection of favorite recipes from the
Friends of UCSD *Healthcare*
and the **UCSD Cancer Center Associates**

With scenic photographs by Greg Lawson
and other San Diego photographers

For information on purchasing
Savoring San Diego—Cookbook of An Evolving Regional Cuisine,
contact:

Savoring San Diego
Friends of UCSD *Healthcare*
200 West Arbor Drive, #8982
San Diego, California 92103-8982
Tel: (619) 543-6499
Fax: (619) 543-2245
www.sandiegocookbook.com
e-mail: ssdcook@ucsd.edu

Proceeds from the sale of **Savoring San Diego** will be used to help
patients and their families at **UCSD Healthcare,** through the many
patient-care projects supported by the **Friends.**

Cover Credits
Design, Wieber Nelson Design
Platter photograph, Alan Watson
Ocean photograph, Greg Lawson
Handpainted platter, Penelope West and Hazel Love
Title, Judith Johnson

ISBN: 0-9636158-1-5
Library of Congress Catalog Card Number: 95-60027

Printed in Hong Kong

TABLE OF CONTENTS

Introduction and Beneficiary   4

Acknowledgements   5

Conversion Tables   8

APPETIZERS AND SALSAS   9

San Diego's Mediterranean Climate — Linda Chisari   10

Menu of Mediterranean Flavors   11

SOUPS   31

Rancho Heritage — Elena Cota   32

Menu for a Patio Barbecue   33

SALADS AND DRESSINGS   53

San Diego Farms — Kitty Morse   54

Buffet Menu for A Salad Luncheon   55

PASTA, RICE AND BREAD   85

A Favorite Trail — Barbara Moore   86

Menu for an Easily Portable Picnic   87

MEAT   107

Celebrating the Border — Quincy Troupe   108

Menu for a Mexican Buffet   109

SAVORING SAN DIEGO • REFLECTIONS ON CAMERA   following 128

SEAFOOD   129

A Boating Tradition — Heather Stevenson and Lowell Lindsay   130

Menu for a Beach or Boating Picnic   131

POULTRY   157

Flavors of the Pacific Rim — Su-Mei Yu   158

Menu for a Taste of Asia   159

VEGETABLES   181

Keeping Health in Perspective — Pam Wischkaemper   182

A Vegetarian Menu   183

DESSERTS AND SWEETS   207

Academic Treasures — Pat JaCoby   208

Menu for a Celebration Dinner   209

INDEX   245

SAVORING SAN DIEGO

INTRODUCTION

In **Savoring San Diego,** we have tried to reflect some of the distinctive aspects of our beautiful and evolving region. We have looked to our climate, our roots, our geography, our neighbors and our population mix. We have given emphasis to recipes which relate to those themes.

Fresh ingredients and great flavor were basic requirements for recipe selection, and each recipe has been carefully evaluated and tested at least twice. Although this is not a "health" book, it reflects a sensible concern for health. We believe that balance, rather than deprivation, is the key to healthy enjoyment of food. Each recipe has been nutritionally analyzed, and every chapter includes low fat selections so that people may create balanced diets in keeping with their individual needs and tastes.

Wherever possible we have acknowledged the many food writers and culinary professionals from whom we drew inspiration. We regret that, inevitably, not all sources were traceable. We hope that our errors of omission will be few and forgiven.

In writing about the West, Wallace Stegner stated that "history builds slowly . . . and understanding of a new country depends upon every sort of report". In its small way, this book is such a report. Using the medium of good food, we have tried to identify and share the nature and pleasures of life in San Diego.

Penelope West, *Editor*
Joany Mosher, *Co-Editor*

COOKBOOK BENEFICIARY

Friends of UCSD *Healthcare* is a volunteer organization dedicated to supporting the programs and facilities of UCSD *Healthcare*—the teaching hospital for the UCSD School of Medicine.

UCSD *Healthcare* is a vital part of the community. It cares for tens of thousands of patients each year, providing a broad spectrum of medical services, including a major cancer center, one of the most comprehensive organ transplant programs in the country, the county's only Level 1 trauma center, a comprehensive eye center and one of the leading regional burn centers in the nation.

Your purchase of this cookbook will help patients and their families at UCSD *Healthcare* through the many patient-care projects supported by the Friends.

Judith Pettitt
President, 1993–1995
Friends of UCSD *Healthcare*

THE COOKBOOK COMMITTEE
1992–1999

Editor and Chairman, Penelope West
Co-Editor and Co-Chairman, Joany Mosher
Recipes, JoAnn Grant
Testing Coordinator, Sally Ashburn
Graphic Design, Cindy Wieber
Index, Joanne Meredith
Transcription, Anna Mitchell
Secretary, Nancy Olmsted Kaehr
Marketing, Priscilla Moxley, Susan Hall
Treasurer, Ellen MacVean

Alida Bracker
Glennalie Coleman
Elena Cota
Judith Feinberg
Laura Galbraith
Stephanie Gildred
Pat JaCoby
Jean Johnson
Judith Johnson
Sima Kashani

Sallye Krause
Lizz Matto
Kelli McCoy
Jean McKee
Lee Millsap
Judith Pettitt
Teddie Pincus
Victoria Powell
Rocío Rivas
Elaine Schneider

Lynne Schulnik
Beth Spooner
Lois Stanton
Barbara Stringer
Virginia Thomas
Tulie Trejo
Mary Wendt
Pam Wischkaemper
Carole Ziegler

SPECIAL THANKS

Friends of UCSD *Healthcare,* the UCSD Cancer Center Associates and the Cookbook Committee would like to extend special thanks to the following, for donating their time and talents to this project:

Nutritional Analysis and Advice:
Barbara Grasse, RD, CDE, Annie Durning-Canty, MS, RD, and **Eva Brzezinski, MS, RD**
Clinical Research Center, UCSD Medical Center

Scenic Photography and Consultant:
Greg Lawson

Cover Photography (platter):
Alan Watson

Cover and Book Design:
Wieber Nelson Design

Divider Page Charcoal Drawings:
Lee Hughes

CONTRIBUTORS AND TESTORS

The Friends of UCSD *Healthcare,* the UCSD Cancer Center Associates and the Cookbook Committee thank everyone who took the time to send us their favorite recipes. All the recipes and ideas received, used or not, helped shape this book. We also thank everyone who participated in the process of testing and evaluating individual recipes.

Doris Achor
Penny Alexander
Susan J. Algert
Antonia Allegra
June Allen
American Heart Association
Prue Arbib
Carolyn Ariza
Leigh Ashburn
Sally Ashburn
Rita Atkinson
Lucy Balistrieri
Mary Bear
Diane Bell
Arlene Berger
Rose Bergner
Sharon Berman
Joseph Bernal
Cindy Black of
   Cindy Black's Restaurant
Irene Bohl
Joe Bolt
Lou Bowles
Helen Boyden
Alida Bracker
Marge Bradner
Jean Brady
Bridget Breitenberg
Judy Buffalo
Mary Bull
Hope Butler
Takako Byars
Diane Canedo
Casa De Pico
Stephenie Caughlin
Bob Cherry of
   La Paloma Restaurant
Linda Chisari
Alice Christiansen
Phyllis Clark
James Cleffi of
   Cafe Japengo
Patricia Clemens
Glennalie Coleman
Anne Coleman
Alma Coles
Bernice Conn
John Connor
Katya Costello
Elena Cota

Ruth Covell
Joanne Crosby
Mary Anne Curray
Clifford Dasco
Shirley Davis
Joel Dimsdale
Annie Durning
Mary DeBrunner
Susan Dramm
Edie Drcar
Mary Jo Dunn
Mary Jane Dunn
Sheila Dym
Mary Elliot
Peggy Elliott
Drew Ellsworth
Marianne Engle
Mary Jo Evans
Diana Eveland
D.Ann Fanestil
Anne-Marie Feenberg
Judith Feinberg
Sallie Fisher
Nancy Fowler
Betty Frazier
Laura Galbraith
Linda Gassenheimer
Audrey Geisel
Joanna Gibbs
Stephanie Gildred
Brenda Goldbaum
The Golden Door
Harris Golden of
   Triangles Restaurant
Myrtle Gordon
Jenna Grant
JoAnn Grant
Barbara Grasse
Judith Green
Edie Greenberg
Dorothy Grier
Cheryl & Dick Gross
Jeanne Grote
Donna Halsey
Katie Haskett
Margaret Hayes
Joan Hayn
Phyllis Hayn
Holly Heaton
Claire Hennum

Jackie Hess
Amanda Huey
Joan Hunsinger
Edie Hunt
John Hunt
Rose Itano
Pat JaCoby
Fran Jenkins
Bonnye F. Johnson
Jean Johnson
Judith Johnson
Sandy Johnson
Jeanne Jones
Valerie Jones
Liz Joyce
Lewis Judd
Sima Kashani
Jane McNeel Keller
Flora L. Kennedy
Joan Kline
Edith Kodmur
Sallye Krause
Joyce Krichman
Hatice Kurdak
Bess Lambron
Rhonda Langley
Greg Lawson
Robert J. Le Ribeus
Judy Lewis
Jean Lindsley
Diana Lombrozo
Donna Long
Donna Lowenstein
Rosemarie Lugmair
Elizabeth G. MacVean
Ellen MacVean
Phyllis Magerman
Rob Magnuson
Mitchell Manning
Dee Marten
Marion Masouredis
Alix Mayhew
Marilyn Maclay
Holly McCormick
Kelli McCoy
Nancie McDermott
Miriam McDonald
Jean McKee
Joanne Meredith
Lee Millsap

Anna Mitchell
Sara Morrow
Chloe Moore
Kitty Morse
Joany Mosher
Robert Mosher
Diane Mounts
Priscilla Moxley
Jenny B. Mudge
Mary Lambron Mumford
Ruth Newmark
Sandra Nichols
Georgette Nicolaou
Edith Nierenberg
Doraine Offerman
Nancy Olmsted
Spencer Olson
Anne Otterson
Eric Otterson
Arlene Paa
Karen Page
Margaret Parks Harris
Jo Ellen Parsons
Judith Pettitt
Teddie Pincus
Vicky Powell
Peggy Preuss
Harriet Price
Project LEAN
Wilda Ramras
Susan Rapaport
Louise Rausa

Rosalind Reinhard
Susan Reisner
Patricia P. Rinaker
Barbara Saltman
Elaine Schneider
Elliot Schulnik
Lynne Schulnik
Jeanne Sebrechts
Roberta Seegmiller
Patricia Sell
Sherry Seymour
Georgina Sham
Betty Shor
Jewel Simons
Lavon Skinker
Evey Solomon
Osa Sommermeyer
Marlene Sorosky
Daphne Spehr
Beth Spooner
Saundra Springfield
Lois Stanton
Carol K. Stark
Dorothy Stevenson
Joanne Stevenson
Barbara Stringer
Jerrie Strom
Susan Stubblefield
Frances Swezey
Birda Tancredi
Eunice Tatarian
Mary Taylor

Elizabeth Taylor-Huey
Miguel O. Tellez
Virginia Thomas
Frances Thompson
Joan Thompson-Smith
Tulie Trejo
L.G. Tucker
Betsy Tyler
Susan S. Ulevitch
Marjorie Van Winkle
Corlyn Vance
Beth Velasques
Helen Wallace
Pat Walsh of
    Brigantine Restaurant
Joan Ward
Isabelle Wasserman
Jane Waterfield
Alice Waters
Pat Weckerly
Penny West
Audrie Westbrook
Maxine E. White
Liz Fong Wills
Russell Wilson
Paula Wolfert
Gina Wright
Su-Mei Yu of
    Saffron Restaurant
Jaime Yuvienco
Carole Ziegler

CONVERSION TABLES

1 cup	=	16 Tablespoons	=	237 ml	=	8 fluid ounces
½ cup	=	8 Tablespoons	=	118 ml	=	4 fluid ounces
⅓ cup	=	5⅓ Tablespoons	=	79 ml	=	2⅔ fluid ounces
¼ cup	=	4 Tablespoons	=	59 ml	=	2 fluid ounces
		1 Tablespoons	=	15 ml		
		1 teaspoon	=	5 ml		

1 pound = 455 grams
1 kilo = 2 pounds, 3 ounces

BUTTER MEASURES

1 stick of butter (U.S.) = ½ cup = 4 ounces = 8 Tablespoons = 115 grams
½ ounce = 1 Tablespoons = 15 grams

OVEN TEMPERATURES

Fahrenheit	Celsius	
225–275 degrees	110–140 degrees	Very Cool
300–325 degrees	150–160 degrees	Cool or slow
350–375 degrees	180–190 degrees	Warm/moderate
400–450 degrees	200–230 degrees	Hot
475–500 degrees	250–260 degrees	Very hot

APPETIZERS AND SALSAS

SAN DIEGO'S MEDITERRANEAN CLIMATE

By Linda Chisari
Landscape Designer

In San Diego, we can take a culinary voyage to Italy, Greece, the south of France, Morocco or Spain, by going into the garden and picking the appropriate ingredients. San Diego is blessed with a Mediterranean climate shared by only four other parts of the world—the Mediterranean basin itself, coastal Chile, the tip of South Africa and southwest Australia. In this warm, summer-dry, winter-wet climate, we can grow the ingredients to 'visit' a different country year round, no passport or traveler's checks required! Travel with me through a year in my garden.

It is February 1 and company is unexpectedly coming for dinner. From the redwood boxes of my vegetable garden, I pick French sorrel, arugula, radicchio, mache, oakleaf lettuce and a few sprigs of parsley and chervil. I pick a colander full of sugar-snap peas and broccoli florets. Dinner will be an early spring combination of cream of sorrel soup followed by stir-fried chicken, snow peas and broccoli. A handful of early Sequoia strawberries, served over vanilla ice cream, completes the dinner.

Now in mid-May, it is still light at 7:30 as I return late from a meeting with a client. On my way to the back door, I collect the last of the peas and broccoli, and the first baby garden beans, carrots and zucchini. With a few pinches of basil and parsley, a nutritionally-balanced pasta primavera is only a boiling pot of linguine away. I pick a lemon and a few sprigs of lemon thyme to complement two dorado fillets, flash-frozen after a fishing trip to the Sea of Cortez in April. Dinner will be ready by 8:15.

In August, friends have invited us to a twilight concert in Seagrove Park and we agree to bring part of the supper. Having picked twenty tomatoes, five cucumbers and two bright orange 'Arian' Dutch peppers that morning, I make a quick trip to the garden for some basil and chives. I mix the diced vegetables with rosemary-infused balsamic vinegar (made by a friend) and some good olive oil. Half of this mixture is puréed with a cup of tomato juice into a smooth first-course gazpacho. The other half is mixed with cubes of yesterday's ciabatta and a cup of basil leaves to make panzanella. Two Galia melons (a wonderful Israeli variety that ripens even in our cool coastal location), still warm from the sun and deeply perfumed, complete our share of the picnic.

It's November, Thanksgiving morning. In the garden, a Santa Ana sun has warmed the herbs; their resinous aromas float in a cloud above my perennial bed, hinting at the scents which will later emanate from the patio as the turkey roasts on the barbecue. I snip lavender, sage and oregano from the flower border, and clip a young branch of rosemary spilling over the brick patio wall. At the kitchen door, I pick Italian parsley from a pot where it grows with calendulas. I hope dinner tastes as good as my hands smell after patting a finely chopped herbal jacket onto the turkey. Next, I pull a few carrots and snip some dill for one vegetable side-dish, and harvest the last four acorn squashes, to cook with a piece of fresh ginger, for a second. Bell peppers, hanging ripely-red and yellow, promise late-fall sweetness when roasted. Lastly, a large 'Lumina' pumpkin, having waited nearly a month on its withered vine, will make a tasty filling for our pumpkin pie.

How lucky I feel to have lived and worked for the last twenty years in the San Diego area where my garden can feed so many senses. Herbs display a pleasing variety of leaf textures in my perennial bed. Their lovely flowers can make a casual bouquet or an attractive garnish. Creeping thyme, chamomile and mints, weaving soft carpets between the flagstones of our garden path, release heady aromas underfoot. A bay laurel tree, kept small by little watering, gives seasoning to winter stews, and provides highly polished, deep green foliage for holiday decorating. Dwarf fruit trees, in large containers on our patio, are both decorative and fruitful.

All these edible plants thrive in San Diego. Many are native to other Mediterranean climates and actually enjoy our similar dry weather. Others take more water and must be irrigated—but they require no more water, when grouped together, than the non-edible plants which usually fill our gardens.

Happily, we can enjoy this bounty every month of the year, as we follow the seasons' produce from our gardens to our kitchens and then onto the table we share with family and friends.

MENU OF MEDITERRANEAN FLAVORS

Chilled Mushrooms Mediterranean, page 15

Baked Eggplant and Garlic Appetizer, page 12

Chicken Stew Provençal with Light Aioli, page 176

Lemon Couscous, page 95

Spinach with Pine Nuts, page 198

Cucumber, Mint and Chive Salad, page 58

Orange and Almond Flourless Cake, page 233

Geranium Cream with Fresh Blackberries, page 215

BAKED EGGPLANT AND GARLIC APPETIZER

Makes ¾ cup of spread

This wonderfully simple and delicious appetizer makes an attractive presentation. The golden slices of baked garlic resemble toasted almonds on top of eggplant halves. Antonia Allegra, food writer, and former Food Editor of *The San Diego Tribune*, created this dish, inspired by the work of her friend, M.F.K. Fisher.

Preparation: 10 minutes
Bake: 1 hour
Cool: 2 hours

	Extra virgin olive oil (approximately ⅓ cup)
1	**medium eggplant, cut in half lengthwise**
2	**heads fresh garlic, peeled and each clove sliced thinly**
	Chopped flat-leaf parsley, for garnish
	Crackers, toast or wedges of pita

1. Preheat oven to 350 degrees. Brush baking sheet with olive oil. Arrange garlic slices on a baking sheet in the shape of the eggplant halves.

2. Coat eggplant surfaces with olive oil. Place them, cut side down, over garlic slices. All garlic slices must be covered or they will burn and become bitter.

3. Bake in oven until eggplant skin begins to shrivel, approximately 45-60 minutes. Turn oven off and cool eggplant in oven, approximately 2 hours.

4. Using a large spatula, gently turn each eggplant half, cut-side up, onto plate, revealing golden slices of toasted garlic. Garnish with chopped parsley.

5. Serve at room temperature with crackers, toast points, or wedges of pita bread, for scooping directly from eggplant shell.

Note: Recipe may be prepared 6-8 hours in advance.

Analysis per serving: Calories: 60   Protein: 0.2g   Carbohydrate: 2g   Fat: 6g   Cholesterol: 0   Fiber: 0   Sodium: 1mg

PEPPER WEDGES WITH TOMATOES AND BASIL

Makes 16 wedges

This do-ahead recipe is a real winner — simple to make, attractive and flavorful.

Preparation: 25 minutes
Cook: 25-30 minutes
Chill: overnight

2	medium cloves garlic, peeled
2	small green onions with tops, cut into 1-inch pieces
4	Italian plum tomatoes or 2 medium tomatoes, seeded and coarsely chopped (1 cup)
3	tablespoons chopped fresh basil or 1 tablespoon dried
2	anchovy fillets, drained, patted dry and chopped
1½-2	tablespoons olive oil
2	tablespoons capers, rinsed
	Freshly ground pepper to taste
2	large bell peppers (1 red and 1 yellow if available)

1. Preheat oven to 375 degrees.

2. In a food processor, mince garlic; add green onions and chop fine. Add tomatoes, basil and anchovies and process until the ingredients are chopped into small pieces. Do not purée. Transfer to a small bowl and stir in oil, capers and pepper.

3. Cut bell peppers in half lengthwise, remove seeds and cut each half into quarters, making 8 wedges per pepper. Fill each wedge with tomato mixture.

4. Place in a shallow baking dish; cover with foil and bake for 15 minutes. Uncover and bake for 10-15 minutes longer, or until the peppers are tender, but not limp. Cool to room temperature. Refrigerate overnight. Bring to room temperature before serving.

This recipe comes from Marlene Sorosky, cookbook author and founding member of the International Association of Cooking Professionals, and is adapted with her permission.

Analysis per serving: Calories: 79   Protein: 2g   Carbohydrate: 7g   Fat: 6g   Cholesterol: 2mg   Fiber: 2g   Sodium: 81mg

TURKISH LENTIL FINGERS

Serves 10-12

This unusual use of lentils makes a tasty and healthy appetizer. Red lentils are available in some supermarkets and all Middle-Eastern markets. They take less cooking time than the more common green lentils.

Preparation: 40-45 minutes

1	cup red lentils
2½-3½	cups water
¾	cup fine-grain bulgur
¼	cup olive oil
1	onion, minced
1½	tablespoons tomato paste
1	cup finely minced green onions, green and white parts
2	teaspoons paprika
2-3	teaspoons cumin
	Salt and cayenne pepper to taste
	Chopped parsley, for garnish

1. In a medium-sized saucepan, cook lentils in 2½ cups water until tender but not mushy, approximately 10 minutes. Add more water if necessary. When lentils are tender and water is almost absorbed, stir in bulgur and boil another 2 minutes. Remove from heat and let sit until bulgur has softened.

2. In a medium-sized skillet, heat oil and sauté onion until softened. Mix in tomato paste and remove from heat.

3. In a large bowl, combine lentil-bulgur mixture, onion-tomato mixture, minced green onions, paprika and cumin. Knead into a paste, season to taste and let cool. Form tablespoonfuls of mixture into small oval shapes, and arrange on a platter and sprinkle with chopped parsley. Chill well before serving.

Analysis per serving: Calories: 122 Protein: 5g Carbohydrate: 16g Fat: 5g Cholesterol: 0 Fiber: 4.1g Sodium: 42mg

CHILLED MUSHROOMS MEDITERRANEAN

Serves 6-8

The flavors released by the slow simmering of fresh herbs and spices is the secret of this recipe. The mushrooms become deliciously fragrant and aromatic. Serve as a starter with crusty French bread.

Preparation: 20-30 minutes
Cook: 20-30 minutes
Chill: 2-3 hours

3	tablespoons olive oil, divided
1	large onion, coarsely chopped
2	carrots, coarsely chopped
5	ounces dry white wine
12	coriander seeds
	Salt to taste
½	teaspoon freshly ground pepper
	Bouquet garni of 2 sprigs parsley, 2 sprigs thyme, 2 bay leaves, 1 stalk coarsely chopped celery
1	clove garlic, finely minced
1	pound button mushrooms, trimmed
½	pound tomatoes, peeled, seeded and coarsely chopped
2	tablespoons fresh lemon juice
2	tablespoons chopped parsley, for garnish

1. In a large heavy-bottomed saucepan, heat 2 tablespoons of the oil, and sauté onions and carrots until they are soft and golden. Add a little of the white wine (just enough to moisten), then add coriander seeds, salt, pepper, bouquet garni and garlic. Simmer gently for 2-3 minutes.

2. Add mushrooms and tomatoes and stir gently to coat with liquid. Moisten with wine as needed, being careful not to add too much liquid at this stage because mushrooms will create liquid as they cook. Simmer uncovered for 15-20 minutes. Taste and adjust seasonings. Remove from heat. Transfer to a serving bowl and allow to cool.

3. Remove bouquet garni, and add remaining 1 tablespoon olive oil and lemon juice. Sprinkle with freshly chopped parsley and chill.

4. Serve on lettuce-lined salad plates.

Note: A bouquet garni consists of herbs and/or spices which are tied together in a 4-inch square of cheesecloth, so that they release their flavors during cooking, and are easily and completely removed before serving.

Analysis per serving: Calories: 141   Protein: 2g   Carbohydrate: 9g   Fat: 10.5g   Cholesterol: 0   Fiber: 2g   Sodium: 151mg

MARINATED DILL-SEED CARROTS

Makes 2 pints

Preparation: 30 minutes
Marinate: 24 hours

1	**pound carrots, cut into 3½x½-inch sticks**
1	**small onion, cut into strips**
1	**red bell pepper, cut into thin strips**
1½	**cups cider vinegar**
⅓	**cup sugar**
2	**cloves garlic, crushed slightly**
2	**tablespoons dill seed**
¾	**teaspoon salt**

1. Blanch carrots in boiling water for 1 minute; drain. Pour cold water over carrots and drain well. Pat dry.

2. Combine onions, bell pepper, vinegar, sugar, garlic, dill seed and salt in a non-reactive pan (stainless steel or enamel, not aluminum), and cook over moderate heat for approximately 2 minutes.

3. Pack carrots and cooked vegetables into a large jar, gradually filling jar with vinegar solution to cover vegetables.

4. Marinate in refrigerator for a minimum of 24 hours. Can be kept up to one week.

Note: Recipe may be doubled or quadrupled.

Analysis for 2 pints: Calories: 475   Protein: 8g   Carbohydrate: 141g   Fat: 3g   Cholesterol: 0   Fiber: 15.7g   Sodium: 1682mg

CALIFORNIA BLACK OLIVE CAVIAR

Makes 1¾ cups
Serves 6-8 as hors d'oeuvres

What could be easier than this spread? It is great for beach or boat picnics.

Preparation: 10 minutes
Chill: 3 hours

1½	**cups finely chopped black ripe olives**
1½	**tablespoons anchovy paste**
2	**teaspoons lemon juice**
½	**teaspoon lemon zest**
1	**teaspoon olive oil**
2	**tablespoons finely chopped green onion**

1. In a medium bowl, combine all ingredients and mix well. Chill at least 3 hours.

2. Serve with crackers or thin slices of French bread.

Analysis per serving: Calories: 135   Protein: 4g   Carbohydrate: 6g   Fat: 12g   Cholesterol: 9mg   Fiber: 3g   Sodium: 684mg

RANCHO DEL SOL GUACAMOLE

Makes approximately 2 cups

This recipe was created by Fran Jenkins, food writer, teacher and consultant. It is our favorite guacamole.

Preparation: 15 minutes

4	tablespoons white onion, chopped
2-3	green serrano or jalapeño chiles, seeded and coarsely chopped
4	tablespoons cilantro, coarsely chopped
½	teaspoon salt, or to taste
2	large ripe avocados, mashed
2	tablespoons lemon juice
1	large tomato, finely chopped (about ¾ cup)
	Chopped cilantro, for garnish
	Chopped tomato, for garnish

1. In a blender or food processor, process onion, chiles, cilantro and salt to a smooth paste. Transfer to a bowl.

2. Add mashed avocado to paste and mix well with a spoon. Stir in lemon juice and chopped tomato.

3. Serve immediately at room temperature, garnished with cilantro and tomato. Accompany with tortilla chips.

Note: If preparing in advance, cover so that plastic wrap touches the top of the dip. Refrigerate up to 4 hours. Return to room temperature before serving.

Analysis per serving: Calories: 83   Protein: 1g   Carbohydrate: 5g   Fat: 7.5g   Cholesterol: 0   Fiber: 1.8g   Sodium: 274mg

WINTER SQUASH SPREAD WITH GARLIC AND CILANTRO

Serves 6-8

People love this healthy appetizer dip. It can be made early in the day, stored in a bowl and transferred to a decorative dish or platter just before serving.

Preparation: 30 minutes
Chill: 1 hour

2-3	**pounds winter squash (pumpkin, Hubbard or banana squash)**
1	**teaspoon caraway seeds or toasted sesame seeds**
2-3	**medium cloves garlic, minced**
¼	**teaspoon hot pepper sauce**
2	**tablespoons fresh lemon juice**
	Salt to taste (optional)
2	**tablespoons extra virgin olive oil**
2	**tablespoons chopped cilantro**
	Sprigs of cilantro, for garnish
	Toasted pita triangles

1.   Preheat oven to 350 degrees.

2.   Cut squash in half, remove seeds and strings. Place on an oiled pan and bake until tender, approximately 20 minutes.

3.   Scoop cooked flesh into a bowl and coarsely mash with a fork. There should be about 5-6 cups.

4.   Add caraway seeds, garlic, hot pepper sauce, lemon juice, salt, if desired, and 1 tablespoon of olive oil. Mix well and chill.

5.   To serve, place mixture in a shallow bowl and garnish with chopped cilantro. Drizzle remaining 1 tablespoon oil on top and decorate with cilantro sprigs. Serve with toasted pita triangles.

Note: To prepare toasted pita triangles, cut pita into eighths and bake in a 350-degree oven until just crisp, approximately 8-10 minutes.

Analysis per serving: Calories: 117   Protein: 1g   Carbohydrate: 13g   Fat: 8g   Cholesterol: 0   Fiber: 3.8g   Sodium: 3mg
(excluding salt to taste)

WILD MUSHROOM AND HAZELNUT PÂTÉ

Makes 2 cups; serves 6

This quick microwave pâté improves on standing, and can be made up to a week in advance—an ideal appetizer for holiday parties.

Preparation: 40 minutes
Chill: overnight

2	tablespoons unsalted butter
1/2	cup thinly sliced green onions
8	ounces mixed wild mushrooms (such as chanterelle, porcini, or shiitake), sliced
8	ounces white or brown mushrooms, sliced
2	tablespoons sherry, Madeira or brandy
1/2	cup sour cream or plain nonfat yogurt
1/2	teaspoon salt
1/2	teaspoon freshly ground black pepper
1/2	teaspoon freshly grated nutmeg
1/2	cup coarsely chopped hazelnuts
2	tablespoons chopped chives
2	tablespoons finely chopped parsley, divided

1. Place butter and green onions in a 2-quart microwavable dish, and microwave, uncovered, on High for 2 minutes.

2. Mix in mushrooms and microwave, uncovered, on High for 5-8 minutes. Mushrooms should cook down and become slightly darker.

3. Transfer mixture to a food processor. Add sherry and sour cream, then salt, pepper and nutmeg. Process until almost smooth. Add nuts, chives and 1 tablespoon of parsley. Process only to mix (2 or 3 pulses), do not purée into paste.

4. Place mixture in a serving bowl or storage jar and chill overnight. May be kept up to 1 week in refrigerator.

5. To serve, garnish with remaining 1 tablespoon parsley and have toast points, crackers, or thinly sliced baguette rounds available.

Note: You may use any combination of mushrooms. The more wild varieties used, the better the flavor, but it will be more expensive. However, all domestic or common mushrooms make a good pâté.

Analysis per serving: Calories: 146   Protein: 4g   Carbohydrate: 11g   Fat: 10g   Cholesterol: 5mg   Fiber: 1g   Sodium: 232mg

APPETIZERS and SALSAS

SPICED VEGETARIAN PÂTÉ

Makes 1½ pounds
Serves approximately 30

Perfect for a buffet, this meatless pâté has a very rich taste. The flavors intensify over time.

Preparation: 40 minutes
Chill: 3 hours

1	tablespoon sesame oil
4	cloves garlic, minced
2	large onions, chopped
8	ounces mushrooms, sliced
1	pound walnuts (4 cups)
2	hard-cooked eggs
	Tamari soy sauce to taste
	Freshly ground black pepper to taste
1	tablespoon fenugreek powder
¼	teaspoon sage
	Lettuce leaves, for garnish
	Chopped parsley or dill, for garnish

1. In a frying pan, heat oil and sauté garlic, onions and mushrooms until onions are soft and golden and mushrooms are cooked.

2. In a food processor, combine mushroom mixture, walnuts, hard-cooked eggs, tamari, fenugreek and sage; process until finely chopped and well mixed. Taste and if necessary adjust seasonings.

3. Spoon into an attractive bowl or mold, packing down firmly. Chill for 3 hours or more.

4. Serve the pâté in a bowl or invert onto a lettuce-lined plate and sprinkle with parsley or dill. Accompany with crackers or thinly sliced party rye.

Note: Tamari soy sauce and fenugreek powder may be found in health food stores or gourmet supermarkets.

Analysis per serving: Calories: 110 Protein: 5g Carbohydrate: 4g Fat: 9g Cholesterol: 14mg Fiber: 4g Sodium: 38mg

NO-FRY TORTILLA CHIPS

Makes 12 cups; serves 6

Use these lowfat, no cholesterol tortilla chips to enjoy the healthy and delicious dips or salsas presented in this book.

Preparation: 15 minutes

12   corn tortillas or 10 flour tortillas, 10-inch size
**   Salt or other spices (optional)**

1.   Preheat oven to 500 degrees.

2.   Immerse tortillas, one at a time, in water. Let drain briefly, then lay flat.

3.   If desired, sprinkle tops lightly with salt or other spices. Cut each tortilla into 6 or 8 wedges.

4.   Cover a non-stick baking pan with a single layer of tortilla wedges, salt side up. Place close together but do not overlap.

5.   Bake for approximately 5 minutes. Turn with a spatula; then continue to bake until golden brown and crisp, approximately 3 more minutes for corn tortillas and 1 minute for flour tortillas. Watch carefully to avoid scorching. Store in an air-tight container until ready to serve.

This recipe is adapted, with permission, from *The UCSD Healthy Diet for Diabetes*, by Susan Algert, Barbara Grasse, Annie Durning; Copyright © 1990; Houghton Mifflin Company.

Analysis per serving for corn tortillas: Calories: 134   Protein: 4g   Carbohydrate: 26g   Fat: 2g   Cholesterol: 0   Fiber: 3.1g
        Sodium: 107mg

Analysis per serving for flour tortillas: Calories: 158   Protein: 4g   Carbohydrate: 29g   Fat: 3g   Cholesterol: 0   Fiber: 1.3g
        Sodium: 107mg

APPETIZERS and SALSAS

OLIVES IN ROSEMARY-SCENTED OIL

Makes approximately 4 cups

The rosemary-scented oil in this recipe may be prepared in larger quantity for use in salad dressings. Poured into decorative bottles, it makes a lovely gift.

Preparation: 15 minutes

¼	**cup extra virgin olive oil**
6-8	**rosemary sprigs, about 2 inches long**
1	**clove garlic, crushed**
1	**pound black olives, preferably Niçoise**
	Freshly ground pepper

1. In a small heavy saucepan, heat oil until it sizzles when a rosemary leaf is dropped in it. Reduce heat to low, and carefully add rosemary sprigs and garlic. Cook for 2 minutes then set aside for at least 10 minutes, to develop flavor.

2. Strain oil through a sieve into a bowl, pressing the rosemary with a spoon to extract as much oil as possible.

3. Place olives in a bowl, pour on rosemary oil and toss. Allow to stand for 24 hours.

4   To serve, lift olives out of oil, place in an attractive serving bowl. Season to taste with salt and pepper and garnish with a few sprigs of rosemary. Reserve remaining rosemary oil for use on salads or steamed vegetables.

Analysis per serving: Calories: 83 Protein: 0.3g Carbohydrate: 2g Fat: 8.5g Cholesterol: 0 Fiber: 0 Sodium: 327mg

SCALLOP CEVICHE

Serves 6-8

Preparation: 15 minutes
Marinate: 24 hours

2	**pounds scallops, bay or sea**
1	**large red onion, very thinly sliced**
1	**tablespoon white wine vinegar**
1	**cup fresh lime juice**
2	**tablespoons fresh lemon juice**
	Pinch of cayenne pepper, or hot dried ground chiles, to taste
⅓	**cup chopped cilantro or flat-leaf parsley**
	Lettuce leaves

1. Rinse and drain scallops. Quarter large sea scallops.

2. Combine all ingredients, except lettuce, in an enameled, ceramic or glass container. Cover with plastic wrap and marinate in refrigerator for at least 24 hours.

3. Drain and serve on chilled lettuce-lined plates with toast or toasted pita triangles.

Analysis per serving: Calories: 120 Protein: 20g Carbohydrate: 8g Fat: 1g Cholesterol: 37mg Fiber: 1g Sodium: 184mg

CEVICHE DOLSA

Serves 8

Ceviche will hold for several days in the refrigerator. This recipe has a wonderful blend of flavors.

Preparation: 30 minutes
Marinate: 8 hours

1-2	pounds corvina or white sea bass fillets
4	large lemons, zest and juice
2	medium tomatoes, seeded and diced
10	green onions, chopped
1	bunch of cilantro, minced
1	cup small tender peas, cooked
1	jalapeño and 2 serrano chiles, seeded and finely diced
12	ounces tomato juice
¼	cup ketchup
1	tablespoon dried oregano
1	teaspoon freshly ground black pepper
	Pinch of salt
¼	cup vegetable oil
2	tablespoons white vinegar
1	tablespoon hot pepper sauce
20	small pimiento-stuffed green olives
8	lettuce leaves
16	avocado slices
	Corn tortilla chips (optional)

1. Dice corvina fillets; place in a glass dish and completely cover with lemon juice and zest. Cover with plastic wrap and marinate in refrigerator for at least 8 hours or overnight.

2. Remove fish from marinade and squeeze gently with your hands to drain. Set fish aside. Discard marinade.

3. In a large bowl, combine tomatoes, onions, cilantro, peas, chiles, tomato juice, ketchup, oregano, pepper, salt, vegetable oil, vinegar, hot sauce and green olives. Add fish and mix gently. Adjust chile and lemon juice to taste. Cover and chill in refrigerator until ready to serve.

4. Serve on a lettuce leaf on individual plates. Garnish with 2 avocado slices. Include corn tortilla chips, if desired.

Analysis per serving: Calories: 304 Protein: 26g Carbohydrate: 22g Fat: 13g Cholesterol: 60mg Fiber: 5g Sodium: 625 mg

STIR-FRIED SHRIMP WITH TWO SAUCES

Makes 4 appetizer servings

In this tasty dish, half of the shrimp is seasoned with wine and garlic, and the other half with a tangy sauce spiced with chili paste. Increase the broccoli to turn this easy appetizer into a main course. This recipe may also be made using scallops instead of shrimp.

Preparation: 35 minutes
Marinate: 30 minutes

¾	pound medium, raw shrimp, peeled and deveined
2	teaspoons cornstarch
1	teaspoon sesame oil
	Pinch of white pepper
3	tablespoons ketchup
2	teaspoons rice vinegar or lemon juice
½-1	teaspoon Asian chili paste
1	cup broccoli flowers
1	tablespoon salad oil
1	teaspoon minced or pressed garlic
1	tablespoon Shao Hsing wine or sherry
	Pinch of white pepper

1. Rinse shrimp briefly, pat dry. In a small bowl, combine cornstarch, sesame oil, and white pepper. Add shrimp and stir to coat. Cover and marinate in refrigerator for 30 minutes.

2. In a small bowl, mix together ketchup, rice vinegar and chili paste. Set aside.

3. In a medium-sized saucepan, bring 2 inches of water to a boil. Add broccoli and simmer until tender-crisp, approximately 1½ minutes. Drain broccoli, rinse under cold water until cool, then drain again. Arrange broccoli in the center of a serving platter, set aside.

4. Place a wok or 10-12-inch skillet over high heat. When pan is hot, add oil and swirl to coat surface. Add garlic and shrimp and stir-fry until the shrimp turn pink, approximately 2 minutes. Remove half the shrimp and the garlic; set aside. To remaining shrimp in pan, add wine and a pinch of white pepper. Stir to coat completely, then place on the side of the platter with the broccoli.

5. Return reserved shrimp to the pan. Add chili sauce, stirring to coat and heat through, approximately 1 minute. Spoon shrimp and sauce onto the other side of the platter.

This recipe was contributed by Project LEAN, an organization dedicated to educating consumers to make healthy food choices.

Analysis per serving: Calories: 156 Protein: 19g Carbohydrate: 7g Fat: 6g Cholesterol: 166mg Fiber: 1g Sodium: 320mg

STEAMED CHICKEN AND SHRIMP DIM SUM

Makes 50 bundles

Preparation: 1 hour
Cook: 12-14 minutes

5	ounces chopped frozen spinach, thawed and drained well
1	8-ounce can water chestnuts, drained and minced
6	ounces boneless chicken, minced
6	ounces raw, peeled and deveined shrimp, minced
3	green onions, minced
1	tablespoon minced fresh ginger
1	tablespoon low-sodium soy sauce
1	egg
¼	teaspoon chili oil
1	tablespoon hoisin sauce
1	package gyoza or wonton wrappers (approximately 55 wrappers)
	Finely shredded cabbage
	Dipping Sauce (below)

1. In a medium-sized bowl, combine spinach, water chestnuts, chicken, shrimp, onions, ginger, soy sauce, egg, chili oil and hoisin sauce and mix well.

2. Place ½ teaspoon of the mixture in the center of a gyoza wrapper. Bring all outside edges up around filling to form a bundle, leaving top open to show filling. Repeat with remaining wrappers and filling.

3. Place bundles in a single layer in a steamer and steam 12-14 minutes. Keep warm. Repeat until all bundles are steamed.

4. To serve, place shredded cabbage on a platter, set a small bowl of dipping sauce in the center and surround with chicken and shrimp bundles.

DIPPING SAUCE

⅓	cup low-sodium soy sauce
¼	cup rice vinegar
1	tablespoon sesame oil
2-4	drops hot pepper sauce

1. Combine all ingredients in a small bowl and whisk until well mixed.

Note: If gyoza wrappers are not available, substitute wonton wrappers cut into circles, using a 3-inch cookie cutter.

Analysis per serving of 5 bundles: Calories: 77   Protein: 3g   Carbohydrate: 14g   Fat: 1g   Cholesterol: 9mg   Fiber: 1g   Sodium: 80mg

CHICKEN SATAY

Serves 12

In this recipe, the chicken should be sliced very thin so that it will be easy to thread on skewers. The satay can also be served as an entrée for 4-6 people.

Preparation: 20 minutes
Marinate: 3 hours
Grill: 15 minutes

6	chicken breast halves, boned and skinned
2	tablespoons canola oil
2	tablespoons coconut milk
½	cup low-sodium soy sauce
¼	cup rice vinegar
3	tablespoons minced onion
1	teaspoon minced garlic
¼	cup peanut butter
⅛	teaspoon salt
⅛	teaspoon cayenne pepper
	Wooden skewers

1. Cut chicken into thin strips and place in a shallow bowl.

2. Place remaining ingredients in a blender and mix at high speed. Pour mixture over chicken, and marinate at least 3 hours or overnight.

3. Preheat broiler. Thread drained chicken strips on skewers (for appetizers, place only 1 piece per skewer). Reserve marinade. Broil until light brown on both sides. Place on a serving platter.

4. In a small pan, heat marinade to a boil. For appetizers, serve in a small bowl for dipping. For an entrée, pour heated marinade over chicken.

Note: This dish may also be prepared on the barbecue.

Analysis per serving: Calories: 131 Protein: 15g Carbohydrate: 3g Fat: 7g Cholesterol: 33mg Fiber: 0.4g Sodium: 56mg

CRANBERRY, CHILE AND CILANTRO SALSA

Serves 8-10

This salsa has a hint of sweet, a hint of sour and lots of spice!

Preparation: 20 minutes

12	ounces fresh cranberries
1	large clove garlic, minced
4	tablespoons finely chopped fresh cilantro
1-2	jalapeño chiles, seeded and minced
3	green onions, minced
½	cup sugar
⅓	cup fresh lime juice
	Freshly ground black pepper

1. In a large saucepan, boil 1 quart of water. Add cranberries and cook for 1-2 minutes. Drain well and transfer to a bowl. Add garlic, cilantro, chiles and green onion.

2. Mix gently with a fork mashing some of the cranberries to a pulp against the side of the bowl. Add sugar, lime juice and pepper to taste. Refrigerate until serving time.

Analysis per serving: Calories: 56 Protein: 0.2g Carbohydrate: 15g Fat: 0 Cholesterol: 0 Fiber: 0.15g Sodium: 1mg

GREEN CUCUMBER SALSA

Makes approximately 2½ cups

Preparation: 20 minutes

2	large cucumbers, peeled, seeded and chopped
½	cup diced red bell pepper
¼	cup seeded and chopped, mild green chile pepper
2	tablespoons chopped cilantro
2	tablespoons wine vinegar
1	jalapeño pepper, seeded and minced
1	teaspoon salt
1	teaspoon minced garlic
1	teaspoon sugar

1. Reserve half the chopped cucumber and half the red bell pepper.

2. In a blender, purée remaining ingredients until smooth. Transfer to a bowl, and add reserved vegetables. Serve with raw vegetables or grilled main dishes.

The recipe comes from *Pleasures of the Palate* by Harris Golden, spa cuisine consultant for San Diego's Triangles Restaurant, and former Food Director/Executive chef for Elizabeth Arden's Maine Chance, in Phoenix.

Analysis per serving: Calories: 3 Protein: 0.1g Carbohydrate: 1g Fat: 0.02g Cholesterol: 0 Fiber: 0.2g Sodium: 57mg

APPETIZERS and SALSAS

SOUTHWEST SALSA

Makes 2½ cups

Preparation: 15 minutes
Chill: 1 hour

2	cups tomatoes, peeled (optional), seeded, chopped and drained
¼	cup seeded, chopped chile peppers (Anaheim or poblano)
3	tablespoons chopped cilantro
2	tablespoons red wine vinegar
¼	teaspoon salt
¼	teaspoon sugar
½	teaspoon minced garlic
1	jalapeño pepper, seeded and minced

1. Mix all ingredients in a glass bowl.

2. Refrigerate for at least 1 hour or several days to blend and intensify flavors.

Adapted, with permission, from *Pleasures of the Palate*, by Harris Golden; Copyright © 1989; published by Golden's Kitchen.

Analysis per tablespoon serving: Calories: 5 Protein: 0   Carbohydrate: 1g Fat: 0 Cholesterol: 0 Fiber: 0.2g Sodium: 18mg

MOROCCAN PEPPERS SALSA

Makes approximately 2 cups; serves 4-6

This recipe, submitted by food writer and teacher, Antonia Allegra, is from her late friend, noted author M.F.K. Fisher, who said, "I don't know why this is so good; nobody has ever told me why it disappears so fast."

Preparation: 10 minutes
Cook: 20 minutes

2	large bell peppers (green, red, yellow or a mix of colors), seeded, deveined and each cut into 6-10 strips
4	large cloves garlic, peeled
	Salt to taste (about ¼ teaspoon)
1	cup olive oil
¼	cup vinegar
2	pinches ground coriander

1. Place all ingredients in a medium-sized sauté pan, and cook very slowly over low heat until peppers are done, approximately 20 minutes.

2. Spoon into a clean jar with a tight lid, and cool before storing in refrigerator. May be stored up to one week.

3. Drain peppers and serve with crusty bread.

Analysis per serving: Calories: 338 Protein: 0.3g Carbohydrate: 5g Fat: 12g Cholesterol: 0 Fiber: 0.2g Sodium: 92mg

CREAMY TOMATILLO SALSA

Serves 8-10

Serve also as a dip for tortilla chips; this is a wonderful condiment for anything grilled or poached.

Preparation: 15 minutes
Chill: 30 minutes

12	medium tomatillos, husks removed
1	small red onion, or other sweet variety
1-3	serrano chiles, seeded, or to taste
½	cup fresh cilantro
1-2	tablespoons sour cream
	Salt and pepper to taste (optional)

1. Bring a large pot of water to a boil, add tomatillos and blanch for 1-2 minutes. Drain.

2. Place onion, chiles and cilantro in a food processor and pulse until finely chopped. Add tomatillos and mix until puréed; then add sour cream to thicken to desired consistency. Season to taste. Chill.

3. Prepare meat, fish or poultry and when ready to serve, generously spoon salsa over entrée. Serve remaining salsa separately.

Analysis per serving: Calories: 43 Protein: 2g Carbohydrate: 8g Fat: 0.8g Cholesterol: 1mg Fiber: 1.1g Sodium: 19mg

PAPAYA AND TOMATO SALSA

Serves 10

Preparation: 30-40 minutes
Chill: 4 hours

2	yellow or red bell peppers, oven-charred, peeled, seeded and chopped
2	serrano or jalapeño chiles, seeded and finely minced
4	large ripe tomatoes, peeled, seeded and chopped
1	small red onion, finely chopped
1	large lime, juiced
2	tablespoons olive oil
½	cup fresh cilantro, chopped
	Freshly ground pepper to taste
2	papayas, ripe but firm, peeled, seeded and cut into small dice

1. In a medium-sized serving bowl, mix together all ingredients except papayas. Cover and chill for at least 4 hours.

2. Just before serving, add papaya. Serve as a dip with chips or with grilled foods.

Note: To char and peel peppers, place on a barbecue grill or under an oven broiler and grill until blackened, turning to char uniformly. Place in a plastic bag for 10 minutes, then peel off the skin.

Analysis per serving: Calories: 84 Protein: 1g Carbohydrate: 12g Fat: 4g Cholesterol: 0 Fiber: 2g Sodium: 89mg

LOQUAT CHUTNEY

Makes 6-8 cups

The productive and attractive loquat tree is drought-resistant and especially well-suited to San Diego's mild, dry climate. This recipe was a prize-winner at the San Diego County Fair. It can be served with cold meats and curries, or as an appetizer with cream cheese and crackers.

Preparation: 30 minutes
Cook: 30 minutes

2	**cups sugar**
1	**cup brown sugar**
1	**cup cider vinegar**
1½	**tablespoons minced fresh ginger, or 1½ teaspoons ground**
1	**teaspoon ground cardamom, or allspice**
½	**teaspoon salt**
½	**teaspoon dry mustard**
2	**small hot chile peppers, fresh or dried, chopped and seeded**
½	**cup finely diced onion**
½	**cup finely diced bell pepper**
½	**lime, chopped, including rind**
1	**clove garlic, mashed**
1	**cup raisins**
8-10	**cups loquats, peeled, seeded and cut into small pieces**

1. In a large saucepan, combine all ingredients except loquats, and bring to a boil; reduce to a simmer. Add fruit, about 2 cups at a time, stirring. Simmer approximately 30 minutes until fruit is thoroughly cooked.

2. Spoon into sterilized jars and seal.

Note: The recipe can be easily halved, and the chutney will keep in unsealed jars in the refrigerator for several weeks.

Analysis per serving: Calories: 35   Protein: 0.13g   Carbohydrate: 9.5g   Fat: 0   Cholesterol: 0   Fiber: 0.5g   Sodium: 13mg

SOUPS

SAVORING SAN DIEGO

RANCHO COOKING

By Elena Cota
Certified Home Economist

The family history of Elena Casanova Cota is rooted in the rancho period of California history. Following Mexico's independence from Spain, the California missions were secularized and their lands divided among prominent Spanish-Mexican dons, who established large cattle ranches throughout the state. Elena's mother was born on a ranch in Julian at the time of the local Gold Rush of the 1870s. The rancho era of San Diego's development began its decline with the great drought of the 1860s, which destroyed vast herds of cattle. Elena Cota passes on to her students the traditions of Spanish/Mexican cooking, learned from her mother.

Rancho cooking in the olden times ("en los tiempos de antes", as my mother would say) and modern Ranch Cooking have similarities: hospitality, outdoor cooking, abundance of fresh fruits and vegetables, open fires and pits. The main differences are methods and modern equipment.

Cooking in the 1800s consisted of iron kettles over open fires, fireplaces or simple wood stoves. Meat for special occasions or large affairs was prepared underneath the ground. The pit was dug, a fire was made inside the pit; rocks were placed and allowed to heat. The meat was seasoned, wrapped in clean sheets, then in burlap sacks, and placed on the hot rocks. The pit was then covered with dirt and allowed to cook all night. While the meat cooked, there was much merriment taking place around the pit. This method is still used by many today.

To barbecue in those "olden times", a side of beef, a goat or a pig was placed between two crudely made tripods, periodically turned for even cooking and gently "mopped" with a marinade or sauce. Today's methods are more sophisticated in that the rotation of meat may be done electrically.

Flour tortillas used to be made on a wood stove and bread was usually baked in a beehive-shaped oven. An authentic beehive-shaped oven may still be seen at Casa de Estudillo in Old Town, the birthplace of San Diego.

Salsas were made on a daily basis and fruits and vegetables were to be found in the ranch garden. Preservation of foods was by salting, drying, canning or, if there was snow, by freezing.

In the past, hospitality was shared, because in many instances survival depended on being neighborly, even though a neighbor was several miles away. Cooking and baking was done with the simple thought of feeding the family. With today's availability of ingredients, modern methods and lifestyle needs, we are witnessing a restoration in food preparation to the simplicity of the past, where emphasis is on the freshness of fruits and vegetables, and ease and healthiness in their preparation.

This is the story my mother, Nina Ruis Casanova, told us over and over again, and I, in turn, have told my children and grandchildren.

MENU FOR A PATIO BARBECUE

Rancho del Sol Guacamole, page 17

Southwest Salsa, page 28

No-Fry Tortilla Chips, page 21

Baja Chicken and Lime Soup, page 39

San Diego Seafood Kebabs, page 143

or

Butterflied Leg of Lamb with Herb Marinade, page 122

Rosemary-Roasted Onions, page 196

Almond-Crusted Broccoli and Spinach Casserole, page 204

Fiesta Salad with Cumin Dressing, page 60

Fresh Plum Cake, page 238

Double-Baked Caramel Pears with Ice Cream, page 216

SOUPS

CHILLED SPINACH-TARRAGON SOUP

Serves 8-10

Delicious anytime, this soup, from chef Lisa Stalker of San Diego's Crest Cafe, makes an elegant treat for a pre-Summer Pops picnic.

Preparation: 35 minutes
Simmer: 50 minutes
Chill: 4 hours

½	**cup unsalted butter**
2	**large onions, halved crosswise and thinly sliced**
5	**large cloves garlic, crushed**
14-16	**ounces fresh spinach, rinsed and stalks trimmed**
4	**cups chicken stock, defatted**
1	**potato, peeled and cut into 8-10 pieces**
1	**cup fresh flat-leaf parsley**
1	**tablespoon fresh lemon juice**
2	**teaspoons dried tarragon**
1	**teaspoon freshly ground black pepper**
	Pinch of cayenne pepper
	Fresh tarragon leaves, for garnish

1. In a heavy medium-sized soup pot, melt butter over medium heat. Add onions and garlic, cover and cook for 15 minutes, stirring occasionally. Add spinach, stir well and cook for 5 minutes, covered.

2. Add chicken stock, potato, parsley, lemon juice, tarragon, black and cayenne peppers. Reduce heat, cover and simmer for 50 minutes.

3. In a food processor or blender, purée soup in small batches until smooth. Allow to cool and refrigerate for at least 4 hours.

4. To serve, ladle into bowls and garnish with tarragon leaves.

Analysis per serving: Calories: 64   Protein: 4g   Carbohydrate: 10g   Fat: 1g   Cholesterol: 1g   Fiber: 2.4g   Sodium: 343mg

CHILLED AVOCADO SOUP

Serves 6-8

This delicious soup, from the kitchen of chef Pat Weckerly, is very rich, so be sure to serve it with a light meal, such as baked or grilled fish and steamed vegetables.

Preparation: 25 minutes
Chill: 2½ hours

2	teaspoons butter
1	small onion, minced
1	carrot peeled and minced
2	small celery stalks, stringed and minced
1	clove garlic, minced
4	cups chicken stock
1	cup heavy cream
2	large avocados
1	tablespoon lime juice
	Freshly ground black pepper
2½	tablespoons chopped cilantro

1. In a large saucepan, melt butter; add onion, carrot, celery and garlic and sauté until soft and transparent. Add stock and bring to a boil. Remove from heat and cool to room temperature. Stir in cream and chill for at least 2 hours.

2. Peel and dice avocado into ¼-inch pieces. Whisk into chilled broth until soup is slightly thickened. Add lime juice and season to taste with pepper. Mix in cilantro and chill well.

Analysis per serving: Calories: 218   Protein: 4g   Carbohydrate: 7g   Fat: 20g   Cholesterol: 43mg   Fiber: 2g   Sodium: 427mg

SOUPS

CHILLED CARROT AND ORANGE SOUP

Serves 4

Preparation: 15 minutes
Simmer: 1 hour
Chill: 3-4 hours

2	tablespoons butter
1	pound young carrots, peeled and thinly sliced
1	onion, finely sliced
2	pints low-sodium or homemade chicken stock
½	teaspoon sugar
	Juice of 4 oranges, strained
4	ounces half-and-half
	Chopped chives, for garnish

1. Melt butter in a heavy-bottomed saucepan and cook carrots and onions, stirring occasionally, until onion is transparent and carrots are soft, but not browned, approximately 5-7 minutes.

2. Stir in stock and add sugar. Bring to a boil, cover and simmer for approximately 1 hour.

3. Remove from heat, transfer to a food processor or blender, and process until smooth. Add orange juice and half-and-half, blending to mix. Cool, then chill in refrigerator for several hours. Serve garnished with chopped chives.

Analysis per serving: Calories: 222 Protein: 5g Carbohydrate: 23g Fat: 11g Cholesterol: 26mg Fiber: 4g Sodium: 1154mg

CHILLED PAPAYA SOUP

Serves 4

Preparation: 15 minutes
Chill: 1 hour

2	large ripe Hawaiian papayas, peeled and cut into large cubes, reserving some for garnish
½	cup plain lowfat yogurt (do not use nonfat)
3-4	tablespoons fresh lime juice
2	tablespoons honey (do not use strongly flavored honey)
1	cup ginger ale, or lemon/lime carbonated soda
	Plain lowfat yogurt, for garnish
4	sprigs of mint, for garnish

1. In a food processor, blend papaya, yogurt, lime juice and honey until smooth. Add ½ cup of the ginger ale and continue processing until blended. Chill in a large bowl.

2. Just before serving, add remaining ½ cup ginger ale and mix well. Ladle into individual glass bowls or mugs. Garnish each serving with 1 tablespoon of yogurt and 2-3 small cubes of fresh papaya and a sprig of mint.

Analysis per serving: Calories: 162 Protein: 4g Carbohydrate: 38g Fat: 1g Cholesterol: 3mg Fiber: 5g Sodium: 45mg

WHITE GAZPACHO

Serves 8

A variation on regular gazpacho, this recipe was contributed by Beth Spooner, food consultant, teacher and caterer in San Diego.

Preparation: 30 minutes
Chill: 24 hours

2	cloves garlic
3	medium cucumbers, peeled, seeded and cut into chunks
3	cups chicken broth or stock, defatted
2	cups drained yogurt (see Note below), or 1 cup plain yogurt and 1 cup sour cream
1	cup sour cream
3	tablespoons white vinegar
1	teaspoon salt
2	teaspoons white pepper
2-4	tablespoons vodka or gin (optional)
2	teaspoons butter
3	ounces slivered, blanched almonds
3	large ripe tomatoes, peeled, seeded and chopped
6-8	green onions, sliced
½	cup parsley, finely chopped
1	cucumber finely chopped, for garnish

1. In a food processor, mince garlic; add cucumbers, ½ cup broth and purée until smooth. Remove to a large bowl and stir in remaining broth.

2. In a separate bowl, mix drained yogurt and sour cream together (or 1 cup plain yogurt and 2 cups sour cream). Thin with a little of the cucumber-broth mixture, then blend all the yogurt and cucumber mixtures together. Add vinegar, salt, pepper and vodka and chill overnight.

3. In a small skillet, melt butter and sauté almonds until well toasted.

4. To serve, ladle soup into chilled bowls. Garnish with chopped tomatoes, green onions, parsley and cucumber. Sprinkle generously with toasted almonds.

Note on draining yogurt: If time permits, drain yogurt for 24 hours before using. Use 1 quart of plain yogurt mixed with 1 tablespoon salt; pour this into a fine colander lined with cheesecloth, and refrigerate in a bowl overnight. The salt pulls the extra moisture and makes it more the consistency of sour cream.

Analysis per serving: Calories: 230 Protein: 10g Carbohydrate: 16gm Fat: 14g Cholesterol: 16mg Fiber: 3g Sodium: 903mg

EASY AGNOLOTTI SOUP

Serves 6

A "Cat in the Hat" favorite, according to Audrey Geisel, whose husband, "Dr. Seuss", loved this recipe. Agnolotti are half-moon-shaped stuffed pasta.

Preparation: 35 minutes

1	tablespoon olive oil
1	medium onion, chopped
½	cup diced carrot
2	teaspoons minced garlic
3½	cups chicken broth
4	ounces agnolotti (or tortellini)
1	cup chopped escarole or fresh spinach
½	cup frozen green peas
2	tablespoons freshly grated Parmesan cheese
2	tablespoons prepared pesto

1. In a large saucepan, heat oil over medium heat. Add onion, carrot and garlic; cook, stirring frequently, until onion is transparent, approximately 3 minutes.

2. Add chicken broth and bring to a boil. Stir in agnolotti, return to a boil; reduce heat and simmer until agnolotti is cooked, approximately 5-8 minutes. Stir in escarole and peas and heat through.

3. To serve, ladle into individual bowls and garnish each with 1 teaspoon Parmesan cheese and 1 teaspoon pesto.

Analysis per serving: Calories: 182   Protein: 8g   Carbohydrate: 21g   Fat: 7g   Cholesterol: 2mg   Fiber: 2g   Sodium: 509mg

BAJA CHICKEN AND LIME SOUP

Serves 8

Preparation: 30 minutes
Cook: 40 minutes

4	chicken breast halves
10	cups vegetable broth or low-sodium chicken broth
3	cloves garlic
½	medium onion
3	sprigs of cilantro
1	teaspoon dried oregano
1	clove
1	1-inch long stick cinnamon
½	teaspoon ground cumin
1	teaspoon olive oil
½	cup chopped red onion
⅓	cup chopped green bell pepper
⅓	cup chopped yellow bell pepper
2	cups chopped tomatoes, peeled and seeded
8	key limes (or Mexican limes), 4 sliced and 4 halved
1	avocado, sliced
	Sprigs of cilantro, for garnish

1. In a large cooking pot, place chicken, broth, garlic, onion and cilantro; bring to a boil. Cover, reduce heat and simmer 30-35 minutes or until chicken is tender. Strain stock and set aside. Shred chicken and discard vegetables.

2. In a small dry frying pan, toast oregano, clove, cinnamon and cumin over medium-high heat for 3-4 minutes. Combine spices in a blender with ½ cup reserved chicken stock. Process to a purée.

3. In a large soup pot, heat oil, add onions and sauté until transparent. Add bell peppers and sauté for 3 minutes. Add tomatoes and cook for approximately 6 minutes, stirring frequently. Add puréed spices and remaining chicken broth; bring to a boil. Add 4 sliced limes and shredded chicken; cover and cook over medium heat for 8-10 minutes.

4. To serve, place slice of lime in the bottom of each bowl and ladle soup into bowl. Pass avocado, lime halves and cilantro sprigs separately, to garnish.

Analysis per serving: Calories: 164   Protein: 18g   Carbohydrate: 9g   Fat: 7g   Cholesterol: 33mg   Fiber: 2g   Sodium: 108mg

SPICY SHRIMP SOUP WITH LEMONGRASS AND LIME

Serves 6

To adapt this popular Thai recipe, we offer substitutes for the less familiar ingredients. However, we think it is worth the trip to an Asian market to find the lemongrass and kaffir lime leaves. Like fresh ginger, they can be used frozen. Buy a supply, wrap tightly, and keep on hand in the freezer. We are indebted to Su-Mei Yu, owner of Saffron Restaurant, and Nancie McDermott, author of the cookbook, *Real Thai*, for help with this recipe.

Preparation: 20 minutes
Cook: 35 minutes

2	stalks fresh lemongrass or 2-3 slices of lime zest
2	tablespoons peanut oil
2	dried red chiles or 1 teaspoon hot red pepper flakes
5	cloves garlic
2	shallots
	Cheesecloth and twine to form a bouquet garni
1	pound large uncooked shrimp, shelled and deveined (save 6-7 shells)
7	cups chicken stock
3-4	slices fresh ginger
2-3	kaffir lime leaves or 2-3 slices of lime zest
8	ounces canned straw mushrooms, drained and rinsed well, or 8 ounces fresh oyster mushrooms
1	tablespoon fish sauce (available at Asian markets) or soy sauce and salt to taste
1-2	tablespoons sugar
1-2	serrano chiles, finely chopped
	Juice of 2-3 limes to taste
	Sprigs of cilantro, for garnish

1. Cut the grassy tops off the lemongrass, leaving a stalk about 6 inches. Peel off outer leaves and remove the woody root section at the base. Using the back of a heavy knife, bruise stalks by pounding at about 2-inch intervals, turning the stalk to bruise all sides.

2. In a large pan, heat 1 tablespoon of the peanut oil, and when hot, stir-fry red chiles, garlic and shallots until aromatic. Remove and tie them in a small piece of cheesecloth to form a bouquet garni. Set aside.

3. Adding a little extra oil to pan if necessary, stir-fry reserved shrimp shells until they turn pink. Add stock, bouquet garni, ginger, kaffir lime leaves and lemongrass. Cover and cook slowly for 30 minutes. Remove shells. The recipe may be prepared ahead to this point and set aside.

4. Before serving, bring stock infusion to a quick boil. Add shrimp and mushrooms. Season with fish sauce, sugar and serrano chiles. Cook until shrimp turn pink. Remove from heat, and immediately add lime juice to taste. Serve garnished with cilantro.

Analysis per serving: Calories: 178 Protein: 19g Carbohydrate: 10g Fat: 7g Cholesterol: 108mg Fiber: 1g Sodium: 1226mg

SAN DIEGO CIOPPINO

Serves 6

Preparation: 20-25 minutes
Cook: 30 minutes

12	clams, well scrubbed
12	mussels, well scrubbed
3	cups dry white wine, divided
1/4	cup olive oil
1	medium onion, finely chopped
4	cloves garlic, minced
1	medium green bell pepper, coarsely chopped
2	pounds tomatoes, peeled, seeded and chopped
3	ounces tomato paste
1	teaspoon freshly ground black pepper
1/4	teaspoon cumin
1	tablespoon oregano
3	tablespoons finely chopped fresh basil or 1 1/2 teaspoons dried
1/2	cup clam juice (or, to reduce sodium, substitute water)
2	pounds fresh white fish, such as halibut, rock cod, red snapper or sea bass, cut into large pieces
3/4	pound scallops
3/4	pound raw shrimp, shelled and deveined
6	1-pound cocktail-sized crab claws
	Chopped fresh cilantro and sun-dried tomatoes, for garnish

1. In a large pot, combine clams and mussels; add 1 cup of the wine; cover and steam over medium heat for 5-6 minutes, or until clams and mussels open. Remove shellfish, discarding any that do not open. Strain stock through a cheesecloth and reserve.

2. In an 8-quart casserole or Dutch oven, heat oil. Add onion, garlic and green pepper, and sauté over medium heat, stirring occasionally, until vegetables start to soften, approximately 5 minutes.

3. Add tomatoes, tomato paste, remaining 2 cups of wine, pepper, cumin, herbs, clam juice and reserved stock. Partially cover and simmer for 20 minutes. Add fish, scallops, shrimp and crab claws. Simmer for approximately 5 minutes or until all seafood is cooked. Do not stir. Add clams and mussels and heat for an additional minute.

4. Sprinkle with cilantro and sun-dried tomatoes and serve immediately from cooking pot into large bowls. Accompany with crusty bread.

Adapted, with permission, from *The UCSD Healthy Diet for Diabetes*, by Susan Algert, Barbara Grasse, Annie Durning; Copyright © 1990; Houghton Mifflin Company.

Analysis per serving: Calories: 751 Protein: 103g Carbohydrate: 21g Fat: 19g Cholesterol: 417mg Fiber: 4g Sodium: 1144mg

ASIAN-SPICED SOUP WITH SCALLOP AND SHRIMP DUMPLINGS

Serves 8

This delicious soup, has intriguing contrasts in flavor and texture. Despite the number of ingredients, the preparation is simple and it may partly be prepared in advance.

Preparation: 30 minutes
Cook: 25 minutes

	Scallop and Shrimp Dumplings (below)
6	**cups homemade or low-sodium chicken broth**

FLAVORINGS

2	**teaspoons grated fresh ginger**
2	**teaspoons grated lemon zest**
2	**teaspoons lemon juice**
2	**teaspoons minced garlic**
¼	**teaspoon five-spice powder**
2	**teaspoons low-sodium soy sauce**
2	**teaspoons chili oil**
1	**tablespoon rice vinegar**
2	**teaspoons dry sherry**
3	**tablespoons finely chopped cilantro**
1	**teaspoon cornstarch mixed with 1 teaspoon water**
	Vegetable oil
4	**large mushrooms, thinly sliced**
2	**small green onions, thinly sliced, for garnish**
2	**tablespoons finely chopped cilantro, for garnish**

1. Prepare dumplings and refrigerate until ready to serve.

2. Place stock in a large saucepan and add flavorings. Bring to a boil; reduce heat; cover and simmer for 15 minutes. Combine cornstarch-water paste with a little of the simmering liquid, then blend into soup to thicken slightly; strain. The soup may be prepared ahead to this point, and refrigerated or frozen.

3. Shortly before serving, heat oil in a small skillet, and sauté mushrooms for approximately 4 minutes. Set aside.

4. When ready to serve, bring soup to a boil and add mushrooms. Drop in prepared Scallop and Shrimp Dumplings, and cook for approximately 1 minute, or until warmed through. Ladle into soup bowls and garnish with green onions and cilantro.

Continued on next page

SCALLOP AND SHRIMP DUMPLINGS

1	teaspoon sesame oil
1	slice white bread
½	teaspoon grated fresh ginger
¼	pound scallops
¼	pound raw shrimp, shelled and deveined

1. In a food processor, combine all ingredients and purée until smooth. With a melon baller, scoop out about 16 1-inch balls (dumplings). Cover with plastic wrap and refrigerate.

Analysis per serving: Calories: 66   Protein: 6g   Carbohydrate: 3g   Fat: 3g   Cholesterol: 13mg   Fiber: 0.6g   Sodium: 665mg

MAZATLAN SHRIMP CHOWDER WITH CORN

Serves 6-8

Be ready for guests to want seconds of this easily prepared chowder. It is also great to take along in a large thermos for a tailgate party.

Preparation: 30-40 minutes

2	tablespoons vegetable oil
1	medium onion, finely chopped
1	medium green bell pepper, seeded, deveined and finely chopped
1	poblano chile, roasted, peeled, seeded, deveined and finely chopped
3	cups fresh corn, cut from cob
2	cups chicken stock
1	cup half-and-half or whole milk
¾	pound medium uncooked shrimp, peeled, deveined and cut into ½-inch slices
	Freshly ground black pepper
¼	cup chopped cilantro leaves
	Sprigs of cilantro, for garnish

1. In a large soup pot, heat oil over medium-high heat. Add onion and sauté until transparent, but not browned. Add bell pepper and chile and continue cooking for another 3-4 minutes.

2. In a food processor, purée 2 cups of the corn and add to pot. Stir in chicken stock and half-and-half and simmer for 3 minutes.

3. Add remaining 1 cup of corn and shrimp slices and let simmer gently until the shrimp are just cooked through, approximately 1-2 minutes. Season with black pepper to taste, and chopped cilantro.

4. To serve, ladle soup into large bowls and garnish with a sprig of cilantro.

Note: As an alternative to poblano chile, use a canned whole green chile, rinsed, patted dry and finely chopped.

Analysis per serving: Calories: 342   Protein: 13g   Carbohydrate: 51g   Fat: 11g   Cholesterol: 54mg   Fiber: 8g   Sodium: 260mg

SOUPS

ROASTED SUMMER VEGETABLE SOUP WITH HERBS

Serves 4-6

Preparation: 20 minutes
Cook: 1½ hours

2	large eggplants
2	large onions, unpeeled
2	large red bell peppers
4	medium plum tomatoes, cut in half
2	tablespoons olive oil
5½	cups chicken broth or stock
1	tablespoon diced canned chipotle chiles
1	teaspoon dried oregano
1	teaspoon dried thyme
1	tablespoon minced fresh basil
¼	cup red wine vinegar
	Freshly ground black pepper
	Several small basil leaves, for garnish

1. Preheat oven to 450 degrees and brush a large shallow roasting pan with oil.

2. Pierce skins of eggplants, onions and bell peppers with a sharp knife and brush all vegetables with oil. Roast for approximately 1 hour, or until eggplant is completely softened, turning vegetables as they brown. When cool enough to handle, remove stems and skins from eggplant, skin onions and remove skins and seeds from peppers.

3. Place vegetables in a large saucepan with 3 cups of the broth, chile, oregano, thyme and basil. Bring to a boil, reduce heat, cover and simmer, for 25 minutes, stirring frequently.

4. In a blender or food processor, purée soup until very smooth. Strain back into saucepan. Add vinegar and remaining broth to achieve desired consistency. Add ground pepper to taste and reheat.

5. To serve, ladle into large shallow bowls and garnish with basil leaves.

Analysis per serving: Calories: 149 Protein: 7g Carbohydrate: 18g Fat: 6g Cholesterol: 0 Fiber: 4.1g Sodium: 813mg

SUMMER SQUASH AND CARROT SOUP WITH LEMON AND BASIL

Serves 6

Preparation: 25 minutes
Cook: 10-15 minutes

2	tablespoons olive oil
1	large sweet onion, finely chopped
2	cloves garlic, chopped
4	cups low-sodium chicken broth or chicken stock
3	medium summer squash, coarsely shredded
3	medium zucchini, coarsely shredded
2	medium carrots, peeled and coarsely shredded
	Grated zest of one medium lemon
5	tablespoons coarsely shredded fresh basil
6	basil leaves, for garnish
	Freshly ground black pepper to taste

1. In a large saucepan, heat oil; add onions and garlic and sauté over low heat until transparent, approximately 5-7 minutes.

2. Add chicken broth, squash, zucchini, carrot, lemon zest and shredded basil. Cook until vegetables are tender but still slightly firm, approximately 5-8 minutes. Season to taste with pepper.

3. Serve in bowls garnished with a basil leaf.

Analysis per serving: Calories: 114   Protein: 6g   Carbohydrate: 11g   Fat: 6g   Cholesterol: 0   Fiber: 3.4g   Sodium: 499mg

CARROT AND POTATO SOUP WITH CHERVIL

Serves 4-6

Preparation: 30 minutes
Cook: 40-45 minutes

2	tablespoons butter
1	large onion, chopped
1¼	cups peeled, sliced potatoes
1¼	cups shredded carrots
	Freshly ground black pepper to taste
	Pinch of sugar
3	cups defatted chicken stock
1	tablespoon chopped parsley
2	tablespoons chopped chervil
	Paper-thin slices of carrot, for garnish
	Chervil leaves, for garnish

1. In a large pot, melt butter; add onions and sauté for 5 minutes over medium heat until transparent. Take care to avoid burning. Add potatoes and carrots, and cook uncovered for 5 minutes. Add sugar and pepper to taste, cover and simmer for 10 minutes. Add chicken stock and continue simmering for 20 minutes.

2. In a food processor or blender, purée soup in batches until very smooth.

3. Return to pot and reheat. Stir in parsley and chervil. Serve hot, garnished with carrot slices and chervil leaves.

Analysis per serving: Calories: 112 Protein: 4g Carbohydrate: 14g Fat: 5g Cholesterol: 10mg Fiber: 1.7g Sodium: 438mg

FRENCH COUNTRY SOUP

This recipe is a special favorite. It was taught by James Beard at the first Celebrity Cooking Series sponsored by the UCSD Medical Center Auxiliary.

Serves 10

Preparation: 1 hour 10 minutes

4	**tablespoons olive oil**
2	**onions, sliced**
4	**tomatoes, peeled, seeded and chopped**
1	**pound green beans, sliced**
1	**cup cooked dried white beans (also available in cans)**
4	**zucchini, sliced**
3	**medium potatoes, peeled and diced**
2½	**quarts water**
¼	**cup chopped celery leaves**
½	**pound vermicelli or fine noodles**
	Freshly ground black pepper
	Pistou (below)
	Grated Parmesan cheese, for garnish

1. In a large soup pot, heat olive oil and cook onions until soft and golden.

2. Add tomatoes, green beans, white beans, zucchini and potatoes; stir well. Add water and celery leaves and bring to a boil. Lower heat and simmer for 10 minutes.

3. Add vermicelli and pepper and simmer until tender. The mixture should be fairly thick.

4. Meanwhile, prepare pistou.

5. When soup is ready, pour into a tureen, and stir in the pistou. Serve in large bowls, accompanied by a bowl of grated Parmesan cheese.

PISTOU

4	**large cloves garlic, coarsely chopped**
2	**cups fresh basil leaves, finely chopped**
1	**teaspoon salt**
⅓	**cup olive oil**
3	**tablespoons grated Gruyère cheese**

1. In a mortar and pestle, blender or food processor, grind garlic, basil and salt to a purée. Add olive oil, a little at a time, blending thoroughly, until thick and smooth. Mix in grated cheese.

Hint: Home-prepared white beans need advance preparation (follow package directions). However, they can be cooked in large quantity and frozen for use as needed.

Analysis per serving: Calories: 289   Protein: 8g   Carbohydrate: 36g   Fat: 14g   Cholesterol: 21mg   Fiber: 5g   Sodium: 184mg

BACON-FLAVORED SWEET CORN CHOWDER WITH WILD RICE

Serves 6

This soup may be made one day ahead and refrigerated. Before serving, slowly bring to a simmer.

Preparation: 45 minutes

3	lean bacon slices, chopped
1/2	onion, diced
5	ears fresh sweet white corn
4 1/2	cups chicken broth
2	teaspoons minced fresh thyme
1	bay leaf
2	tablespoons cornstarch mixed with 2 tablespoons water
2	cups buttermilk
1/4	cup raw wild rice, cooked
	Freshly ground black pepper to taste
2	tablespoons chopped chives or parsley, for garnish

1. In a large heavy saucepan, cook bacon until crisp. Reduce heat, add onion and sauté until tender, approximately 3-4 minutes. Pour off fat.

2. Meanwhile, cut corn off cobs and set aside. Break cobs into pieces.

3. Add broth, corn cobs, thyme and bay leaf to saucepan and simmer, covered, for 20 minutes. Remove cobs.

4. Add cornstarch-water mixture to soup, and mix well. Add corn kernels, buttermilk and rice; increase heat, bringing soup to a boil, stirring until slightly thickened. Lower heat and simmer for approximately 5 minutes. Season with pepper.

5. To serve, ladle soup into shallow bowls and garnish with chives or parsley.

Analysis per serving: Calories: 217 Protein: 12g Carbohydrate: 36g Fat: 4g Cholesterol: 6 mg Fiber: 3g Sodium: 725mg

OLD TOWN BLACK BEAN SOUP

Serves 10-12

Preparation: 30-40 minutes
Soak: overnight
Cook: 3-3½ hours

1	pound dried black beans
	Water to cover
1	pound carrots, peeled and chopped
1	bunch celery, stringed and chopped (with leaves)
2	large onions, chopped
3	large cloves garlic, mashed
1	small jalapeño chile, seeded and minced
	Grated zest of 1 large lemon
1	bay leaf
4	quarts chicken broth
6-8	black peppercorns
1	large lemon, thinly sliced, for garnish
	Chopped cilantro, for garnish
3	tablespoons minced green onion, for garnish

1. Wash and pick over beans, place in a large bowl and cover by 2 inches of water. Soak overnight. Drain well. (Alternatively, in a large pot, cover beans by 2 inches of water; bring to a boil and cook for 1 minute. Remove from heat, cover, and set aside for 1 hour. Drain well.)

2. Place beans in a large soup pot with carrots, celery, onions, garlic, lemon zest, bay leaf, chicken broth and peppercorns. Cover and bring to a boil over high heat. As soon as mixture boils, turn heat to very low and simmer, uncovered, for 2½-3 hours, or until beans are very tender. Remove bay leaf.

3. Purée soup, in batches if necessary, until fairly smooth; return to pot. Place over medium heat. Add lemon juice, salt to taste and more pepper, if desired. Bring to serving temperature, stirring often to prevent scorching.

4. To serve, ladle into heated bowls and garnish with lemon slices, cilantro and green onion.

Hint: For a more textured soup, purée only half the amount, leaving half as whole beans.

Analysis per serving: Calories: 254 Protein: 19g Carbohydrate: 39g Fat: 3g Cholesterol: 0 Fiber: 10.4g Sodium: 1287mg

PUMPKIN SOUP WITH GREEN VEGETABLE GARNISH

Serves 4

Preparation: 40 minutes

1	**whole pumpkin or winter squash (about 2 pounds)**
1	**cup lowfat milk**
	White pepper to taste
	Freshly grated nutmeg
1	**tablespoon butter**
	Green Vegetable Garnish (below)
	Finely chopped fresh parsley, for garnish

1. Halve pumpkin, scoop out seeds and stringy fibers. Remove rind and dice flesh. In a saucepan, cook pumpkin in 1 ½ cups water until soft. Remove pumpkin from the liquid, keeping the liquid steaming in the pan. Add extra water to make the quantity up to 2 cups.

2. In a food processor or blender, purée pumpkin pulp and return purée to pan with reserved steaming liquid. Simmer for 4 minutes, stirring often. Add milk and simmer over low heat for 5 minutes, stirring often. Season with white pepper and nutmeg.

3. While pumpkin cooks, prepare Green Vegetable Garnish. When ready to serve, gently reheat soup. Remove from heat and stir in butter. Ladle into individual bowls and top each with Green Vegetable Garnish. Sprinkle with parsley.

GREEN VEGETABLE GARNISH

2	**tablespoons butter**
2	**leeks, white and light green parts, rinsed thoroughly and sliced**
2	**lettuce leaves, cut into thin strips**
2	**tablespoons water**
½	**cup frozen peas, thawed**

1. In a skillet, melt butter until foamy. Add leeks and reduce heat to low. Cover and cook for 3 minutes. Add 2 tablespoons water and cook for 5 minutes longer, stirring occasionally, until tender but not browned. Add lettuce and peas; cook just until lettuce is tender and peas are hot. Taste and adjust seasoning. Set aside.

Analysis per serving: Calories: 204   Protein: 6g   Carbohydrate: 26g   Fat: 10g   Cholesterol: 26mg   Fiber: 2g   Sodium: 130mg

CURRIED SQUASH SOUP

Serves 6-8

Preparation: 20 minutes
Cook: 1 hour 15 minutes

2½-3	pounds butternut squash or banana squash
2	tablespoons butter
½	cup chopped onion
2	cloves garlic, chopped
2	teaspoons chopped cilantro
½	teaspoon hot curry powder or more to taste
¼	teaspoon ground cumin
½	teaspoon cinnamon
½	teaspoon ground ginger
¼	teaspoon dry mustard
	Pinch of cayenne pepper
½-¾	cup freshly squeezed orange juice
1	tablespoon lemon juice
3	cups chicken stock
	Sour cream or plain yogurt, for garnish
	Extra cilantro, for garnish

1. Preheat oven to 375 degrees.

2. Halve squash lengthwise, remove seeds and stringy fibers. Bake, cut side down, on an oiled cookie sheet for 45 minutes, or until soft.

3. Scoop out pulp of squash (there should be about 2 cups) and purée in a food processor or blender. If necessary, strain to remove any stringy fibers.

4. In a large pot, melt butter until foamy. Add onion, garlic, cilantro, curry, cumin, cinnamon, ginger, mustard and cayenne pepper. Mix well and cook until onions are transparent. Add orange juice, squash purée, lemon juice and chicken stock. Stir well and simmer for 30 minutes. Adjust seasoning.

5. To serve, ladle into bowls and top each serving with a spoonful of sour cream or yogurt and a little freshly chopped cilantro.

Analysis per serving: Calories: 143   Protein: 6g   Carbohydrate: 26g   Fat: 3g   Cholesterol: 6mg   Fiber: 3.5g   Sodium: 449mg

HEARTY LENTIL SOUP WITH WINTER SQUASH AND FENNEL

Serves 4

This substantial vegetable soup makes a meal in itself, accompanied by crusty sourdough bread and a green salad.

Preparation: 20-25 minutes
Cook: 1 hour

¼	**cup extra virgin olive oil**
1	**onion, finely diced**
1	**small fennel bulb**
1	**cup lentils**
1	**teaspoon fennel seeds**
5	**cups water or chicken stock, homemade or canned, and defatted**
½	**pound winter squash, butternut or pumpkin, peeled and cut into medium dice**
	Freshly ground black pepper
	Parsley, for garnish

1. In a large soup pot, heat olive oil over medium heat. Add onion and sauté for approximately 10 minutes.

2. Remove and discard stalks of fennel bulb. Finely chop feathery tops; set aside. Cut bulb into medium dice (there should be about 1½ cups). Add diced bulb to onion and sauté for another 5 minutes, stirring occasionally.

3. To onion mixture, add lentils, fennel seeds and water or chicken stock; bring to a boil. Lower heat, partially cover and simmer gently for 30 minutes. Add squash and continue cooking for another 20 minutes or until vegetables are tender. Add chopped fennel tops and cook for a few minutes longer.

4. Just before serving, season with pepper. Ladle into bowls and garnish with chopped parsley. If soup is too thick, thin with some chicken stock.

Analysis per serving: Calories: 383 Protein: 21g Carbohydrate: 41g Fat: 16g Cholesterol: 0 Fiber: 8.7g Sodium: 1010mg

SALADS AND DRESSINGS

SAVORING SAN DIEGO

SAN DIEGO FARMS

by Kitty Morse
Author, *The California Farm Cookbook*; published by Pelican

Few consumers are aware that in 1992 alone, agriculture contributed over 1 billion dollars to the local economy, or that San Diego County ranks third in California in the number of small farms. Thanks to the unique topography, which nurtures a variety of micro-climates, nowhere is this agricultural bounty more apparent than in the North County, where I have lived since 1979.

After a winter rain, I love to travel the lesser-known roads which slice deep into "farm country" towards Fallbrook, Valley Center and Rainbow, feasting my eyes on the velvety green countryside. On the outskirts of my hometown of Vista, extensive orchards of citrus line the roads winding through the canyons. Groves of avocado trees, their limbs bowing under the weight of Bacon, Hass or Fuertes, cling to the rock-strewn hills. In the fall, exotic Fuyu and Hachiya persimmons dot the deep green foliage like bright orange ornaments, and macadamia trees are laden with grape-like bunches of mahogany shells, holding North County's prized crop of macadamia nuts.

I love to shop at local farmstands for juicy Valencia oranges, locally-grown grapefruit, and candy-sweet tangerines. Often, a few varieties of winter squash or vine-ripened heirloom tomatoes will catch my culinary fancy. In late spring, I look forward to the first crop of sweet white corn, picked hourly, from the fields behind one of my favorite farmstands. During berry season, I make daily stops to purchase basketfuls of sun-ripened strawberries or blackberries.

The bounty of the North County is also in the spotlight at the farmers' markets held weekly in Vista, Oceanside and Escondido, among other cities. Every Saturday morning finds me rubbing elbows with the hundreds of eager shoppers who crowd the Vista market, the grand-daddy of farmers' markets in San Diego County. I stroll along, selecting produce from displays piled high with freshly-picked vegetables and fruit, sampling here a slice of honey-tasting melon, there a mouthful of refreshing cherimoya or custard-like sapote. Vendors patiently answer my persistent queries, helping me to distinguish among a rainbow of fiery chiles, or pungent tropical guavas.

I formulate my weekly menus as I browse through the market. A feathery bunch of fresh dill and a cluster of sugary beets serve as the inspiration for a refreshing Russian borscht; a few sprigs of French tarragon will find their way into my French grandmother's tarragon-scented salad dressing. Crisp, finger-sized cucumbers will get pickled the way my husband prefers, in a sweet and sour vinaigrette.

Finally, my market basket overflowing with produce, freshly-laid eggs, and a jar or two of eucalyptus honey, I linger in front of one of the flower stands to contemplate the colorful display. This Saturday, like most others, a kaleidoscopic armload of freshly cut flowers will infuse our home all week long with the spirit of the market.

MENU FOR A BUFFET SALAD LUNCHEON

Green Onion Quiche, page 203

Scallops with Tomato and Corn Salsa, page 135

Brown Rice Salad with Mandarin Oranges, page 69

Warm Chicken and Black Bean Salad with Lime Vinaigrette, page 79

Broccoli and Grape Salad, page 65

Minted Citrus Salad, page 65

Gazpacho Salad with Herb Dressing, page 61

Yogurt Dinner Rolls with Herbs, page 106

Rosemary Bread, page 104

Guiltless Chocolate Cake with Orange Liqueur Frosting, page 229

Apricot-Orange Ice, page 211

SALADS and DRESSINGS

SPINACH AND SALAD GREENS WITH MACADAMIA NUTS

Serves 4-6

Preparation: 15-20 minutes

20-25	baby spinach leaves
¼	pound small, firm mushrooms
	Freshly ground pepper
2	teaspoons lemon juice
½	cup alfalfa sprouts
8-10	lettuce leaves (romaine, cos, red leaf or butter)
	Small head radicchio or about 6 leaves of good size
3	ounces macadamia nuts
	Vinaigrette Piquante (below)

1. Wash spinach, removing stems from each leaf; spin or pat dry, and chill.

2. Remove stalks from mushrooms. Cut caps into thin slices and season with pepper and a little lemon juice. Let stand for about 15 minutes before using.

3. Break lettuce and radicchio into small pieces and chill until crisp.

4. Cut nuts into thin slices. Place in a 350-degree oven and bake until golden, or toast them in a dry frying pan until lightly colored, approximately 8 minutes. Be careful not to scorch.

5. In a large bowl, combine spinach, mushrooms, alfalfa and lettuce and toss with 3-4 tablespoons of vinaigrette. Scatter nuts over the top. Serve at once.

VINAIGRETTE PIQUANTE

Makes ½ cup

4	tablespoons extra virgin olive oil
1	tablespoon Worcestershire sauce
1	tablespoon white wine vinegar
	Freshly ground black pepper

1. Whisk together oil, Worcestershire sauce and vinegar, or place in a jar with a tight-fitting lid and shake vigorously. Add pepper to taste.

Analysis per serving: Calories: 200 Protein: 3g Carbohydrate: 5g Fat: 20g Cholesterol: 0 Fiber: 2.4g Sodium: 25mg

ROMAINE SALAD WITH RED CHILI DRESSING AND HERBED CROUTONS

Serves 4

Preparation: 20 minutes

½	**cup Herbed Croutons (below)**
½	**cup Red Chili Dressing (below)**
1	**head romaine lettuce**
½	**cup freshly grated Parmesan cheese**

1. Prepare croutons and dressing; set aside.

2. Wash lettuce thoroughly, spin or pat dry, and break into pieces. In large bowl, toss lettuce with ⅓-½ cup Red Chili Dressing.

3. Arrange on individual salad plates; divide croutons among the dishes and sprinkle Parmesan cheese on top.

HERBED CROUTONS

1½-2	**tablespoons olive oil**
1½	**teaspoons dried herbs, such as oregano, tarragon or basil**
	Pepper to taste
	Garlic salt (optional)
	Day-old sourdough or French bread, crusts removed, cut into ½-inch cubes (about 1 cup)

1. Preheat oven to 375 degrees.

2. Place oil, herbs and seasoning in a shallow bowl. Add bread cubes and toss to coat.

3. Bake for approximately 10 minutes or until they are crispy and brown. Cool.

RED CHILI DRESSING

Makes 2 cups

2	**cloves garlic, cut into pieces**
3	**anchovy fillets, cut up**
2	**tablespoons Worcestershire sauce**
2	**tablespoons Dijon mustard**
1	**tablespoon red chili powder (mild or hot according to taste)**
1	**teaspoon paprika**
2	**tablespoons lemon juice, freshly squeezed**
2	**tablespoons cider vinegar**
1	**cup olive oil**

1. In a food processor or blender, combine all ingredients except olive oil. With the machine running, slowly drip in oil. Store extra dressing for later use.

Adapted, with permission, from *Santa Fe Lite and Spicy Recipes* by Joan Stromquist; Copyright © 1992; Tierra Publications.

Analysis per serving: Calories: 157 Protein: 6g Carbohydrate: 5g Fat: 13g Cholesterol: 9mg Fiber: 1g Sodium: 239mg

SALADS and DRESSINGS

WATERCRESS AND BELGIAN ENDIVE SALAD

Serves 6

Preparation: 20 minutes

2	bunches watercress
2	medium-sized Belgian endives
½	cup shredded Gruyère cheese
6	tablespoons slivered almonds, toasted and coarsely chopped
3	tablespoons walnut oil or other good quality oil
2	tablespoons lemon juice
	Salt and freshly ground pepper to taste

1. Remove stems from watercress. Separate endive leaves. Wash and dry greens.

2. Cut endives across in ½-inch lengths and place in a salad bowl together with the watercress. Sprinkle with cheese and nuts.

3. Place oil, lemon juice and pepper in a small jar with a tight-fitting lid. Shake vigorously for 10-20 seconds until well combined. Pour immediately over salad; toss lightly and serve.

Analysis per serving: Calories: 159 Protein: 6g Carbohydrate: 7g Fat: 13g Cholesterol: 8mg Fiber: 4g Sodium: 63mg

CUCUMBER, MINT AND CHIVE SALAD

Serves 4

Preparation: 15 minutes
Standing time: 30 minutes
Chill: 1 hour

1	hothouse cucumber, peeled and thinly sliced
¼	teaspoon salt (preferably coarse)
1	teaspoon sugar
1	teaspoon tarragon vinegar
½	cup nonfat plain yogurt
	Freshly ground black pepper, to taste
3	tablespoons chopped chives, divided
2	tablespoons olive oil
2	tablespoons chopped mint

1. Sprinkle cucumber with salt and drain in a colander for half an hour. Rinse off excess salt, pat dry, and place in a shallow dish.

2. In a medium-sized bowl, mix sugar and vinegar together, stir in yogurt, and season with pepper. Add olive oil and 2 tablespoons chopped chives. Pour dressing over cucumber and mix well. Refrigerate for at least 1 hour before serving.

3. To serve, garnish with mint and remaining chives.

Analysis per serving: Calories: 100 Protein: 2.5g Carbohydrate: 8g Fat: 7g Cholesterol: 0 Fiber: 1.6g Sodium: 144mg

JÍCAMA SLAW WITH PEANUT DRESSING

Serves 6

The jícama gives this "slaw" a different twist in this crunchy and refreshing salad. It was created by chef Neil Stuart, formerly of the Pacifica Grill Restaurant.

Preparation: 15-20 minutes
Chill: 1 hour

5	cups peeled, shredded jícama (about 2 medium jícama)
1	large red bell pepper, julienne sliced
½	cup chopped cilantro
¾	cup golden raisins
¾	cup dry roasted peanuts
1	cup Peanut Dressing (below)

1. In a large salad bowl, combine the vegetables, raisins and nuts, mixing well. Toss with Peanut Dressing, and chill for 1 hour before serving.

PEANUT DRESSING

½	cup light mayonnaise
1½	tablespoons white wine vinegar
¾	tablespoon dry mustard
3	tablespoons sugar
2	tablespoons minced red onion
⅛	teaspoon white pepper
¼	cup creamy peanut butter

1. In a medium-sized bowl, combine all ingredients and blend well. Refrigerate until ready to use.

Analysis per serving: Calories: 352   Protein: 9g   Carbohydrate: 42g   Fat: 19g   Cholesterol: 5mg   Fiber: 4.4g   Sodium: 208mg

SALADS and DRESSINGS

FIESTA SALAD WITH CUMIN DRESSING

Serves 6

Preparation: 20-30 minutes
Chill: 1-2 hours

	Enough mixed, crisp greens for 6, in bite-sized pieces
2	cups jícama, peeled and julienne sliced
1	medium red onion, thinly sliced
1	grapefruit, peeled and cut into sections, membranes removed
2	oranges, peeled and cut into sections, membranes removed
½	pound cherry tomatoes, cut in half
1	large avocado
	Cumin Dressing (below)

1. In a large serving bowl, mix greens and jícama. Arrange onion rings on top of greens. Arrange sections of both fruits and the tomatoes on top of onions. Cover and chill for 1-2 hours.

2. To serve, arrange slices of avocado on top of chilled salad. Pour just enough dressing to moisten salad very lightly and toss gently to mix.

CUMIN DRESSING

Makes about ¾ cup

2	tablespoons cider, rice or wine vinegar
2	tablespoons fresh lime juice
½	cup olive oil
1	clove garlic
1	teaspoon freshly ground black pepper, or to taste
½	teaspoon salt
½	teaspoon ground cumin
⅛	teaspoon crushed hot red pepper flakes (optional)

1. Put all ingredients in a blender and process at top speed until smooth and blended.

2. Pour dressing into a small jar with a tight-fitting lid. Let stand at room temperature, or in refrigerator, until time to dress salad. If dressing is chilled, bring to room temperature and shake well before using. Any unused dressing may be kept in the refrigerator for at least one week.

Note: To reduce fat, omit avocado, or use only 1 slice per serving.

Analysis per serving: Calories: 196 Protein: 3g Carbohydrate: 25g Fat: 14g Cholesterol: 0 Fiber: 3.9g Sodium: 99mg

GAZPACHO SALAD WITH HERB DRESSING

Serves 5

Packed with taste and nutrition, this recipe comes from *The UCSD Healthy Diet for Diabetes* - a book full of great recipes, whether you need to watch your diet or not.

Preparation: 30 minutes
Chill: 2 hours

1	large tomato, chopped
1/2	medium cucumber, chopped
1/2	medium green bell pepper, seeded and chopped
1	stalk celery, finely chopped
1/4	cup chopped onion
1/3	cup peeled and chopped jícama
2	tablespoons chopped fresh parsley or fresh cilantro
	Herb Dressing (recipe below)
	Lettuce leaves
	Parsley or cilantro, for garnish

1. Combine all salad ingredients in a shallow dish.

2. Pour dressing over the vegetables; toss gently. Chill for at least 2 hours.

3. Arrange lettuce leaves on a serving platter. Spoon salad over leaves and garnish with parsley or cilantro.

HERB DRESSING

3	tablespoons red wine vinegar
2	tablespoons freshly squeezed lemon juice
1	tablespoon olive oil
1	teaspoon Dijon-style mustard
1/2	teaspoon dried oregano
1	large clove garlic, finely minced

1. Combine vinegar, lemon juice, oil, mustard, oregano and garlic in a small bowl and mix or whisk until thoroughly blended.

Adapted, with permission, from *The UCSD Healthy Diet for Diabetes*, by Susan Algert, Barbara Grasse, Annie Durning; Copyright © 1990; Houghton Mifflin Co.

Analysis per serving: Calories: 50   Protein: 1g   Carbohydrate: 6g   Fat: 3g   Cholesterol: 0   Fiber: 1.3g   Sodium: 38mg

GRILLED EGGPLANT AND SPINACH SALAD

Serves 4

Cindy Black, who contributed this recipe, has extensive international credentials in classical cuisine. She is owner and chef of Cindy Black's Restaurant in La Jolla, where this recipe is a favorite.

Preparation: 35 minutes
Grill: 15 minutes

HOISIN MARINADE DRESSING

Makes 1¾ cups

¼	**cup hoisin sauce**
2	**tablespoons water**
2	**tablespoons rice wine vinegar**
2	**tablespoons light soy sauce**
1	**teaspoon minced garlic**
1	**teaspoon minced fresh ginger**
	Dash of hot red pepper flakes
¼	**teaspoon cracked black pepper**
½	**cup olive oil**
¼	**cup sesame oil**

SALAD

2	**Japanese eggplants, washed and sliced on the diagonal**
6½	**cups spinach leaves, washed and trimmed**
1	**cup radicchio leaves**
12	**asparagus spears, peeled**
3	**tablespoons chopped cilantro, for garnish (optional)**
3	**tablespoons chopped tomato, for garnish (optional)**

1. In a medium-sized bowl, combine hoisin sauce, water, vinegar, soy sauce, garlic, ginger, hot red pepper flakes and black pepper. Slowly whisk in olive and sesame oils.

2. In a shallow bowl, marinate eggplant in ¾ cup of the Hoisin Marinade Dressing for 30 minutes.

3. Meanwhile steam asparagus until just tender, plunge briefly into iced water to stop further cooking. Drain well and pat dry on paper towels. Set aside in refrigerator.

4. Grill or broil eggplant over medium heat until tender. Brush with dressing as you grill, reserving approximately ¾ cup for tossing salad.

5. Toss spinach and radicchio in reserved dressing.

6. To serve, mound tossed salad on large salad plates. Top with grilled eggplant and asparagus. Garnish with cilantro and chopped tomato. Serve immediately.

Analysis per serving: Calories: 436   Protein: 5g   Carbohydrate: 16g   Fat: 42g   Cholesterol: 0   Fiber: 7g   Sodium: 497mg

SWEET RED PEPPER AND FRESH FENNEL SALAD

Serves 6

Preparation: 45 minutes

3	red bell peppers, julienne sliced
3	medium fennel bulbs, julienne sliced
½	cup red onion, julienne sliced
20	Kalamata olives, pitted and chopped to make ½ cup
3-4	tablespoons chopped chives
½	cup pine nuts
6	tablespoons light olive oil
1	tablespoon red wine vinegar
2	tablespoons balsamic vinegar
1	tablespoon Dijon-style mustard
½	teaspoon sugar
	Salt and freshly ground pepper to taste
	Butter lettuce or other mild lettuce leaves
	Chopped flat-leaf parsley, for garnish

1. In a large bowl, combine julienned vegetables, olives and chives. Toss to mix and place salad in refrigerator to keep crisp.

2. Toast pine nuts by placing them in a small dry skillet over medium heat. Stir constantly until toasted to a light brown, approximately 4-5 minutes. (Alternatively, cover a baking sheet with aluminum foil, spread nuts in a single layer and bake at 350 degrees until lightly browned. Stir once or twice, and watch carefully to avoid burning.)

3. In a jar with a tight-fitting lid, place oil, both vinegars, mustard, sugar, salt and pepper. Shake vigorously until well combined. Pour half of the dressing over the salad and toss well. Taste and add more dressing, if desired. Add pine nuts and toss lightly.

4. To serve, line individual plates with lettuce leaves. Spoon salad on top and garnish with chopped parsley.

Note: The term "julienne" can apply to any food which is finely shredded or cut into very thin matchstick-sized strips. To julienne vegetables, first remove unwanted stems, seeds, veins or skins, then slice trimmed vegetables into slivers or matchsticks. In the case of onions, cut into thin rings and cut into thin (curved) strips. The process takes a little more time, but makes for a very elegant presentation.

Analysis per serving: Calories: 186 Protein: 3.5g Carbohydrate: 16g Fat: 14g Cholesterol: 0 Fiber: 6g Sodium: 229mg

CHILLED SPAGHETTI SQUASH SALAD WITH MINT VINAIGRETTE

Serves 6-8

Preparation: 10 minutes
Cook: 6-7 minutes (microwave) or 40 minutes (oven)
Chill: 1 hour

1	**2-pound spaghetti squash**
3	**tablespoons chopped cilantro**
2	**green onions, thinly sliced**
1	**carrot, peeled and chopped**
2	**stalks celery, stringed and chopped**
	Mint Vinaigrette (below)
1	**tomato, chopped, for garnish**
	Sprigs of cilantro, for garnish

1. Stab squash in 3-4 places with a sharp knife. Microwave on High for 6-7 minutes, or bake in a 350-degree oven for approximately 35-40 minutes.

2. Cut squash in half and remove seeds. Scrape inside with a fork to remove spaghetti-like strands. Place in a bowl with cilantro, green onions, carrot, celery, and mix well. Pour vinaigrette over squash, toss and chill.

3. To serve, mound squash salad on lettuce-lined plates and garnish with chopped tomatoes and cilantro sprigs.

MINT VINAIGRETTE

3	**tablespoons extra virgin olive oil**
1	**tablespoon red wine vinegar**
2	**tablespoons chopped fresh mint**
	Salt and freshly ground black pepper to taste

1. In a jar with a tight-fitting lid, combine vinaigrette ingredients and shake vigorously.

Analysis per serving: Calories: 94   Protein: 1g   Carbohydrate: 11g   Fat: 6g   Cholesterol: 0   Fiber: 3.4g   Sodium: 15mg

BROCCOLI AND GRAPE SALAD

Serves 8-10

These ingredients sound like an unlikely combination, but the refreshing taste and contrasting texture will surprise and delight. The recipe can be made ahead and is a great choice for buffets or picnics.

Preparation: 30 minutes

4	cups small broccoli florets
1	cup green seedless grapes, halved
1	cup red seedless grapes, halved
1	cup chopped celery
½	cup dried currants or raisins
2-3	green onions, sliced
6	slices crisp cooked bacon (optional)
1	cup lowfat or fat-free mayonnaise
¼	cup powdered sugar
1	teaspoon rice vinegar
½	cup slivered almonds

1. In a large serving bowl, mix broccoli, grapes, celery, currants, onions and bacon.

2. In a small bowl, or a jar with a tight-fitting lid, blend mayonnaise, sugar and rice vinegar. Pour over salad and toss gently and thoroughly.

3. Toast almonds in oven until golden; cool. Before serving, sprinkle over salad.

Analysis per serving: Calories: 130 Protein: 4g Carbohydrate: 20g Fat: 5g Cholesterol: 32mg Fiber: 3g Sodium: 387mg

MINTED CITRUS SALAD

Serves 6

Preparation: 20 minutes
Standing time: 2 hours

4	medium navel oranges (use blood oranges if available)
2	medium, very ripe lemons
1	small red onion, peeled and thinly sliced
	Freshly ground black pepper
6	leaves fresh mint, finely chopped (or a combination of fresh basil and mint)
2	tablespoons extra virgin olive oil

1. Using a small sharp knife, peel oranges and lemons, so that all peel and pith are removed completely. Work over a bowl to catch and reserve all juices.

2. Slice oranges horizontally, about ¼-inch thick. Slice lemons about ⅛-inch thick, again reserving all juices. Remove and discard seeds.

3. Place oranges on a shallow platter; arrange lemons attractively over them. Pour collected juices over fruit. Arrange sliced onion on top. Grind fresh pepper over all. Sprinkle evenly with chopped mint; then drizzle entire surface with olive oil. Let platter stand for about 2 hours at room temperature to blend flavors before serving.

Analysis per serving: Calories: 96 Protein: 1g Carbohydrate: 14g Fat: 5g Cholesterol: 0 Fiber: 2.7g Sodium: 1mg

WATERMELON AND RED ONION SALAD WITH MINT

Serves 4

This unusual blend of sweet and savory is both colorful and surprisingly good. It can be expanded easily, and makes a good buffet dish or accompaniment to a barbecue.

Preparation: 15 minutes

4	**cups cubed watermelon, preferably seedless or seeded, rind removed**
½	**red onion, thinly sliced, then coarsely chopped**
1	**tablespoon chopped mint**

1. Place watermelon in a bowl and keep chilled.

2. Just before serving, add onion and enough mint to give a good sprinkling of green, and gently toss together.

Analysis per serving: Calories: 63 Protein: 1g Carbohydrate: 14g Fat: 0.7g Cholesterol: 0 Fiber: 1.2g Sodium: 4mg

PEAR AND GORGONZOLA SALAD

Serves 4

Preparation: 15 minutes

1	**head of red leaf lettuce, washed, dried and torn into bite-sized pieces**
¾	**cup chopped walnuts, toasted**
¼	**cup golden raisins**
¾	**cup chopped or crumbled Gorgonzola cheese**
1	**Fresh pear, cored and diced (preferable Bosc pears, but any fresh pear will do)**
	Balsamic Vinaigrette with Herbs (below)

1. Combine all ingredients in a large bowl. Toss with Balsamic Vinaigrette with Herbs. Arrange on individual plates and serve immediately.

Continued on next page

BALSAMIC VINAIGRETTE WITH HERBS

4	tablespoons extra virgin olive oil
2	tablespoons balsamic vinegar
½	teaspoon herbes de Provence
	Freshly ground black pepper to taste

1. Place oil, vinegar and herbs in a jar with a tight-fitting lid; shake until well blended.

Note: Herbes de Provence consists of a combination of dried marjoram, basil, thyme, rosemary, savory and tarragon, which are grown and used extensively in the Provence region of southern France. It may be found in most supermarket spice sections or in specialty stores.

Analysis per serving: Calories: 417 Protein: 12g Carbohydrate: 20g Fat: 34g Cholesterol: 19mg Fiber: 12g Sodium: 359mg

AVOCADO AND PAPAYA SALAD WITH MANGO DRESSING

Serves 8

Preparation: 20 minutes

1	large head of leafy lettuce (such as red leaf), washed and dried
2	large ripe avocados, peeled, quartered and thinly sliced
2	large ripe papayas, peeled, quartered and thinly sliced
1	small red onion, thinly sliced and separated into rings
	Mango Dressing (below)
8	sprigs of mint, for garnish

1. Arrange lettuce on plates. Alternate avocado and papaya slices. Top with onions; chill.
2. Just before serving, drizzle 1 tablespoon Mango Dressing over salad; garnish with mint.

MANGO DRESSING

1	very ripe mango, juice and softened pulp
2	tablespoons dry vermouth
2	tablespoons chopped fresh mint
	Freshly ground pepper to taste
¾	cup light olive oil

1. Squeeze mango in your hand to soften. Cut off one end and squeeze mango over a small bowl to extract juice. Add the vermouth, mint and pepper.
2. Whisk in olive oil until smooth and well blended.

Note: Avocados are harvested year-round, as different varieties reach maturity. Fuerte (harvested November to April) and Reed (June through August) are both excellent. Mango or oranges slices may be substituted for papaya.

Analysis per serving: Calories: 108   Protein: 2g   Carbohydrate: 10g   Fat: 8g   Cholesterol: 0   Fiber: 2.6g   Sodium: 10mg

WHITE BEAN AND TOMATO SALAD

Serves 10-12

For quicker preparation, you may use canned white beans, eliminating Step 1 and reducing the cooking time in Step 3.

Preparation: 20 minutes
Cook: 2 hours
Chill: 3 hours

2	**cups dried white beans**
1/3	**cup plus 1 tablespoon extra virgin olive oil**
2	**large red onions, halved and finely sliced**
8	**large cloves garlic, thinly sliced**
2	**carrots, quartered lengthwise, then cut into 1/8-inch slices**
3	**ripe tomatoes, peeled, seeded and mashed**
1/4	**teaspoon freshly ground black pepper**
2	**teaspoons paprika**
1	**lemon wedge**
2	**tablespoons sugar**
1	**tablespoon minced fresh rosemary**
1	**cup chopped parsley**
1/4	**teaspoon salt**
1	**tablespoon extra virgin olive oil**
1	**tablespoon balsamic vinegar**
	Chopped parsley, for garnish
	Lemon wedges, for garnish

1. Place beans in a large pot, with enough water to cover by at least 3 inches. Soak overnight. Drain water and cover again with cold water. Bring to a boil; cover and simmer for 20 minutes. Drain.

2. In a large heavy pan, heat 1/3 cup olive oil. Sauté onions, garlic and carrots for 20 minutes, stirring frequently. Add tomatoes, stir and cook for another 3 minutes. Add 2 cups hot water, pepper, paprika, lemon wedge and sugar; bring to a boil.

3. Add beans, cover and simmer for 1 1/2 hours or until beans are tender. Add small amounts of water, as needed, to maintain water level. Add rosemary and parsley and simmer for an additional 10 minutes. Remove from heat, drain, cool and chill for several hours. Taste for seasonings; add salt if necessary.

4. To serve, spoon into a large serving dish; drizzle remaining 1 tablespoon of olive oil and balsamic vinegar over beans; sprinkle with parsley and garnish with lemon wedges.

Hint: Do not salt beans while they soak or cook, as it tends to toughen them.

Analysis per serving: Calories: 352   Protein: 14g   Carbohydrate: 47g   Fat: 14g   Cholesterol: 0   Fiber: 3g   Sodium: 117mg

BROWN RICE SALAD WITH MANDARIN ORANGES

Serves 6

This is a good recipe for a buffet luncheon and may be prepared ahead. Fresh oranges may be used instead of canned mandarin oranges, but the taste of mandarin oranges is very good in this dish. Canned lychees may also be substituted for the oranges with equally good results.

Preparation: 10 minutes
Cook: 45 minutes
Chill: 2 hours

2½	cups chicken stock
1	cup brown rice, washed and drained
3	tablespoons fresh lemon juice
2	tablespoons olive oil
1	cup finely chopped celery, strings removed
3	tablespoons minced green onions
3	tablespoons chopped fresh parsley
¼	cup sour cream
2	teaspoons Dijon mustard
¼	teaspoon pepper, or to taste
½	cup coarsely chopped pecans
1	11-ounce can mandarin oranges (or 2 fresh oranges, peeled, pith removed and segmented)
	Boston or romaine lettuce
	A few reserved mandarin orange segments or fresh orange slices, for garnish
¼	cup pecan halves, for garnish

1. In a heavy, medium-sized saucepan, bring stock to a boil. Add rice, cover and reduce heat to low. Simmer until liquid is absorbed, approximately 45 minutes.

2. In a large bowl, combine rice with lemon juice and olive oil, tossing well. Add celery, green onion, parsley, sour cream, mustard and pepper to taste; toss well. Stir in chopped pecans and mandarin oranges, reserving a few segments for garnish. (If using fresh oranges, halve segments and remove seeds.) Cover with plastic wrap and refrigerate for at least 2 hours.

3. About 15 minutes before serving, remove salad from refrigerator. Arrange washed lettuce leaves on large platter. Mound rice onto lettuce and garnish with reserved mandarin segments (or fresh orange slices) and pecan halves.

Analysis per serving: Calories: 270 Protein: 6g Carbohydrate: 31g Fat: 14g Cholesterol: 4mg Fiber: 3g Sodium: 391mg

SALADS and DRESSINGS

KASHA SALAD WITH FRUIT AND NUTS

10 (½-cup) servings

This high-fiber salad makes a good buffet dish. The kasha and fruit flavors complement each other nicely.

Preparation: 20-25 minutes
Chill 1-2 hours

1	cup whole kasha or bulgur
1½	cups chicken broth
	Orange Vinaigrette (below)
¾	cup chopped dried apricots
1	medium-sized red apple, cored and diced
2	tablespoons slivered almonds, toasted
¼	cup raisins
	Chopped parsley or chives, for garnish
	Butter lettuce leaves, rinsed and crisped

1. Combine kasha and chicken broth in a 2- to 3-quart pan. Bring to a boil, cover and cook over low heat, without stirring, until kasha is tender and liquid is absorbed, about 10-15 minutes. Remove lid and let cool without stirring. Transfer to a salad bowl.

2. Add Orange Vinaigrette, apricots, apple, almonds and raisins; mix gently. Chill well.

3. To serve, spoon salad onto lettuce-lined plates or a serving platter.

ORANGE VINAIGRETTE

1	teaspoon grated orange zest
½	cup orange juice
2	tablespoons olive oil
2	tablespoons water
1	tablespoon cider or balsamic vinegar
1	teaspoon honey

1. In a small bowl, whisk together all ingredients, and set aside.

Analysis per serving: Calories: 146 Protein: 4g Carbohydrate: 26g Fat: 4g Cholesterol: 0 Fiber: 3.3g Sodium: 118mg

SALAD OF NEW POTATOES, ARUGULA AND MINT

Serves 8

This recipe offers a fresh way with an old favorite.

Preparation: 15 minutes
Cook: 10-15 minutes

2	pounds small-to-medium new potatoes, washed and quartered, skin on
3	ounces arugula, stems trimmed
1	ounce fresh mint leaves
	Balsamic Vinaigrette Dijonnaise (below)

1. Steam potatoes until very slightly crunchy, approximately 10 minutes. Be careful not to over-cook. Cool, but do not chill. Potatoes should be warm or at room temperature.

2. Just before serving, toss potatoes, arugula and mint in enough Balsamic Vinaigrette to coat potatoes and greens. Serve immediately.

BALSAMIC VINAIGRETTE DIJONNAISE

¼	cup red or white wine vinegar
2	tablespoons balsamic vinegar
2	tablespoons Dijon mustard
½	cup extra virgin olive oil
	Freshly ground black pepper to taste

1. Measure vinegars into a small bowl. Beat mustard into vinegar with a fork or whisk. Add olive oil slowly, beating until smooth. Season to taste with pepper. Refrigerate extra dressing for other use.

Analysis per serving: Calories: 233 Protein: 2.5g Carbohydrate: 26g Fat: 14g Cholesterol: 0 Fiber: 1.9g Sodium: 58mg

ROASTED NEW POTATO SALAD WITH ROSEMARY AND SHALLOTS

Serves 4-6

Preparation: 10-15 minutes
Bake: 40 minutes
Cool: 45 minutes

3	medium shallots
1	tablespoon fresh rosemary leaves
2	teaspoons fresh thyme leaves
1/4	teaspoon black pepper
1/8	teaspoon cayenne pepper
1/3	cup extra virgin olive oil
1/4	cup firmly packed fresh parsley leaves
3	pounds small new potatoes, well scrubbed
1 1/2	tablespoons lemon juice
	Chopped parsley, for garnish

1. Preheat oven to 425 degrees. Adjust oven rack to lowest position.

2. In a food processor, with motor running, drop in shallots and process until minced. Add rosemary, thyme, black and cayenne peppers and pulse until minced. Add olive oil and mix. Lastly add parsley and pulse to mince.

3. Quarter potatoes and pat dry with paper towels.

4. Pour herbed oil mixture into a 13x10-inch shallow baking pan. Add potatoes and turn to coat all sides completely with oil mixture. Roast 35-40 minutes, turning potatoes twice, until evenly browned and soft when pierced with a knife.

5. Remove and cool to room temperature. Taste and adjust seasoning. Sprinkle lemon juice over potatoes, toss gently and thoroughly. Garnish with chopped parsley and serve.

Analysis per serving: Calories: 308   Protein: 4g   Carbohydrate: 47g   Fat: 12g   Cholesterol: 0   Fiber: 3.5g   Sodium: 10mg

GRILLED SCALLOP SALAD WITH LIME CILANTRO DRESSING

Serves 4

Preparation: 15 minutes
Marinate: 1 hour
Grill: 5 minutes

1	cup orange juice, freshly squeezed
4	tablespoons chopped fresh basil
1¼-1½	pounds fresh sea scallops, rinsed
4-6	cups mixed salad greens
	Lime Cilantro Dressing (below)
3	Roma tomatoes, thinly sliced
16-20	thin slices hothouse cucumber
4	sprigs of cilantro, for garnish

1. Combine orange juice and basil in a medium-sized bowl. Add scallops and marinate for at least 1 hour at room temperature.

2. Grill scallops on a hot grill for 2 minutes each side.

3. In a large bowl, toss greens with Lime Cilantro Dressing.

4. To serve, place dressed greens on four salad plates. Attractively arrange grilled scallops, tomatoes and cucumber on greens. Garnish with sprigs of cilantro.

LIME CILANTRO DRESSING

2	tablespoons freshly squeezed lime juice
½	tablespoon minced cilantro
1	serrano chile, seeded and minced
1	large clove garlic, minced
1	shallot, minced
1	tablespoon chili paste (found in Asian markets)
2	tablespoons rice vinegar
½	cup vegetable oil
¼	cup sugar

1. Combine all ingredients in a jar with a tight-fitting lid; shake vigorously.

Adapted, with permission, from *Santa Fe Lite and Spicy*, by Joan Stromquist; Copyright © 1992; Tierra Publications.

Analysis per serving: Calories: 524 Protein: 35g Carbohydrate: 32g Fat: 30g Cholesterol: 47mg Fiber: 3g Sodium: 564mg

MARINATED SHRIMP AND CORN SALAD

Serves 8

This unusual salad, perfect for a buffet, combines marinated shrimp with an attractive corn and bell pepper salad. For a picnic, prepare and store each salad separately, and combine on a platter just before serving.

Preparation: 30 minutes (may be prepared a day ahead)

MARINATED SHRIMP WITH CHIVES

1	tablespoon Dijon-style mustard
3	tablespoons fresh lemon juice
3	tablespoons chopped fresh chives
	Salt and freshly ground pepper to taste (optional)
½	cup olive oil
1	pound raw shrimp, shelled and deveined

1. In a medium-sized bowl, whisk together the mustard, lemon juice and chives. Add the oil in a thin stream, whisking constantly until mixture is emulsified.

2. In a large saucepan of boiling water, cook shrimp for 1 minute or until pink; drain.

3. Add shrimp to dressing and toss to coat well. Cover and chill for 1-24 hours, stirring occasionally.

CORN AND BELL PEPPER SALAD

2	tablespoons olive oil
2	cups fresh corn cut from the cob (or 2 cups frozen corn)
½	cup diced green bell pepper
1	large clove garlic, minced
¼	teaspoon ground cumin
	Salt and pepper to taste (optional)
2	green onions, thinly sliced
1	teaspoon fresh lemon juice, or more to taste

1. In a large skillet, heat oil and add corn, bell pepper, garlic, cumin, salt and pepper. Cook over medium heat for 3 minutes. Stir in green onions and cook for 1 minute, then stir in lemon juice and remove from heat.

2. Transfer salad to a bowl and cool to room temperature. May be refrigerated for 1 day. Bring to room temperature before serving.

FINAL ASSEMBLY

1	pound tomatoes, seeded and chopped
¼	teaspoon sugar
1	tablespoon olive oil
	Salt and pepper to taste
2	avocados
2	tablespoons lemon juice
	Sprigs of parsley, for garnish

Continued on next page

1. In a bowl, toss tomatoes with sugar, olive oil, salt and pepper; set aside for 20 minutes.

2. Meanwhile, peel avocados and halve lengthwise. Thinly slice each half crosswise and fan them attractively on a serving platter. Sprinkle with lemon juice.

3. Remove shrimp from dressing with a slotted spoon and arrange in the center of the platter. Reserve chive dressing.

4. Arrange corn-pepper salad and tomato mixture decoratively on the platter; garnish with parsley sprigs and pass chive dressing separately.

Adapted, with permission, from *Gourmet*. Copyright © 1988 by the Conde Nast Publications, Inc.

Analysis per serving: Calories: 277 Protein: 13g Carbohydrate: 13g Fat: 20g Cholesterol: 87mg Fiber: 2g Sodium: 117mg

CHICKEN COUSCOUS SALAD

Serves 6

Preparation: 30-40 minutes
Cook: 15 minutes

⅔	cup chicken broth
½	cup orange juice
	Grated zest of 1 orange
⅓	cup raisins
½	teaspoon ground cumin
¾	cup couscous
4	cups cubed, cooked chicken
3	large green onions, thinly sliced
2	stalks celery, stringed and thinly sliced
½	medium red bell pepper, minced
1	small pickling cucumber, peeled and minced
1	tablespoon safflower oil
2	tablespoons balsamic vinegar
	Cayenne pepper
	Romaine lettuce leaves, shredded
	Chopped mint, for garnish

1. In a large saucepan, combine broth, orange juice, zest, raisins and cumin; bring to a boil. Remove from heat. Add couscous and stir. Cover and set aside until liquid is absorbed, approximately 10 minutes.

2. Place mixture in a large bowl. Add chicken, green onion, bell pepper, celery and cucumber. Mix oil and vinegar in a small bowl and pour over couscous mixture. Stir lightly with a fork. Season with cayenne pepper.

3. To serve; line individual plates with lettuce and spoon couscous mixture on top. Garnish with chopped mint.

Analysis per serving: Calories: 310 Protein: 33g Carbohydrate: 29g Fat: 6g Cholesterol: 73mg Fiber: 2g Sodium: 168mg

ASIAN-FLAVORED CHICKEN SALAD

Serves 4-6

This is a delicious do-ahead recipe that can be quickly assembled at the last minute. Szechwan peppercorns may be found in Asian or specialty food stores. They are not very hot or spicy, but have an unusual and interesting flavor, especially when lightly toasted.

Preparation: 20 minutes (not including time to cook and chill chicken)

4	**tablespoons soy sauce**
2	**tablespoons honey**
1-2	**large cloves garlic**
½	**teaspoon salt**
1	**teaspoon Szechwan peppercorns (do not substitute regular black peppercorns)**
4-5	**large slices fresh ginger, peeled and finely minced**
2-3	**green onions, minced**
½-1	**teaspoon crushed hot red pepper flakes**
3	**tablespoons canola oil**
1	**head romaine or head lettuce**
1	**3-pound chicken, cooked, boned, skinned and cut into bite-sized pieces**
	Nasturtium flowers or julienne-sliced red bell pepper, for garnish

1. In a medium-sized bowl, combine soy, honey, garlic and salt. Cover and set aside.

2. In a dry hot skillet, toast Szechwan peppercorns until they give off their aroma; crush slightly. In a small pan, combine peppercorns with ginger, green onions, red pepper flakes and oil. Cover and set aside.

3. Shortly before serving, cut lettuce into ½-inch strips and arrange on a large platter. Scatter chicken pieces over lettuce.

4. Heat peppercorn-ginger mixture over medium-low heat, and allow to bubble gently for approximately 1 minute. Pour immediately into honey-soy mixture and mix well. Pour over prepared chicken platter. Garnish salad with nasturtium flowers or julienne red bell peppers and serve.

Analysis per serving: Calories: 252 Protein: 25g Carbohydrate: 11g   Fat: 12g   Cholesterol: 66mg Fiber: 1g Sodium: 741mg

VIETNAMESE CHICKEN SALAD

Serves 6

Preparation: 30-45 minutes

2	**pounds boneless chicken breast (turkey breast may be substituted)**
1	**bunch green onions**
1	**tablespoon minced fresh ginger**
1½	**teaspoons salt, divided**
1	**teaspoon pepper, divided**
⅔	**cup salad oil**
⅔	**cup lemon juice**
2	**teaspoons sugar**
1	**cabbage, approximately 1½ -2 pounds**
2	**tablespoons coarsely chopped fresh mint**
2	**tablespoons coarsely chopped fresh basil**
	Fresh cilantro leaves, for garnish

1. Thinly slice chicken, then cut into matchstick-sized strips. Cut the green tops of the onions into 2-inch lengths, then cut each piece lengthwise into thin strips; set aside.

2. Finely chop white part of onions and combine with chicken, ginger, 1 teaspoon of the salt, and ½ teaspoon of the pepper in a large bowl.

3. Heat a wok or skillet over high heat; add 1 tablespoon of the oil. Divide chicken mixture into 4 batches and cook one batch at a time. When oil is hot add first batch. Cook, stirring constantly, until chicken is no longer pink, about 2 minutes. Remove from pan. Add more oil to pan if needed, and cook remaining 3 batches of chicken. Cool, cover, and chill.

4. In a small bowl, stir together lemon juice, sugar, remaining salad oil, and remaining ½ teaspoon salt and pepper.

5. Finely shred cabbage with a knife. Just before serving, mix cabbage, chilled chicken mixture, green onion strips, mint, basil and dressing. Garnish with cilantro leaves and serve at once.

Note: After about 10 minutes, cabbage begins to wilt and loose its crunchiness; some people prefer it like this.

Analysis per serving: Calories: 390 Protein: 34g Carbohydrate: 5g Fat: 26g Cholesterol: 83mg Fiber: 1g Sodium: 980mg

SALADS and DRESSINGS

GRILLED CHICKEN SALAD WITH CITRUS SALSA

Serves 4

Using tomatillos and citrus adds a unique accent in this colorful main-course salad.

Preparation: 25 minutes
Marinate: 30 minutes
Grill: 10 minutes

	Citrus Salsa (below)
¼	**cup fresh lime juice**
¼	**cup extra virgin olive oil**
2	**dashes tequila (optional)**
1	**jalapeño chile, seeded and thinly sliced**
4	**chicken breast halves, boned, skinned and trimmed of fat**
	Freshly ground pepper
4	**handfuls mesclun or other mixed greens**

1. Prepare Citrus Salsa and set aside to allow flavors to blend while preparing the chicken.

2. In a shallow glass dish large enough to hold chicken breasts, combine lime juice, olive oil, tequila and jalapeño slices. Season chicken with pepper and place in the marinade, turning to coat both sides. Marinate for at least 30 minutes.

3. Remove chicken from marinade. Cook on a hot grill (or cast iron skillet) for approximately 5 minutes on each side or until cooked through. Remove and let stand for 5 minutes.

4. To serve, divide and mound the greens on four plates. Slice chicken breasts diagonally (one breast for each plate) and arrange on top of the greens. Spoon Citrus Salsa over breast meat and serve immediately. Serve any extra salsa in a separate bowl.

CITRUS SALSA

4	**tomatillos**
1	**navel orange, peeled, sectioned, and cut into ¼-inch pieces**
1	**small pink grapefruit, peeled, sectioned, and cut into ¼-inch pieces**
4	**green onions, thinly sliced**
10	**yellow and/or red cherry tomatoes, seeded and diced**
1	**tablespoon fresh lime juice**
1	**tablespoon olive oil**
	Grated zest of ½ orange and ½ lime
¼	**cup chopped fresh cilantro**
1	**jalapeño chile, seeded and diced**
1½	**teaspoons tequila (optional)**
	Salt and freshly ground pepper

1. Discard tomatillo husks; rinse tomatillos in hot water to remove sticky film; dry and dice.

2. In a medium-sized bowl, combine all ingredients. Mix well and allow to stand for one hour before using.

Analysis per serving: Calories: 205   Protein: 14g Carbohydrate: 1g Fat: 14g Cholesterol: 66mg   Fiber: 4g   Sodium: 284mg

WARM CHICKEN AND BLACK BEAN SALAD WITH LIME VINAIGRETTE

Serves 2

Served with sour dough bread and white wine, this dish makes a complete meal.

Preparation: 30 minutes
Cook: 10-15 minutes

	Lime Vinaigrette (below)
2	**small chicken breast halves, boned and skinned (approximately 8 ounces)**
2	**teaspoons olive oil**
1	**8-ounce can black beans, rinsed and drained**
3	**cups romaine lettuce, cut into bite-sized strips**
½	**red bell pepper, cut into thin slices**
2	**tablespoons chopped fresh cilantro**

1. Prepare Lime Vinaigrette in a large salad bowl.

2. Put chicken breasts on a plate, and drizzle 1 tablespoon of the Vinaigrette over breasts. Turn to coat and marinate for 10-15 minutes.

3. In a large skillet, heat 1 teaspoon of the oil; add chicken and cook over medium-high heat for 3-4 minutes per side, or until chicken is golden brown and center is cooked. Remove from skillet; reserve pan juices.

4. In salad bowl with Vinaigrette, add remaining teaspoon of oil, black beans, romaine lettuce, bell pepper and cilantro. Toss gently to mix and coat. Using a slotted spoon to drain off excess dressing, lift out salad and arrange on individual plates.

5. Slice chicken into thin strips and drizzle with pan drippings. Arrange over salad, and serve immediately.

Note: Black beans may be heated in the microwave and added warm to the salad, if preferred.

LIME VINAIGRETTE

2½	**tablespoons olive oil**
1½	**tablespoons fresh lime juice**
¼	**teaspoon minced garlic**
⅛	**teaspoon pepper**
⅛	**teaspoon ground cumin**

1. In a large bowl, whisk vinaigrette ingredients until blended.

Analysis per serving: Calories: 494 Protein: 45g Carbohydrate: 25g Fat: 24g Cholesterol: 96mg Fiber: 6g Sodium: 359mg

ASIAN PEAR AND SMOKED TURKEY SALAD

Serves 8-10

Preparation: 30-40 minutes
Chill: 1-2 hours

4	large Asian pears
2	pounds smoked turkey breast, cubed or sliced into thick strips
1½	cups coarsely chopped celery
½	cup finely diced red bell pepper
1	cup toasted pecan pieces
	Freshly ground black pepper to taste
1½	cups plain nonfat or lowfat yogurt or light sour cream
1½	cups brown sugar or light corn syrup
1	cup crumbled blue cheese or Roquefort cheese
	Lettuce, watercress, and/or radicchio leaves
1	Asian pear, peeled and thinly sliced, for garnish
	Red bell pepper strips, for garnish
	Sprigs of watercress, for garnish

1. Peel and core 3 of the Asian pears, and dice into ¾-inch cubes. In a large bowl, combine cubed Asian pears, turkey, celery, red pepper and pecans. Season to taste with pepper.

2. In a medium-sized bowl, combine yogurt, sugar and cheese. Add to turkey mixture and toss. Cover and chill for 1-2 hours.

3. Peel and core remaining pear, and cut into thin slices. To serve, place greens on individual plates and mound salad on top. Garnish with pear slices, red pepper strips and watercress.

Analysis per serving: Calories: 306 Protein: 33g Carbohydrate: 15g Fat: 13g Cholesterol: 90mg Fiber: 2g Sodium: 253mg

TURKEY, WILD RICE AND CRANBERRY SALAD

Serves 6

This recipe from Chula Vista's award-winning cook, Tulie Trejo, is a delicious way to use cooked turkey during the holiday season. This attractive salad, which may be prepared ahead, would make an excellent lunch or picnic entrée.

Preparation: 40 minutes
Cook: 1 hour

3	cups, plus 1 tablespoon, water
1	cup wild rice
1/2	teaspoon salt
1	cup cranberries
1	tablespoon sugar
1/2	cup diced carrot
1/4	cup olive oil
2	teaspoons fresh lemon juice
1	small clove garlic, minced
	Salt and pepper to taste
3/4	pound cooked turkey, shredded (about 2 cups)
1/2	cup chopped celery
1/2	cup chopped fresh parsley
1/2	cup chopped red onion
1/4	cup raisins (preferably golden)
	Green leaf lettuce

1. In a heavy medium-sized saucepan, bring 3 cups water, wild rice and salt to a boil. Cover and cook over medium-low heat until rice is tender and water is absorbed, approximately 55 minutes. Set aside, and let rice cool completely.

2. Meanwhile, in a heavy saucepan, combine cranberries and remaining 1 tablespoon water. Cook over medium heat, stirring constantly, until cranberries just begin to soften, approximately 2 minutes. Add sugar and cook over high heat until sugar is dissolved and cranberries are tender, approximately 5 minutes. Transfer to a plate and refrigerate until chilled.

3. Steam carrots until tender but crunchy, approximately 5 minutes. Plunge into cold water to stop cooking; drain.

4. In a small bowl, whisk olive oil, lemon juice and garlic until blended. Season dressing with salt and pepper.

5. In a large bowl, combine rice, carrots, turkey, celery, parsley, onion and raisins. Pour dressing on top. Add cranberries and toss thoroughly. Cover and chill. (Can be prepared 8 hours ahead).

6. Line individual plates with lettuce leaves. Divide salad among plates and serve.

Analysis per serving: Calories: 308 Protein: 19g Carbohydrate: 34g Fat: 12g Cholesterol: 36mg Fiber: 1g Sodium: 246mg

BUTTERMILK HERB DRESSING

Makes 1 cup

This is an excellent and healthy salad dressing. It may be stored in the refrigerator for about one week.

Preparation: 10-15 minutes
Chill: 2-24 hours

1	**cup buttermilk**
1	**tablespoon prepared mustard, Dijon or whole-grain**
1	**teaspoon minced onion**
½	**teaspoon dried dill weed**
1	**tablespoon finely chopped parsley**
1	**medium clove garlic, minced**
2	**drops hot pepper sauce**
	Freshly ground black pepper to taste

1. Combine all ingredients in a jar with a tight-fitting lid. Cover and shake vigorously to blend.

2. Chill overnight or for several hours.

3. Shake well again before serving.

This is a thin dressing. If preferred, add mayonnaise or plain yogurt to thicken it to desired consistency.

Adapted with permission, from *The American Heart Association Cookbook*, 5th edition; Copyright ©1991; Random House Inc.

Analysis per serving: Calories: 8   Protein: 1g   Carbohydrate: 1g   Fat: 0   Cholesterol: 0.6mg   Fiber: 0.2g   Sodium: 41mg

LOWFAT CREAMY GARLIC DRESSING

Makes 1½ cups

This low-calorie dressing is equally good as a dip or spooned onto crisp hearts of lettuce. It may also be used on hot vegetables.

Preparation: 5 minutes
Chill: 2 hours

4	**large cloves garlic, finely minced**
1	**cup plain nonfat yogurt**
½	**cup reduced-calorie mayonnaise**
½	**teaspoon Dijon-style mustard**

1. In a medium-sized bowl, combine all ingredients and mix well. Chill for at least 2 hours before using.

Adapted with permission, from *The UCSD Healthy Diet for Diabetes*, by Susan Algert, Barbara Grasse, Annie Durning; Copyright © 1990; Houghton Mifflin Co.

Analysis per serving: Calories: 39   Protein: 1g   Carbohydrate: 2g   Fat: 3g   Cholesterol: 4mg   Fiber: 0   Sodium: 20mg

CUCUMBER DRESSING WITH JALAPEÑO AND DILL

Makes 1½ cups

This tangy dressing is best made with hothouse cucumbers. The addition of jalapeño chile gives it a real bite. Toss with mixed salad greens and serve with cold cuts for lunch or with grilled meat at a barbecue.

Preparation: 12-15 minutes

1	**cup seeded and coarsely chopped unpeeled cucumber**
2	**tablespoons chopped fresh dill**
2	**cloves garlic**
½	**jalapeño chile, seeded or ¼ teaspoon hot pepper sauce**
1	**tablespoon lemon juice**
¾	**cup plain or natural yogurt**
1	**tablespoon extra virgin olive oil**
¼	**teaspoon salt**
1	**teaspoon sugar**
	Salad greens

1. Remove all seeds from jalapeño chile and finely chop.

2. In a blender or food processor, combine cucumber, dill, garlic and 1 teaspoon of the jalapeño, reserving the rest to add later, if a hotter taste is desired. Process to a pulp.

3. Add lemon juice, yogurt, olive oil, salt and sugar and process again until smooth. Test for flavor and add more jalapeño or dill, to taste. Refrigerate until ready to use.

Note: This quantity is sufficient for approximately 12 cups of salad greens.

Analysis per serving: Calories: 12 Protein: 0.4g Carbohydrate: 1g Fat: 1g Cholesterol: 0.4mg Fiber: 0 Sodium: 28mg

SOY AND SESAME SEED DRESSING

Makes about 1 cup

A healthy, tasty salad dressing choice from chef Harris Golden, cookbook author and spa cuisine consultant to San Diego's Triangles Restaurant.

Preparation: 5 minutes

⅓	**cup rice vinegar**
⅓	**cup light sesame seed oil**
3	**tablespoons soy sauce**
1	**tablespoon honey**
1	**teaspoon minced garlic**
1	**tablespoon toasted sesame seeds**

1. In a medium-sized jar with a tight-fitting lid, combine all ingredients and shake vigorously to blend well. Serve chilled or at room temperature.

Analysis per serving: Calories: 49 Protein: 0.2g Carbohydrate: 2g Fat: 5g Cholesterol: 0 Fiber: 0.1g Sodium: 193mg

SALADS and DRESSINGS

ASIAN FRUIT JUICE DRESSING

Makes 1 cup

This dressing works well on any meat or grilled vegetables, and on fruit and vegetable salads. Contributed by Su-Mei Yu, caterer and owner of San Diego's Saffron Restaurant, the recipe demonstrates the healthy influence of Pacific Rim cooking.

Preparation: 5-10 minutes

½	cup concentrated frozen apple juice, thawed
½	cup concentrated frozen pineapple juice, thawed
	Juice of 1 lime
	Juice of one sweet Valencia orange
1	tablespoon fresh ginger
1	tablespoon seeded, minced serrano chile
1	teaspoon minced garlic
1	tablespoon minced lemongrass or grated lemon zest

1. Thaw, but do not dilute, the frozen apple and pineapple juices.

2. Combine all ingredients in a large jar. Refrigerate until ready to use.

Analysis per tablespoon: Calories: 24   Protein: 0.1g   Carbohydrate: 6g   Fat: 0   Cholesterol: 0   Fiber: 0   Sodium: 2.5mg

ROQUEFORT CHEESE DRESSING

Makes 2 cups or sixteen 2-tablespoon servings

In this recipe, San Diegan Jeanne Jones, food writer and syndicated columnist, demonstrates her skill at creating lighter versions of favorite but richer dishes. Serve with a salad of mixed greens (lettuces, radicchio, watercress, arugula) and sprinkle with toasted walnuts.

Preparation: 10 minutes

1	cup buttermilk
½	cup silken soft tofu
1½	teaspoons canola oil
1½	teaspoons freshly squeezed lemon juice
1	clove garlic, quartered
¼	teaspoon freshly ground black pepper
3	ounces Roquefort cheese (about ⅓ cup, packed), crumbled

1. In a blender or food processor, combine all ingredients, except Roquefort cheese, and blend until smooth. Pour into a bowl; mix well, and stir in cheese.

2. Store, tightly covered, in refrigerator.

Analysis for total salad per serving: Calories: 66   Protein: 3g   Carbohydrate: 3g   Fat: 6g   Cholesterol: 1mg   Fiber: 1g   Sodium: 35mg

PASTA, RICE AND BREAD

A FAVORITE TRAIL

by Barbara Moore, naturalist and author

Early seafarers called it Punta de los Arboles, or Pine Hill. It was the only landmark with visible trees from the southern tip of Baja California to Central California. Torrey pine trees grow only here, in the Del Mar area, and on Santa Rosa Island near Santa Barbara.

Early San Diegans came to Pine Hill to collect firewood by cutting down the trees. By the 1850s, scientists recognized that these trees were unique and the rarest pine tree in America. But not until the 1880s was it realized that the trees were sorely in need of protection; and this led to the establishment of what is now known as the Torrey Pines State Reserve. With 1500 acres, it is one of the truly unique and most beautiful places in Southern California, an oasis in the midst of a growing metropolis. From any of its trails, there are spectacular views of the ocean, rugged red bluffs, wind-blown Torrey pine trees, and in spring, hundreds of varieties of wildflowers.

My favorite combination of trails starts on the Beach Trail. There are few trees on this part of the Reserve. Instead, you walk through an elfin forest called the coastal sage scrub. This plant community has a variety of shrubby plants that bloom at various times of the year and are adapted to living in semi-aridity. They have small thick leaves that can store water.

After a quick detour to Red Bluff, you start heading down the trail on gentle switchbacks, all the time seeing the Pacific in one of its many moods. In winter, you might see California gray whales swimming past on their southward migration to the warm lagoons of Baja California. Sometimes there are pods of Pacific bottlenose dolphins surfing in the breakers; at other times you might see a raft of sleeping California sea lions.

Before the trail starts heading down to the beach, there is a junction. A side trail will take you out to Yucca Point, which looks down on Flat Rock, sometimes called Bathtub Rock. You might notice the rectangular hole in it. There are several tales about the creation of the hole. The most logical is that the Army Corps of Engineers made it to test some geological theory. Another is that, in the last century, a Welsh coalminer found a seam of coal (there is some poor-quality coal there) and decided to mine and sell it to San Diegans. The third story, and the one I like best, is that, in the days of long dresses and bloomers, female swimmers had difficulties in the surf, so some gentlemen created the hole so that ladies could bathe safely.

The Big Basin Trail heads off toward the trees and crosses a small bridge over a small ravine that washes into Big Basin. After the first rains of winter, you'll start seeing several species of ferns popping out. Later, there will be bright yellow sea dahlias and lavender Mariposa lilies. As you walk up some stairs past a lone Torrey pine, you might notice a clump within the tree that looks a bit like a nest. It is an aberrant growth called a "witch's broom". Scientists don't agree on the cause. It may be a virus, or a genetic anomaly. It is not, however, a nest; and there are several other trees within the Reserve that have similar growths.

Just past the lone tree, another detour takes you to the Razor Point overlook, where you can look down on the jagged cliffs and, perhaps, see some California brown pelicans diving for fish, or gliding along just at your eye level.

The trail continues uphill and along a deep canyon called the Canyon of the Swifts. The canyon was formed by a branch of the Rose Canyon Fault known as the Carmel Valley Fault. There are several overlooks where you can sit and watch for nesting owls and white-throated swifts in the wind-sculpted caves.

Recently, a new Rim Trail along the side was built and gives the hiker a thrilling view of the canyon. The trail meets up with the Beach Trail again, and you may retrace your steps back to the Lodge. The fine small museum there is interactive and depicts the plant and animal life of Torrey Pines State Reserve and the coastal sage-scrub community.

Although you can't picnic in the Reserve, there are picnic tables at the bottom of the hill, next to the beach. Body surfing is popular there as well as strolling along the beach. At extremely low winter tides, you can walk south to La Jolla or North to Encinitas.

There are many special places in San Diego, but Torrey Pines State Reserve is among the very best.

MENU FOR AN EASILY PORTABLE PICNIC

Marinated Dill-Seed Carrots, page 16

Turkish Lentil Fingers, page 14

California Black Olive Caviar, page 16

Moroccan Peppers Salsa, page 28

Braided Herb Bread, page 105

Sausage and Leek Pie, page 128

or

Pasta with Fresh Basil and Marinated Tomatoes, page 90

Lemon Herb Tea Bread, page 239

Rosemary Shortbread Cookies, page 243

Fresh Fruit

PASTA WITH GREEN OLIVES, ARUGULA AND ESCAROLE

Serves 4-5

This dish is best when served hot, but may also be served at room temperature, making it a good picnic dish.

Preparation: 15-20 minutes
Cook: 15 minutes

¾	pound tubular pasta such as rigatoni, ziti or mostaccioli
6	tablespoons olive oil
4	large cloves garlic, minced
1	onion, halved and sliced
1	cup green olives, chopped
½-¾	head escarole, coarsely chopped
1	cup coarsely chopped arugula
½	cup chopped flat-leaf parsley
¼	teaspoon hot red pepper flakes
	Salt and freshly ground black pepper to taste
	Parmesan cheese, grated

1. In a large pot, bring 4-6 quarts water to a boil. Add pasta and cook until tender but still slightly firm, approximately 8-10 minutes.

2. While pasta cooks, slowly sauté garlic and onion in a large frying pan over low heat, until soft and transparent (do not brown). Add olives, escarole, arugula and parsley. Cook over low heat until wilted, approximately 5 minutes.

3. Drain pasta and immediately toss together with sauce in a large serving bowl. Pass cheese separately.

Analysis per serving: Calories: 489 Protein: 13g Carbohydrate: 60g Fat: 22g Cholesterol: 3 mg Fiber: 4g Sodium: 785mg

PENNE WITH EGGPLANT AND VEGETABLES

Serves 6

Fresh herbs and vegetables make this a colorful main course and an appealing vegetarian selection. The optional crushed red pepper adds a touch of fire.

Preparation: 1 hour
Cook: 30 minutes

2	**fresh, firm eggplants (about 12 ounces each), peeled and cut into ½-inch cubes**
½	**teaspoon salt**
3	**tablespoons extra virgin olive oil**
2	**red onions, diced into ½-inch pieces**
4	**large cloves garlic, minced**
1	**pound penne**
1	**medium zucchini, diced into ½-inch pieces**
1	**medium yellow summer squash, diced into ½-inch pieces**
1	**large red bell pepper, diced into ½-inch pieces**
2	**teaspoons balsamic vinegar**
⅓	**cup freshly grated Parmesan cheese, at room temperature**
¼	**cup fresh basil leaves, julienne sliced**
¼	**cup fresh mint leaves, julienne sliced**
	Hot red pepper flakes (optional)

1. To draw out excess fluid from eggplant, sprinkle it with salt, and allow to drain for 30 minutes in a colander, or on paper towels. Rinse salt from eggplant with cold water. Drain again in a colander, but do not pat dry.

2. In a large non-stick skillet, heat oil over medium-high heat. Add eggplant and onions. Sauté until heated through, approximately 3 minutes, stirring only occasionally. Add garlic and gently toss together. Cook until eggplant is almost tender, but still holds its shape, approximately 1 more minute. Remove from heat and set aside.

3. In a large pot, bring 4-6 quarts water to a boil and cook penne until tender but still slightly firm, approximately 8-10 minutes. Add zucchini, yellow squash and red bell pepper. When boiling resumes, stir well and quickly drain, reserving cooking liquid. Remove pasta and vegetables to a large serving dish.

4. In a measuring cup, combine ⅓ cup pasta-cooking liquid and balsamic vinegar. Pour over pasta and toss. Add eggplant mixture and combine gently. Sprinkle with cheese, herbs and red pepper flakes. Toss gently and serve immediately.

Analysis per serving: Calories: 281   Protein: 9g   Carbohydrate: 41g   Fat: 9g   Cholesterol: 4mg   Fiber: 5g   Sodium: 139mg

PASTA, RICE and BREAD

PASTA WITH FRESH BASIL AND MARINATED TOMATOES

Serves 4

Preparation: 10 minutes
Marinate: 45 minutes
Cook: 10 minutes

2	**large ripe tomatoes**
4	**oil-packed sun-dried tomatoes, drained and chopped**
1	**clove garlic, minced**
¼	**cup extra virgin olive oil**
	Freshly ground black pepper
¾	**pound dry penne or garganelle (quill-shaped pastas)**
2	**cups coarsely chopped fresh basil leaves**

1. Halve fresh tomatoes, squeeze out seeds, and coarsely chop.

2. In a large serving bowl, combine the fresh and sun-dried tomatoes, garlic and oil. Season with freshly ground pepper. Set aside and marinate for about 45 minutes at room temperature, stirring occasionally. Do not allow to marinate any longer.

3. In a large pot, bring 4-6 quarts water to a boil and cook pasta until just tender, 8-10 minutes. Drain well and while still hot, toss with tomato mixture.

4. Add basil and toss again. Serve warm immediately or serve at room temperature.

Analysis per serving: Calories: 486 Protein: 13g Carbohydrate: 74g Fat: 17g Cholesterol: 0 Fiber: 4.5g Sodium: 5mg

LINGUINE WITH BAKED TOMATOES

Serves 6-8

Preparation: 20-30 minutes
Bake: 1 hour

1	**cup coarsely chopped flat-leaf parsley, divided**
8	**tablespoons olive oil, divided**
6	**medium to large cloves garlic, minced**
2-2½	**pounds Roma tomatoes, firm-ripe (at least 16 medium-sized)**
	Freshly ground black pepper
1	**pound dry linguine**
2	**tablespoons butter, softened**
⅔	**cup fresh chopped basil or 3 tablespoons dried basil, crumbled**
	Parmesan cheese, freshly grated (optional)

1. Preheat oven to 425 degrees.

2. In a small bowl, mix ½ cup of the parsley, 3 tablespoons of the olive oil and all of the garlic and set aside.

Continued on next page

3. Cut tomatoes in half lengthwise, and place, cut side up, in a baking dish or pan large enough to hold them in one layer. Spoon parsley mixture over tomatoes and pat down; then, drizzle with 3 more tablespoons olive oil. Sprinkle with pepper. Bake for 1 hour.

4. Twenty minutes before tomatoes are done, bring 4-6 quarts water to a boil in a large pot. Add linguine and cook until just tender, approximately 8-10 minutes. Drain.

5. In a large warmed serving bowl, place butter, remaining ½ cup parsley and 2 tablespoons oil, basil and 6 baked tomato halves, skins removed and tomatoes coarsely mashed. Mix in pasta. Gently mix in remaining baked tomatoes and all pan juices.

6. Serve with grated Parmesan cheese.

Analysis per serving: Calories: 408 Protein: 9g Carbohydrate: 48g Fat: 21g Cholesterol: 8mg Fiber: 4g Sodium: 77mg

PASTA WITH SPINACH, TOMATOES AND GREEK OLIVE SAUCE

Serves 4-6

Preparation: 10 minutes
Cook: 15-20 minutes

¼   **cup extra virgin olive oil**
3   **cloves garlic, minced**
½   **teaspoon hot red pepper flakes**
1   **35-ounce can peeled Italian plum tomatoes, drained and coarsely chopped, or 2 pounds fresh tomatoes, peeled, seeded and chopped**
½   **cup Kalamata or brine-cured olives**
¼   **teaspoon sugar**
¼   **teaspoon fresh ground black pepper**
1   **pound fresh rigatoni or gnochetti rigati**
2   **cups washed, trimmed and coarsely chopped fresh spinach**
    Freshly grated Parmesan and Romano cheese

1. In a large skillet, combine olive oil, garlic and pepper flakes. Cook gently for approximately 3 minutes. Add tomatoes, olives, sugar and pepper, and simmer, over medium-high heat, for approximately 15 minutes. Set aside.

2. Place spinach in a large mixing bowl. Set aside.

3. Meanwhile in a large pot, bring 4-6 quarts water to a boil. Add pasta and cook until just tender, approximately 8-10 minutes. Drain well and toss with spinach. Pour sauce over pasta and toss gently.

4. To serve, transfer pasta to a serving dish and sprinkle with grated cheese.

Analysis per serving: Calories: 226 Protein: 6g Carbohydrate: 28g Fat: 11g Cholesterol: 25g Fiber: 34g Sodium: 51mg

SHRIMP WITH ORZO AND SUN-DRIED TOMATOES

Serves 4

This dish may easily be expanded to serve more people. The use of orzo, a rice-shaped pasta, and the variety of flavors, make it a crowd-pleaser — an excellent choice for a large group.

Preparation: 30 minutes
Cook: 20 minutes

1½	cups orzo (a rice-shaped pasta)
3	tablespoons chopped fresh basil
3	tablespoons olive oil, divided
2	tablespoons butter
1½	tablespoons minced shallots
½	cup drained and chopped canned plum tomatoes
1-2	tablespoons minced garlic
2	teaspoons fresh oregano
1	pound large raw shrimp, shelled and deveined
6	sun-dried tomatoes in oil, chopped
½	cup brine-cured black olives (Kalamata) pitted, and drained
7	ounces feta cheese, crumbled
	Freshly ground pepper

1. Bring a large pot of water to a boil. Add orzo and cook for 8 minutes.

2. Drain and transfer orzo to a large oven-proof serving bowl. Add basil and toss with 1 tablespoon olive oil. Cover and keep warm.

3. In a large skillet, melt butter in remaining 2 tablespoons oil. Add shallots and cook until soft. Stir in tomatoes, garlic and oregano; mix well. Add shrimp and sun-dried tomatoes and cook until shrimp turns pink. Sprinkle with olives, feta cheese and pepper to taste.

4. To serve, spoon shrimp mixture over orzo and serve at once.

Analysis per serving: Calories: 494 Protein: 30g Carbohydrate: 30g Fat: 29g Cholesterol: 225mg Fiber: 1g Sodium: 918mg

PASTA WITH SUN-DRIED TOMATO PESTO

Serves 4-6

Preparation: 5-10 minutes
Cook: 10 minutes

1	**pound fresh pasta of choice**
	Sun-Dried Tomato Pesto (below)
	Flat-leaf parsley, chopped, for garnish

1. In a large pot, bring 4-6 quarts of water to a boil and cook pasta until just tender, but still slightly firm, approximately 8-10 minutes.

2. Meanwhile, prepare Sun-Dried Tomato Pesto.

3. Drain pasta, and immediately stir in one half (about 1 cup) of the Sun-Dried Tomato Pesto recipe, and serve. Remaining pesto may be stored covered in refrigerator. See note below.

SUN-DRIED TOMATO PESTO

Makes about 2 cups

¾	**cup oil-packed sun-dried tomatoes, drained and coarsely chopped**
¾	**cup coarsely chopped black olives**
2	**large cloves garlic, mashed with the side of a knife**
1	**cup chopped parsley, packed tightly**
½	**cup pine nuts**
½	**cup extra virgin olive oil (oil from the sun-dried tomatoes may be used)**

1. Put tomatoes, olives, garlic, parsley, pine nuts and olive oil in a blender and pulse to a fine mince.

Note: Pesto will keep, covered, in the refrigerator for up to 3 weeks. It may also be spread on crackers or on lightly toasted Italian or French bread and served as an appetizer.

Analysis per serving: Calories: 534 Protein: 12g Carbohydrate: 56g Fat: 31g Cholesterol: 65mg Fiber: 7g Sodium: 535mg

SPINACH, EGGPLANT AND RED PEPPER LASAGNA

Serves 6

Preparation: 1 hour
Bake: 45-60 minutes
Standing time: 10 minutes

SPINACH FILLING

20	ounces spinach, stems removed
1	tablespoon minced garlic
2	large egg whites
1/4	teaspoon salt
1/4	teaspoon freshly ground nutmeg
1/4	teaspoon black pepper

EGGPLANT-PEPPER FILLING

1	tablespoon olive oil
1	cup minced red onion
1	tablespoon minced garlic
1	large eggplant (at least 1 pound), peeled and cut into 1/2-inch cubes
1	large red bell pepper, seeded and coarsely chopped
1/4	teaspoon sugar
1/4	teaspoon hot red pepper flakes
1	cup tomato sauce (preferably homemade)
4	tablespoons chopped fresh basil
10-12	lasagna noodles
6	ounces thinly sliced part-skim mozzarella cheese
4-5	ounces soft goat cheese
1/4	cup freshly grated Parmesan cheese
3	tablespoons slivered fresh basil, for garnish

1. To make spinach filling, wash spinach leaves, dry in a dish towel or salad spinner, then mince. In a medium bowl, toss together spinach, garlic, egg whites, salt, nutmeg and black pepper. Set aside.

2. To make eggplant-pepper filling, heat oil in a non-stick sauté pan on medium-high. Add red onion, garlic, eggplant, bell pepper, sugar and pepper flakes. Cook for approximately 4-5 minutes, stirring occasionally. Stir in tomato sauce and heat thoroughly. Remove from heat and stir in basil. Set aside.

3. Cook lasagna noodles in a large pot of slowly boiling water until tender. Drain and rinse in cold water.

4. Preheat oven to 375 degrees. Oil a 13x9-inch lasagna pan.

5. Divide noodles into 3 groups; divide fillings, mozzarella and goat cheese in two parts each.

6. To assemble lasagna, place one group of noodles in the pan and layer the first half of the fillings and cheese in the following sequence: spinach filling, mozzarella slices pressed gently into spinach, eggplant-pepper filling, and goat cheese dotted over the surface. Add

Continued on next page

second group of noodles and repeat the filling sequence. Top with remaining noodles. Press down gently to settle the layers. Spread tomato sauce evenly over the top, and sprinkle on Parmesan cheese.

7. Bake until lightly browned and bubbling around the edges, approximately 45-60 minutes. Remove from oven and allow to sit for 10 minutes before serving. Garnish with basil.

Analysis per serving: Calories: 628 Protein: 33g Carbohydrate: 73g Fat: 25g Cholesterol: 52mg Fiber:8g Sodium: 1830mg

LEMON COUSCOUS

Serves 6

This recipe for couscous, from the famous Golden Door spa in Escondido, makes a tasty accompaniment to roast chicken, lamb or barbecued fish. Couscous is a tiny Moroccan pasta made from semolina, and is available in the rice section of most supermarkets.

Preparation: 15 minutes
Cook: 10 minutes

2	cups couscous
2¼	cups chicken stock
3	tablespoons lemon juice
1	tablespoon minced fresh ginger
1	teaspoon ground coriander
1	teaspoon ground cumin
⅛	teaspoon saffron threads
2	tablespoons chopped fresh mint
2	tablespoons chopped fresh parsley
1	tablespoon extra virgin olive oil
2	teaspoons grated lemon zest

1. In a blender, combine stock, lemon juice, ginger, coriander, cumin and saffron. Mix well.

2. Pour mixture into a saucepan and heat to boiling. Add couscous and cook, covered, for 3 minutes. Remove from heat; let stand for 5 minutes, covered.

3. When ready to serve, add mint, parsley, oil and lemon zest; toss gently with a fork and spoon into a serving dish.

Analysis per serving: Calories: 173 Protein: 6g Carbohydrate: 30g Fat: 3g Cholesterol: 0 Fiber: 5.6g Sodium: 252mg

MEXICAN GREEN RICE

Serves 6

Preparation: 20 minutes
Cook: 30 minutes

1	bunch fresh spinach (¹/₂ pound), washed, stemmed, patted dry and coarsely chopped
1	bunch cilantro (or parsley), coarsely chopped
3	green onions, coarsely chopped
1	poblano chile, seeded and coarsely chopped
2	cloves garlic, coarsely chopped
	Juice of 1 lemon
3	cups chicken stock, divided
¹/₃	cup olive oil
1	small white onion, minced
2	cups converted rice
	Freshly ground black pepper to taste
	Additional chopped green onions, for garnish

1. In a food processor or blender, combine spinach, cilantro, green onions, chile, garlic, lemon juice and 1 cup of the stock. Blend until completely smooth. Set aside.

2. In a large heavy saucepan, heat olive oil; add onion and sauté until transparent. Add rice and cook for 1 minute, stirring. Add the blended vegetable mixture and bring to a boil.

3. In a separate pan, bring remaining 2 cups chicken stock to a boil, and add to rice mixture. Season with pepper. Cover and simmer over very low heat for 30 minutes.

4. To serve, remove to a serving dish and decorate with chopped green onions.

Hint: To reduce fat content, use chicken stock instead of oil to cook onions and rice.

Analysis per serving: Calories: 260 Protein: 9g Carbohydrate: 26g Fat: 14g Cholesterol: 2mg Fiber: 3g Sodium: 808mg

MANGO RICE WITH ALMONDS

Serves 8-10

This refreshing dish is a perfect accompaniment to any grilled meat, poultry or fish, and goes well with many Asian entrées. It is from Jerrie Strom, cooking teacher and former Food Editor of *San Diego Home/Garden*.

Preparation: 30 minutes
Cook: 5-6 minutes

3	tablespoons butter
5	cups cooked rice (2¹/₂ cups raw)
6-8	ounces fresh or canned mango, peeled and chopped, or substitute spiced peaches
1	cup slivered almonds, toasted

1. In a large skillet, melt butter and sauté cooked rice until heated through. Add chopped mango and sauté for 3 more minutes. Rice may be kept warm in the oven in a covered serving dish.

Continued on next page

2.	To serve, remove to a serving bowl and sprinkle with toasted almonds.

Note: For a dramatic effect, prepare rice in a buttered mold. Turn out and decorate with mango slices and an edible flower or two.

Analysis per serving: Calories: 244   Protein: 5g   Carbohydrate: 35g   Fat: 10g   Cholesterol: 9mg   Fiber: 3g   Sodium: 39mg

EDIBLE FLOWERS

When using flowers in salads or as garnish, be sure that they are edible. The following are some edible flowers found in San Diego gardens and elsewhere.

Calendula	**Hibiscus**	**Nasturtium**
Chive blossom	**Honeysuckle**	**Passion flower**
Chrysanthemum	**Impatiens**	**Rose**
Daylily	**Johnny-Jump-Up**	**Salvia**
Geranium	**Lavender**	**Yucca blossom**
Herb blossoms	**Marigold**	

RICE WITH ASIAN SPICES

Serves 6-8

This rice dish, from food writer and cooking teacher, Marlene Sorosky, is simple to prepare and excellent served with barbecued flank steak. The recipe may be expanded easily to serve a crowd.

Preparation: 5 minutes
Cook: 20-25 minutes

1½	cups rice
4	tablespoons canola oil or other vegetable oil
½	cup golden raisins
½	teaspoon turmeric
½	teaspoon curry powder
1½	tablespoons soy sauce
3	cups chicken stock

1.	In a medium-sized saucepan or flame-proof casserole, mix rice, oil, raisins, turmeric, curry powder and soy sauce. Blend well.

2.	In a separate pan, bring chicken stock to a boil, and pour into rice mixture. Cover and cook on low heat 20 minutes or until liquid is absorbed and rice is tender.

Analysis per serving: Calories: 235   Protein: 5g   Carbohydrate: 37g   Fat: 8g   Cholesterol: 0   Fiber: 0.4g   Sodium: 487mg

RISOTTO WITH ASPARAGUS AND MUSHROOMS

Serves 6

Preparation: 20 minutes
Cook: 30-40 minutes

5-7	cups chicken broth or homemade chicken stock, defatted
5	tablespoons olive oil, divided
1	tablespoon butter
2	cups Italian arborio rice
2-3	large cloves garlic, minced
12-15	thin asparagus spears, cut into 2-inch lengths
1/2	pound mushrooms, sliced
1	small head radicchio
	Large bunch of fresh basil leaves
3/4	cup dry white wine
3/4-1	cup freshly grated Parmesan cheese
	Freshly ground black pepper
	Flat-leaf parsley, for garnish

1. In a covered saucepan, heat chicken broth and keep hot throughout procedure.

2. In a large heavy pot, heat 3 tablespoons of the olive oil with butter. Add rice and sauté for 2-3 minutes over medium-high heat until entirely coated and glistening. Stir frequently, being careful not to let the rice brown.

3. Begin adding hot chicken broth to rice, 1/2 cup at a time (a soup ladle makes this easier). Cook each addition, uncovered, over medium-high heat, until liquid is absorbed; then add next 1/2 cup of broth. Stir frequently to prevent rice from sticking. Repeat this process until rice is cooked but still a little firm, approximately 30 minutes.

4. While rice is cooking, prepare vegetables. In a sauté pan, heat remaining 2 tablespoons olive oil and sauté garlic for 1-2 minutes; do not brown. Add asparagus and sauté for 3 minutes, or until just tender. Add mushrooms and continue to sauté for another 3 minutes.

5. Thinly slice radicchio and add to the vegetables, cooking for another 2-3 minutes until only slightly limp. Take off the heat. Slice basil leaves into slivers and stir into mixture. Set aside until rice is cooked.

6. When rice is just tender and slightly creamy, add white wine and cook until it is absorbed, stirring frequently. Mix in Parmesan cheese and season with freshly ground pepper. Stir in vegetables, garnish with parsley and pass additional Parmesan cheese separately.

Note: Any type of mushroom or a mixture of mushrooms may be used. Porcini mushrooms are especially good in this dish. Sautéed shrimp may be added for a more substantial meal.

Analysis per serving: Calories: 562 Protein: 28g Carbohydrate: 58g Fat: 22g Cholesterol: 22mg Fiber: 2g Sodium: 2174mg

CALIFORNIA WILD RICE PILAF

Serves 10

Preparation: 10 minutes
Cook: 45 minutes
Cool: 2 hours

1½	**cups wild rice**
5½	**cups chicken stock**
½	**cup pecan halves**
½	**cup golden raisins**
4	**green onions, thinly sliced**
2	**tablespoons grated orange zest**
⅓	**cup orange juice**
2	**tablespoons olive oil**
2	**tablespoons chopped mint or cilantro**
	Freshly ground black pepper to taste

1. Rinse rice under cold water until water runs clear. In a large saucepan, combine chicken stock and rice; bring to a boil. Lower heat, cover, and simmer for 45 minutes or until opened and softened. Drain well.

2. Place rice in a serving bowl and stir in pecans, raisins and onions.

3. In a small bowl, combine orange zest, orange juice, oil, mint or cilantro and pepper to taste. Pour over rice and toss gently. Cool and serve at room temperature.

Adapted, with permission, from *The UCSD Healthy Diet for Diabetes*, by Susan Algert, Barbara Grasse, Annie Durning; Copyright © 1990; published by Houghton Mifflin Co.

Analysis per serving: Calories: 215   Protein: 10g   Carbohydrate: 27g   Fat: 8g   Cholesterol: 2mg   Fiber: 2g   Sodium: 875mg

BROWN RICE AND LENTIL PILAF

Serves 4-6

Preparation: 10 minutes
Cook: 50-60 minutes

3	**tablespoons olive oil, divided**
1/2	**medium onion, chopped**
1	**cup brown rice**
2 1/2	**cups water or vegetable stock**
1/4	**teaspoon cinnamon**
1	**tablespoon tomato paste (optional)**
1/4	**cup lentils**
1	**teaspoon salt**
1/2	**cup pine nuts, sunflower seeds or chopped almonds, lightly toasted**
1/2	**cup raisins**

1. In a large skillet, heat 2 tablespoons of the oil, and sauté onion until soft. Add rice and cook, stirring, for several minutes.

2. In a small bowl, combine water, cinnamon and tomato paste. Add this mixture and lentils, to rice. Bring to a boil, cover tightly, turn heat very low and simmer for 30 minutes.

3. Preheat oven to 350 degrees.

4. Stir salt, nuts and raisins into rice.

5. Coat baking dish with the remaining tablespoon of oil and 1 tablespoon of hot water. Pour in rice mixture. Cover and bake for 50-60 minutes.

Analysis per serving: Calories: 289   Protein: 7g   Carbohydrate: 38g   Fat: 15g   Cholesterol: 0   Fiber: 3.1g   Sodium: 190mg

SPICED BASMATI PILAF WITH NUTS AND DRIED FRUIT

Serves 6-8

Preparation: 30 minutes
Cook: 20-25 minutes

2	cups Basmati rice
2	tablespoons vegetable oil
1	stick cinnamon
2	bay leaves
4	cardamom seeds, shells removed
	Small pinch of salt
4	cups water
2	tablespoons almonds, finely chopped
2	tablespoons pistachios, finely chopped
4	dried apricots, finely chopped
2	tablespoons raisins
	Zest of two oranges

1. Wash rice very well until water runs clear. Soak in cold water for half an hour.

2. In a heavy saucepan heat oil, add cinnamon stick, bay leaves and cardamom. Sauté for 1 minute. Add drained rice and sauté gently to evaporate any water. Add salt and water; mix gently with a fork.

3. Cook on medium heat, uncovered, until water is almost all absorbed. Then cover and cook on low heat for a few minutes until dry and well cooked. Do not stir rice while cooking, or the grains will break and become sticky.

4. Add nuts, apricots, raisins, and orange zest; mix gently with a fork. Serve hot.

Analysis per serving: Calories: 262   Protein: 5g   Carbohydrate: 47g   Fat: 6g   Cholesterol: 0   Fiber: 1.8g   Sodium: 593mg

PASTA, RICE and BREAD

THAI FRIED RICE WITH CHICKEN

Serves 4

This versatile recipe can also be made with shrimp, julienne of duck, beef or sliced squid. Fish sauce and fresh herbs are essential. Having all ingredients ready is the secret to quick and easy preparation of this one-dish meal.

Preparation: 15-20 minutes
Cook: 30-35 minutes

1½-1⅔ cups jasmine or long grain rice (4-5 cups cooked)
2-2½ tablespoons vegetable oil
2-3 tablespoons seeded and finely chopped fresh chile (Anaheim or jalapeño), seeded
4 tablespoons finely chopped onion
2 tablespoons minced garlic
¾ pound chicken breast, boned, skinned and julienne sliced
¼ cup chopped green bell pepper
¼ cup chopped red bell pepper
¼ cup coarsely chopped green onion
3 eggs, beaten
3 tablespoons soy sauce
1½ tablespoons fish sauce (available in Asian markets)
1 tablespoon sugar
¼ cup coarsely chopped fresh herbs (basil, mint or cilantro)

1. Cook rice according to directions and keep warm.

2. Heat a wok or large skillet; add oil and when hot, sauté chile, onion and garlic until softened. Add chicken and sauté for approximately 5 minutes. Add bell peppers and green onion, and sauté for approximately 2 minutes more.

3. Add eggs and stir until cooked. Stir in warm rice, then soy sauce, fish sauce and sugar, blending well. Remove from heat and gently fold in fresh herbs. Serve at once.

Analysis per serving: Calories: 585 Protein: 26g Carbohydrate: 85 Fat: 15g Cholesterol: 194mg Fiber: 4g   Sodium: 1016mg

POLENTA WITH SUN-DRIED TOMATOES AND MUSHROOMS

Serves 8-10

This delicious accompaniment for broiled and roasted meats, fish or poultry comes from Anne Otterson, founding director of The Perfect Pan Cooking School. It can be prepared in advance up to step 6; then slipped into the oven for the final baking.

Preparation: 1 hour (including cooking polenta)
Bake: 30-35 minutes

6	cups water
2	teaspoons salt, or to taste
2	cups polenta (coarse cornmeal)
3	tablespoons extra virgin olive oil
$\frac{1}{2}$	pound fresh mushrooms, sliced
1-2	ounces dried porcini mushrooms, soaked in hot water, 20-30 minutes, cleaned and drained (reserve soaking liquid)
2-3	ounces sun-dried tomatoes, julienne sliced
$\frac{1}{2}$	cup fresh basil leaves, julienne sliced crosswise
2-3	cloves fresh garlic, chopped
1	cup cream or half-and-half
$\frac{1}{2}$-$\frac{3}{4}$	cup Parmesan cheese, grated

1. In a large pot, bring water to a boil and add salt. Then begin adding polenta very slowly, stirring constantly. (Use a long-handled spoon because polenta, when thick, boils and sputters.) After stirring and boiling for approximately 5 minutes, place pot into a larger pot partially filled with boiling water, and steam polenta, as in a double boiler, for 40-50 minutes, stirring occasionally.

2. Pour hot polenta into a large (12x8½x3-inch) oiled baking pan or sheet. Spread evenly and allow to cool.

3. In a large skillet, heat oil and sauté fresh mushrooms and porcini mushrooms over medium heat, until beginning to brown.

4. Add dried tomatoes, basil and garlic, and sauté for 2 minutes. Remove from heat.

5. Turn out cooled polenta on to a board. Cut horizontally into two layers about a ½ inch thick. This is best done with a length of heavy thread, thin wire or nylon fishing line, using a gentle sawing motion.

6. Place first layer into an oiled, deep baking dish. Top with the mushroom mixture. Sprinkle with half the cream and Parmesan cheese. Top with second layer of polenta and sprinkle with remaining cream and Parmesan.

7. Bake for 30 minutes or until very hot, at 350 degrees. Serve immediately.

Analysis per serving: Calories: 498 Protein: 14g Carbohydrate: 87g Fat: 13g Cholesterol: 15mg Fiber: 16g Sodium: 622mg

ROSEMARY BREAD

Makes 4 dozen rolls or 2 loaves

Preparation: 1 hour; allow time to rise
Bake: 15 minutes (rolls) 30 minutes (loaf)

6	**cups flour**
1	**teaspoon salt**
½	**teaspoon baking soda**
1½	**teaspoons baking powder**
¼	**cup sugar**
3	**tablespoons fresh rosemary, chopped**
½	**cup butter**
1	**envelope dry yeast**
½	**cup lukewarm water**
1¾	**cups buttermilk, 2%**
	Melted butter

1. In a large bowl, sift together flour, salt, soda, baking powder and sugar. Mix in rosemary. Add ½ cup butter and blend into flour mixture, using a pastry blender.

2. Dissolve dry yeast in water; add yeast mixture and buttermilk to flour mixture.

3. Knead dough in a bowl or on a breadboard until ingredients are well mixed (an electric mixer with a dough hook may also be used). Cover tightly with plastic wrap and set in refrigerator until chilled. The dough will keep for up to 5 days. When ready to bake continue according to loaf or roll directions.

4. For loaves, grease two 9x5-inch loaf pans. Divide dough in half to form 2 loaves and put into prepared pans. Make 3 or 4 diagonal cuts across the surface; brush with melted butter; cover with a damp cloth and let rise in a warm place until very light.

5. For rolls, grease a cookie sheet. Divide dough into 4 balls, and roll out each ball into a 9- to 10-inch circle. Cut into 8 pie wedges and roll each up to form a crescent roll. Place on prepared cookie sheet, seam down. Brush with melted butter; cover with a damp cloth and let rise in a warm place until double in volume, approximately 45 minutes.

6. Preheat oven to 375 degrees. Bake loaves for 30 minutes, or rolls for 10-15 minutes, until browned.

Analysis per serving: Calories: 83   Protein: 2g   Carbohydrate: 13.5g   Fat: 2g   Cholesterol: 6mg   Fiber: 1g   Sodium: 86mg

BRAIDED HERB BREAD

Makes 1 large braided loaf   Serves 8-10

Preparation: 20 minutes
Rising time: 3 hours
Bake: 40 minutes

4½-5	cups unbleached flour
1	package active dry yeast
2	tablespoons sugar
2	teaspoons salt
1¼	cups lowfat milk
½	cup butter or margarine
3	eggs
2	tablespoons minced rosemary
1	tablespoon minced thyme
2	tablespoons minced parsley
3	cloves garlic, minced
	Extra virgin olive oil

1. In a large bowl, combine 1½ cups of the flour, yeast, sugar and salt.

2. In a small saucepan, heat milk and butter until very warm (120-130 degrees). Pour into flour-yeast mixture and add 2 eggs. Beat for 2 minutes. Add remaining 3-3½ cups flour to form a stiff dough. If desired, some of the minced herbs may be included in the batter at this stage.

3. Knead for 5 minutes or until smooth and elastic.

4. Place in a greased bowl, cover, and allow to rise until double in volume, approximately 1½ hours.

5. Punch down dough, divide into 4 equal amounts, and shape each part into a strip about 20 inches long. On a similar-length strip of waxed paper, combine rosemary, thyme, parsley and garlic. Roll strips of bread in this mixture.

6. Place 4 strips side by side on a greased baking sheet. Braid by weaving far right strip over and under other strips to far left; then follow with remaining strips. Pinch ends together to seal. Let dough rise until doubled in volume, approximately 45 minutes. Brush with beaten egg.

7. Preheat oven to 375 degrees. Bake for 35-40 minutes, or until golden brown. Cool on a wire rack.

Analysis per serving: Calories: 326   Protein: 9g   Carbohydrate: 46g   Fat: 12g   Cholesterol: 91mg   Fiber: 2g   Sodium: 128mg

YOGURT DINNER ROLLS WITH HERBS

Makes 12

These rolls are easy to make and add a special treat to any menu.

Preparation: 15 minutes
Rising time: 2 hours 10 minutes
Bake: 15 minutes

1	**cup plain lowfat yogurt**
1	**tablespoon margarine**
¼	**cup water**
2	**tablespoons sugar**
1	**package active dry yeast**
1¼	**cups white flour, divided**
1½	**cups whole wheat flour, divided**
¼	**teaspoon baking soda**
1	**egg**
1	**teaspoon dried oregano**
1	**teaspoon dried marjoram**
1	**teaspoon dried basil**
2	**tablespoons grated onion**
	Non-stick vegetable spray

1. In a saucepan, heat together yogurt, margarine, water and sugar until margarine is melted. Set aside and let cool to lukewarm.

2. In a large bowl, combine yeast, ¾ cup of the white flour, ¾ cup of the whole wheat flour and baking soda. Add cooled liquid mixture to yeast-flour mixture and then add egg, herbs and grated onion. Beat at low speed with electric mixer for 30 seconds. Then beat for 3 minutes at high speed.

3. Stir in remaining ½ cup white flour and ¾ cup whole wheat flour. Dough will still be moist and a little sticky. Spray a bowl with non-stick vegetable spray. Place dough in the bowl and turn over once so that all sides are lightly coated with the oil. Set in a draft-free location and let rise until doubled in volume, approximately 1½ hours.

4. Remove dough and place on a floured board; knead lightly. Divide evenly into 12 pieces, form into round balls and place in muffin pans sprayed with non-stick vegetable spray. Cover and let rise for about 40 minutes.

5. Bake at 400 degrees for 12-15 minutes or until nicely browned. Remove from muffin pans immediately. Serve hot or at room temperature.

Variation: Other herbs may be substituted to vary the flavor. Also, some grated cheese may be included in step 2, or sprinkled on top of the muffins 10-15 minutes before they are done. This will, however, increase the calories and fat.

Adapted, with permission, from *The American Heart Association Cookbook*, 5th edition; Copyright © 1991; Random House Inc.

Analysis per serving: Calories: 95 Protein: 3g Carbohydrate: 16 Fat: 2g Cholesterol: 19mg Fiber: 0.6g Sodium: 30 mg

CELEBRATING THE BORDER

A conversation, at home, with acclaimed poet, Quincy Troupe, Professor of American and Caribbean Literature and Creative Writing at the University of California, San Diego.

"In San Diego, we should recognize that we are on the border with a very sophisticated, cultured and proud people, who have a long history. The Mexicans have a lot to offer Americans in art and music. Their art has already impacted us. After all, California used to be Mexico. A lot of Mexican culture has entered this country, besides food, and I see this as very positive. Mexico has great painters, sculptors, and musicians. They have great literature: Carlos Fuentes, Octavio Paz, Juan Ruffo, Jaime Sabines—poets, novelists and essayists—a lot of great plays and an up-and-coming film industry. I also love the museums down there—Tijuana's Cultural Center. I have met many performance artists, painters and poets living there, whom I have got to know in the past four years.

"My first border experience was with a Mexican friend, Theresa Gordon-Sanchez, who lives in Los Angeles: this experience happened before my family and I moved here. Theresa said "Why don't I take you and Margaret (my wife) to Baja—there is this great lobster village, called Puerto Nuevo." So, we got in her car and she drove all the way down, through San Diego to Baja, and another hour to Puerto Nuevo. We left at 9:00 and got there by noon. She took us to this family-owned restaurant, where we sat, looking right at the ocean, while they brought us these lobsters—gigantic lobsters—with rice and beans, and shrimp and huge margaritas. The food was incredible. A mariachi band came up and played just for us, for about 20 minutes; then we gave them a little money. They left and we could hear them as they went up and down the street, playing at other restaurants and on the beach. It was just a marvellous experience.

"It was intriguing to me, and it was one of the reasons I decided to come to live in San Diego; the fact that another country was 30 minutes from my door. Living in Manhattan was a wonderful experience, because you had all these cultures in Manhattan. You could walk down Broadway and hear all these languages spoken any given day. But that's not like crossing a border into another country.

"Now that we live here, my wife and I go across the border a lot, and take our friends. We've taken Toni Morrison there, we've taken Derek Walcott—both of whom are good friends and Nobel prize laureates. And all of them say things like (in Derek's case), 'I'm not going back to Boston; I just want to die here. I don't want to go back!' They had a marvellous time because they discovered the same thing that we did—the great food, the great culture, the kind of sleepiness of this place. You can really forget about being in the United States, because the pace of life, the whole attitude, the way the people are, what you see—it has a totally different feel. It's casual and relaxed. The music is energized. Everybody is energized, including the people eating in the restaurants. In good restaurants in the United States, everything is hushed and very quiet. Down there, it's boisterous. Everyone is into the joy of having this great food, into the joy of being in the sun and looking at the ocean, into the joy of the music being played. It's upbeat, with no pretensions. I like that, and everybody else likes it, too. Also, Mexicans have a strong sense of family and family values and they extend it to other people, once they know you. They go out of their way—and are very generous; they take care of you. Of course, it's about business, but it is also about something else.

"I see myself as a poet who crosses borders. A lot of my concerns are international concerns. In the Cross Fertilization Series that I organize for the Museum of Contemporary Art in San Diego, we bring artists from everywhere and create an evening in which all these different cultures are coming at the audience. You have got to be open to it, and it transforms and transports you. I look at myself as a cultural worker, one who tries to open the community up to different, exciting things. So far, it's been working."

Quincy Troupe is the creative force behind "Artists On The Cutting Edge: Cross Fertilizations", an annual arts festival sponsored by the Museum of Contemporary Art, San Diego.

MENU FOR A MEXICAN BUFFET

Ceviche Dolsa, page 23

Creamy Tomatillo Salsa, page 29

No-fry Tortilla Chips, page 21

Spicy Shrimp with Chicken Cilantro, page 142

Mushroom-Stuffed Green Chiles with Goat Cheese Sauce, page 192

Carne Asada California Style, page 114

Baked Chicken with Ranchero Sauce, page 173

Mexican Green Rice, page 96

Black Beans with Cumin and Vegetables, page 185

Papaya and Tomato Salsa, page 29

Cranberry, Chile and Cilantro Salsa, page 27

Jicama Slaw with Peanut Dressing, page 59

Romaine Salad with Red Chili Dressing, page 57

Caramelized Meringue Ring with Mangos, page 221

Fresh Fruit Platter

MEDITERRANEAN MEATLOAF

Serves 8-10

French-trained UCSD Food Service Chef, Drew Ellsworth, submitted this tasty meatloaf - so quick and easy to make in a food processor. It is very good served with pasta and a tomato sauce or gravy.

Preparation: 25-35 minutes
Bake: 1 hour

1	**pound ground turkey**
1	**pound ground beef**
¼	**cup breadcrumbs, plus 2 tablespoons for topping**
¼	**cup grated Parmesan cheese, plus 2 tablespoons for topping**
1	**egg**
½	**teaspoon salt**
¼	**teaspoon white pepper**
½	**cup coarsely chopped carrot**
½	**cup coarsely chopped onion**
½	**cup coarsely chopped green bell pepper**
½	**cup coarsely chopped celery**
2	**large cloves garlic**
1	**tablespoon dry basil**
1	**tablespoon whole oregano**
1	**tablespoon chopped parsley**
1	**tablespoon thyme**
1	**teaspoon red pepper flakes**
1	**teaspoon fennel seeds**
	Sprigs of parsley, for garnish

1. Preheat oven to 350 degrees.

2. Place all ingredients in a food processor (meats broken up and layered). Chop and grind, using pulse control, just until entire mixture forms a mass. Do not overmix. Chopped vegetables should be recognizable and chunky.

3. Place meatloaf in a 2-quart porcelain baking dish or earthenware terrine. Top with 2 tablespoons breadcrumbs and 2 tablespoons Parmesan cheese. Bake for approximately 1 hour or until the interior temperature reaches 165 degrees.

4. Serve garnished with parsley sprigs.

Note: If mixing by hand, vegetables should be finely chopped or diced.

Analysis per serving: Calories: 194   Protein: 18g   Carbohydrate: 5g   Fat: 11g   Cholesterol: 75mg   Fiber: 1g   Sodium: 215mg

ROAST FILLET OF BEEF WITH CORNICHON-TARRAGON SAUCE

Serves 18

Here is a perfect recipe for that special dinner party. Serve with steamed green vegetables and baby new potatoes for a good contrast with the rich flavor of the sauce.

Preparation: 20 minutes
Bake: 40 minutes
Stand: 15 minutes

3	**fillets of beef (3-4 pounds each), trimmed and tied**
1/3	**cup vegetable oil**
	Freshly ground pepper
	Cornichon-Tarragon Sauce (below)
	Sprigs of fresh tarragon, for garnish

1. Preheat oven to 550 degrees.

2. Rub fillets with oil and season with pepper. Roast in preheated oven for 25 minutes, or until a meat thermometer registers 125 degrees for rare or 130 degrees for medium-rare meat. Transfer to a platter, cover loosely with foil and let stand for 15 minutes.

3. Meanwhile, prepare Cornichon-Tarragon Sauce.

4. To serve, slice meat and arrange on a platter. Spoon some of the Cornichon-Tarragon Sauce onto meat and garnish with sprigs of tarragon. Pass remaining sauce separately.

CORNICHON-TARRAGON SAUCE

Serves 18

1	**cup unsalted butter, softened**
2/3	**cup Dijon-style mustard**
1 1/4	**cups minced shallots**
5	**cups dry white wine**
1/2	**cup minced fresh tarragon leaves or 2 tablespoons dried**
1/3	**cup heavy cream**
	Juices from roasted meat
40	**cornichons, julienne sliced (about 1 cup)**
	Freshly ground pepper to taste

1. In a small bowl, cream together butter and mustard; set aside.

2. In a large saucepan, combine shallots, wine and tarragon; cook until wine is reduced to 1 cup. Add cream and reduce heat to low. Whisk in butter mixture, a little at a time, along with any meat juices that have accumulated from the roast. Add cornichons and season with pepper. Keep warm until ready to serve.

Note: Cornichons are small French pickled gherkins.

Analysis per serving: Calories: 430 Protein: 25g Carbohydrate: 14g Fat: 24g Cholesterol: 85mg Fiber: 1g Sodium: 470mg

PICNIC STEAK WITH RAVIGOTE SAUCE

Serves 6

Preparation: 10-15 minutes
Marinate: overnight
Grill: 10-16 minutes

1½	pounds steak (London broil or flank), trimmed of all fat
2	tablespoons minced garlic
2	tablespoons soy sauce
2	tablespoons red wine vinegar
1	tablespoon canola oil
½	teaspoon hot red pepper flakes
½	teaspoon sugar
	Ravigote Sauce (below)

1. Place meat in a large glass dish. In a blender, combine garlic, soy sauce, vinegar, oil, red pepper flakes and sugar; blend well. Pour over meat and turn to coat. Marinate for 1 hour at room temperature; turn occasionally; cover and refrigerate overnight. Turn from time to time.

2. Prepare a fire in a charcoal grill or preheat an oven broiler. Drain meat and grill on an oiled rack over coals, or broil about 1 inch from the heat. Cook for approximately 5-8 minutes on each side, or until a meat thermometer registers 130 degrees for medium-rare.

3. Transfer steak to a cutting board and let stand for 10 minutes. Slice thinly at a 45-degree angle. Serve with Ravigote Sauce.

Note: Meat may be cooked, but not sliced, and sauce made, a day in advance. Keep covered and chilled.

RAVIGOTE SAUCE

Makes ¾ cup

1	tablespoon Dijon mustard
2	teaspoons white wine vinegar
¼	cup olive oil
⅓	cup finely chopped onion, soaked in water for 3 minutes, drained and squeezed dry
1	tablespoon minced shallot
1	tablespoon snipped fresh chives or minced tops of green onions
2	tablespoons drained capers
2	tablespoons minced fresh parsley
¼	teaspoon dried tarragon, crumbled
	Freshly ground black pepper to taste

1. In a small bowl, whisk mustard and vinegar together, add oil in a slow stream, whisking until emulsified. Stir in onion, shallots, chives, capers, parsley, tarragon and add pepper to taste. Combine well.

Adapted from *Gourmet*. Copyright © 1988 by the Conde Nast Publications, Inc.

Analysis per serving: Calories: 328   Protein: 25g   Carbohydrate: 6g   Fat: 22g   Cholesterol: 60mg   Fiber: 0   Sodium: 461mg

BARBECUED FLANK STEAK WITH PINEAPPLE-GINGER MARINADE

Serves 4-6

Preparation: 5 minutes
Marinate: 2 hours
Grill: 5-10 minutes

1	**flank steak (1-1½ pounds)**
	Pineapple-Ginger Marinade (below)

1. Place flank steak in a glass dish large enough to hold meat and marinade.

2. Pour Pineapple-Ginger Marinade over meat, turning to coat. Cover with plastic wrap and marinate in refrigerator for at least 2 hours.

3. Prepare a fire in a charcoal grill or preheat a gas grill.

4. Barbecue steak on hot grill until meat is cooked rare, approximately 5-10 minutes.

5. To serve, thinly slice meat across the grain. Accompany with a salad and crusty French bread.

PINEAPPLE-GINGER MARINADE

1	**cup pineapple juice**
⅓	**cup soy sauce**
1	**teaspoon molasses**
	Pinch of ground ginger
1	**onion, chopped**
1	**tablespoon canola or other vegetable oil**
1-2	**cloves garlic, crushed**

1. In a small bowl, combine marinade ingredients, blending well.

Note: This marinade is also good with fish or chicken.

Analysis per serving: Calories: 334   Protein: 36g   Carbohydrate: 15g   Fat: 13g   Cholesterol: 101mg   Fiber: 1g   Sodium: 725mg

CARNE ASADA CALIFORNIA STYLE

Serves 6-8

Elena Cota, whose article we feature on rancho cooking, adapted this Carne Asada from an oldtime ranch recipe for barbecued beef.

Preparation: 10-15 minutes
Marinate: 4 hours
Grill: 5-8 minutes

4	**skirt steaks (approximately 2 pounds total)**
	Papaya Seed Marinade (below)
8	**papaya slices, for garnish**
	Sprigs of cilantro, for garnish

1. Place steaks in a large shallow bowl. Prepare marinade and pour over meat. Turn steaks to coat well and sprinkle papaya seeds on top.

2. Cover and marinate in refrigerator for at least 4 hours, turning several times.

3. Prepare a fire in a charcoal grill or preheat a gas grill. Remove steaks from marinade and grill over hot coals to desired doneness.

4. To serve, thinly slice meat against the grain. Garnish with papaya slices and cilantro.

PAPAYA SEED MARINADE

1	**cup raw apple cider, apple jack or beer**
¼	**cup lime juice**
3	**large cloves garlic, minced**
¾	**teaspoon coarsely ground black pepper**
	Seeds of 1 papaya, ground in a food processor

1. In a small bowl, combine apple cider, lime juice, garlic and pepper.

2. Pour marinade over meat, and sprinkle papaya seeds on top to tenderize.

Analysis per serving: Calories: 410   Protein: 18g   Carbohydrate: 7g   Fat: 34g   Cholesterol: 76mg   Fiber: 1.5g   Sodium: 44mg

BARBECUED MEXICAN-STYLE FLANK STEAK

Serves 5-8

Serve this simple ranch-style recipe with warmed flour tortillas and guacamole.

Preparation: 5 minutes
Marinate: 1 hour
Grill: 8 minutes

1   **flank steak (1½-2 pounds)**
     Oregano Marinade (below)
     Sprigs of cilantro, for garnish.

1.   Place steak in a rectangular glass dish. Pierce generously with a fork.

2.   Prepare Oregano Marinade. Pour over steak, turning to coat. Cover and marinate in refrigerator for at least 1 hour.

3.   Prepare a fire in a charcoal grill or preheat a gas grill.

4.   Grill steak over hot coals for 3-4 minutes on each side. Brush again with marinade before turning.

5.   To serve, thinly slice across the grain at a 45-degree angle, and garnish with cilantro.

OREGANO MARINADE

1   **teaspoon dried oregano, crumbled**
1   **clove of garlic, mashed**
1   **tablespoon vinegar**
2   **tablespoons vegetable oil**
     Salt and pepper to taste

1.   In a small bowl, combine oregano, garlic, vinegar and oil, and season with salt and pepper to taste. Mix well.

Analysis per serving: Calories:447 Protein: 47g Carbohydrate: 0   Fat: 27g Cholesterol: 121mg Fiber: 0 Sodium:123mg

MEAT

STIR-FRIED BEEF WITH TOMATO AND ONION

Serves 4-6

Preparation: 20 minutes
Cook: 10-15 minutes

1	tablespoon cornstarch
2	tablespoons sugar
	Salt and freshly ground black pepper to taste
1	tablespoon soy sauce
1	teaspoon sherry or dry white wine
1	flank steak (1-1½ pounds)
2	tablespoons vegetable oil (1 tablespoon canola oil and 1 tablespoon sesame oil)
1	clove garlic, mashed with the side of a knife
1	small onion, coarsely chopped
4-5	green onions, cut into ½-inch lengths
4	medium tomatoes, cut into wedges

1. In a medium-sized bowl, prepare marinade by blending cornstarch, sugar, salt, pepper, soy sauce and sherry or wine.

2. Thinly slice flank steak across the grain, and add to the bowl. Toss meat to coat all sides. Allow to marinate at room temperature for 15 minutes.

3. In a wok or skillet, heat oil and brown the garlic to flavor oil. Remove garlic and discard. Pour off half the oil and reserve. Add chopped onions and cook until transparent. Remove to a platter and keep warm.

4. Return reserved oil to pan and when hot, add meat in batches and stir fry until no longer pink. When meat is cooked, add cooked onions, green onions and tomatoes. Cook for approximately 2 minutes more. Serve immediately with fluffy rice and steamed vegetables.

Analysis per serving: Calories: 293 Protein: 25g Carbohydrate: 10g Fat: 16g Cholesterol: 60mg Fiber: 0.4g Sodium: 227mg

VIETNAMESE LEMONGRASS-SAUTÉED BEEF

Serves 2-4

Lemongrass, ginger and sesame oil blend to give this quick and easy beef dish that distinctly aromatic, Asian flavor. This recipe was contributed by California Project LEAN, an organization educating consumers to make healthful food choices.

Preparation: 20-25 minutes
Marinate: 1 hour
Cook: 10 minutes

8	ounces lean beef (eye of round or top round)

MARINADE

2	teaspoons soy sauce
3	teaspoons wine
1/2	teaspoon sugar
2	teaspoons cornstarch
1	tablespoon water

SAUCE

	Pinch of pepper
1/8	teaspoon sesame oil
1	teaspoon soy sauce
1	teaspoon cornstarch
1/4	cup water

TO STIR FRY

1	teaspoon sesame oil
1	teaspoon peanut oil
4	slices fresh ginger, slivered
1/2	cup coarsely chopped onion
2	green onions, chopped into 1-inch pieces
2	cloves garlic, sliced
1	stalk lemongrass, finely chopped, tough top trimmed off
	Red chile pepper, finely chopped

1. Slice beef at an angle into very thin strips and place in a shallow dish. In a small bowl, combine marinade ingredients and mix well. Pour over beef and toss to coat all sides. Set aside to marinate for 1 hour.

2. In another small bowl, combine sauce ingredients and mix well. Set aside.

3. Heat a non-stick skillet or wok. When hot, add sesame and peanut oil. When oil is hot, sauté ginger, onions, garlic and lemongrass. Drain beef, reserving marinade, and stir-fry until cooked, approximately 6 minutes. Add reserved marinade and sauce. Stir in chopped chile pepper to taste, cook for 1-2 minutes. Serve with steamed rice.

Analysis per serving: Calories: 291   Protein: 38g   Carbohydrate: 13g   Fat: 8g   Cholesterol: 95mg   Fiber: 2g   Sodium: 591mg

KOREAN MARINATED BEEF

Serves 6-8

This dish, contributed by one of the UCSD Medical Center's own chefs, Jaime Yuvienco, has a Pacific Rim flavor.

Preparation: 15 minutes
Marinate: 3 hours
Cook: 5 minutes

2	pounds top round steak
	Korean Marinade (below)
2	tablespoons oil
2	tablespoons finely minced green onions, for garnish

1. Cut beef into paper-thin strips and place in a bowl.

2. Prepare Korean Marinade and pour over beef. Marinate at room temperature for a least 3 hours, or overnight in the refrigerator.

3. Drain meat, reserving marinade. Heat a non-stick skillet or wok; add 2 tablespoons oil. When oil is hot, add meat and sauté in batches, stirring continuously, until cooked.

4. In a small saucepan, heat reserved marinade and boil for 3 minutes. Remove to a small bowl.

5. To serve, place meat on a platter and pass heated sauce separately. Garnish with chopped green onions.

KOREAN MARINADE

2	teaspoons sugar
3	tablespoons soy sauce
3	teaspoons finely chopped green onion
1	teaspoon finely minced garlic
1	teaspoon sesame seed, toasted and ground in a mortar
½	teaspoon chili sauce
1	teaspoon bean paste (available in Asian markets and many supermarkets)
2	teaspoons sesame oil
2	tablespoons rice vinegar

1. In a food processor or blender, combine marinade ingredients, blending well.

Analysis per serving: Calories: 97   Protein: 11g   Carbohydrate: 4g   Fat: 4 g   Cholesterol: 25mg   Fiber: 1g   Sodium: 567mg

GINGER-MUSTARD LAMB RIB CHOPS

Serves 4-6

Preparation: 30 minutes
Cook: 15 minutes

12	lamb rib chops
4	cloves garlic, crushed
¼	teaspoon crushed green peppercorns
1	2-inch piece fresh ginger, peeled and coarsely chopped
2	teaspoons dry vermouth
2	teaspoons fresh lime juice
2	teaspoons white wine vinegar
1	cup Dijon mustard
1	teaspoon honey
	Freshly ground black pepper
2	cups fine whole-wheat breadcrumbs, toasted
8	tablespoons butter, clarified (see Note below)
⅓	cup chopped fresh parsley, for garnish
⅓	cup chopped shallot, for garnish

1. Trim the lamb chops by removing all fat from the tips of the bones, leaving them bare. (Or ask your butcher to French them for you).

2. Crush the garlic and peppercorns and combine in a small saucepan with ginger, vermouth, lime juice and vinegar. Cook over medium-high heat until reduced by half. Add mustard and honey; bring back to a boil and cook, stirring constantly, until slightly reduced, approximately 5-8 minutes. Strain and cool.

3. Season both sides of the chops with pepper. Spread about 1 teaspoon of the ginger-mustard mixture over all surfaces of each chop. Dip chops into breadcrumbs and pat gently so that crumbs coat all sides.

4. In a large skillet, heat half the clarified butter. When hot, add half the chops, and brown on both sides. Remove meat to a platter and keep warm while repeating the process with the remaining butter and chops.

5. To serve, arrange chops on a warmed serving platter; combine parsley and shallots and sprinkle over each chop.

Note: To clarify butter, cut a 4-ounce stick into 8 pieces and place in a heat-proof glass measuring cup. Microwave on High until melted and boiling, approximately 2 minutes. Remove from microwave and let settle. Skim off any foam. Carefully remove the clear yellow liquid, discarding the milky residue in the bottom of the cup. This milky residue is what will turn brown or black and bitter when used in cooking.

Analysis per serving: Calories: 947 Protein: 45g Carbohydrate: 31g Fat: 70g Cholesterol: 209mg Fiber: 1g Sodium: 1485mg

LAMB ROAST WITH CORIANDER SEEDS

Serves 8

The coriander seeds give a delicious flavor to the meat in this recipe.

Preparation: 15 minutes
Roast: 15 minutes per pound

1	**leg of lamb (5-6 pounds)**
1-2	**large cloves garlic, slivered**
2-3	**tablespoons coriander seeds, crushed (see Note)**
	Freshly ground black pepper

1. Preheat oven to 350 degrees.

2. With a small pointed knife, make incisions in the fleshy parts of the leg of lamb about 2 inches apart. Into each incision, put a piece of garlic and about ⅛ teaspoon coriander. Use a chopstick or narrow implement to poke in the crushed seeds.

3. Rub meat with pepper. Place on a rack in a roasting pan, and roast for 15 minutes per pound, or until a meat thermometer registers 145 degrees for medium-rare, or 160 degrees for medium. The meat should be moist and tender. Remove from oven and allow to sit for 10 minutes, to retain juices.

4. To serve, slice thickly so that each slice contains some of the garlic and coriander. Deglaze the pan with a little herbed vinegar and chicken stock and drizzle over the meat. Serve with rice pilaf or new potatoes.

Hint: To crush seeds such as coriander or peppercorns, fold them in plastic wrap and crush with a rolling pin.

Analysis per serving: Calories: 318 Protein: 26g Carbohydrate: 1g Fat: 23g Cholesterol: 104mg Fiber: 0 Sodium: 142mg

ROMAN LAMB WITH ARTICHOKE HEARTS

Serves 4-6

Prosciutto, rosemary and garlic perfume the meat and artichoke hearts in this Roman-inspired casserole recipe from La Jolla food writer and columnist, Marianne Engle.

Preparation: 20-30 minutes
Bake: 2 hours

1	**3-pound boneless lamb shoulder or 4-5 pounds lamb shanks**
	Flour
5	**tablespoons butter**
¼	**pound prosciutto, chopped into small cubes**
3	**cloves garlic, minced**
2	**sprigs fresh rosemary, plus extra sprigs for garnish**
¼	**cup brandy**
1	**cup dry white wine**
2	**packages frozen artichoke hearts, defrosted and patted dry**

1. Preheat oven to 350 degrees.

2. Trim lamb, cut into 1-inch cubes, and dust with flour.

3. In an oven-proof casserole, melt 3 tablespoons of the butter and brown lamb over medium heat. Add prosciutto, 2 cloves of the minced garlic and 1 sprig of rosemary. Pour in brandy and wine. Boil for 3 minutes.

4. Cover casserole and place in preheated oven. Check to make sure that liquid is simmering and not boiling; lower heat if necessary. If liquid evaporates too quickly, add a little more wine or water. Bake until meat is tender, approximately 2 hours.

5. Just before serving, lightly flour defrosted artichoke hearts and brown in remaining 2 tablespoons butter. Keep warm.

6. Cut remaining leaves of second rosemary sprig into little pieces and place in a mortar with remaining garlic clove. Pound them together until they form a paste. Stir into lamb casserole. Add browned artichoke hearts and cook together for 1-2 minutes.

7. Garnish with remaining rosemary sprigs, and serve directly from the casserole.

Analysis per serving: Calories: 658   Protein: 64g   Carbohydrate: 7g   Fat: 35g   Cholesterol: 233mg   Fiber: 0   Sodium: 558mg

MEAT

BUTTERFLIED LEG OF LAMB WITH RED-WINE OR HERB MARINADE

Serves 8-10

Preparation: 5 minutes
Marinate: 24 hours
Grill: 20-30 minutes

1   **leg of lamb (5-6-pounds), butterflied**
        Herb or Red-Wine Marinade (below)

1.   Place lamb in a glass dish large enough to hold meat and marinade. Prick all over with the tip of a sharp knife. Prepare either Herb or Red-Wine Marinade, and pour over lamb, coating meat well. Cover and marinate for 24 hours in refrigerator.

2.   Before cooking, allow meat to come to room temperature.

3.   Preheat oven broiler or prepare a fire in a charcoal grill. Broil about 4 inches from heat for 12-14 minutes each side, or barbecue over hot coals for 10-12 minutes each side. Meat should be medium-rare.

4.   Allow meat to stand for 10 minutes before slicing. Garnish with fresh herbs or parsley.

HERB MARINADE

½   **cup wine vinegar**
1   **cup olive oil**
2   **tablespoons fresh thyme or 2 teaspoons dried**
2   **tablespoons fresh rosemary or 2 teaspoons dried**
2   **tablespoon fresh oregano or 2 teaspoon dried**
½   **cup fresh mint or 1 tablespoon dried**
2   **large cloves garlic**
1   **teaspoon freshly ground black pepper**
        Extra herbs for garnish

RED-WINE MARINADE

2   **cups Burgundy wine**
½   **cup olive oil**
1   **medium onion, finely chopped**
1   **lemon, thinly sliced**
2   **tablespoons finely minced parsley**
2   **tablespoons tarragon vinegar**
1   **tablespoon dried basil, crumbled**
3   **cloves garlic, minced**
½   **teaspoon freshly ground pepper**
1   **bay leaf, crumbled**

1.   In a small bowl, combine all ingredients for marinade of choice, and blend well.

Analysis per serving: Calories: 153   Protein: 7g   Carbohydrate: 0.6g   Fat:14g   Cholesterol: 26mg   Fiber: 0   Sodium:19mg

PORK STIR-FRIED WITH FRESH GINGER

Serves 4

Three years in the Peace Corps in Thailand stimulated San Diegan, Nancie McDermott, to write *Real Thai*, from which this recipe is adapted, with permission.

Preparation: 20 minutes
Cook: 10 minutes

2	**tablespoons vegetable oil**
1	**tablespoon coarsely chopped garlic**
¼	**pound thinly sliced pork**
	Fresh ginger, peeled into thin 2-inch long slices (about ½ cup)
1	**small onion, sliced lengthwise in thick wedges**
1	**tablespoon fish sauce (available in Asian markets and many supermarkets)**
1	**cup fresh small oyster mushrooms or any fresh mushrooms, thinly sliced**
1	**tablespoon soy sauce**
1	**red bell pepper, seeded and julienne sliced**
1	**tablespoon water**
1	**teaspoon sugar**

1. Heat a wok or large deep skillet over medium-high heat. When hot, add oil and swirl to coat the surface. When oil is hot, add garlic and toss briefly, until it just begins to turn golden. Working in batches, add pork and stir-fry for 1-2 minutes, until meat is no longer pink.

2. Stirring and cooking for approximately 1 minute between additions, first add ginger, then add the following combinations of ingredients: onion and fish sauce, mushrooms and soy sauce, and lastly bell pepper, water and sugar. Continue to cook, without stirring, for 1 minute. Adjust the sauce for a pleasing balance of salt and sweet.

3. To serve, mound on a platter with hot cooked rice.

Note: Fish Sauce is the essence of South East Asian cooking, and is called *nam pla* in Thailand, *nuoc nam* in Vietnam and *tuk trey* in Cambodia. Fresh anchovies give this clear thin brown liquid its powerful fishy scent which fades on cooking. Although there is no real substitute, if you cannot obtain it, use a combination of soy sauce and salt to taste.

Analysis per serving: Calories: 170   Protein: 7g   Carbohydrate: 10g   Fat: 12g   Cholesterol: 18mg   Fiber: 2g   Sodium: 267mg

PORK FILLETS IN MUSTARD SAUCE

Serves 6-8

Preparation: 15 minutes
Cook: 10-15 minutes

2	pounds pork tenderloin
	Freshly ground black pepper
5	tablespoons Dijon mustard
1	tablespoon olive oil
1	teaspoon butter
3	teaspoons liquid-packed green peppercorns, drained (see Note)
3	tablespoons heavy cream
3	tablespoons dry white wine
¾	cup sliced button mushrooms (optional)
3	tablespoons chopped fresh parsley

1. Slice pork across the grain in ⅓-inch slices. Sprinkle meat with pepper and spread one side with a little of the mustard.

2. In a non-stick skillet, heat oil and sauté meat on both sides. Add butter to oil, stirring the meat in it. Remove meat to a platter and keep warm.

3. To make sauce, add peppercorns to skillet, crushing them with a wooden spoon. Add remaining mustard, cream, wine and mushrooms. Bring to a boil, then reduce heat and cook for 1 minute. If you wish to increase the quantity of sauce, more cream and wine may be added.

4. To serve, pour sauce over meat and garnish with parsley.

Note: If using dry green peppercorns, soak in hot water for 5 minutes and crush before using.

Analysis per serving: Calories: 199 Protein: 26g Carbohydrate: 1g Fat: 9g Cholesterol: 90mg Fiber: 0 Sodium: 302mg

FOUR-PEPPERCORN PORK ROAST WITH RED-WINE SAUCE

Serves 8-10

Preparation: 15 minutes
Roast: 1½ hours

4-5	**pounds boneless pork loin**
3	**tablespoons butter, softened**
½	**cup flour, divided**
¼	**cup mixed black, green, white and red peppercorns, coarsely crushed**
¼	**cup pan drippings**
2	**cups chicken broth**
1	**cup water**
2-3	**tablespoons red wine**
	Sprigs of rosemary, for garnish

1. Preheat oven to 475 degrees. Pat meat dry with paper towels.

2. In a small bowl, blend butter and ¼ cup of the flour into a paste, and spread over pork. Sprinkle with peppercorns, and press them in lightly.

3. Place meat on a rack in a roasting pan, and roast for 30 minutes. Lower temperature to 325 degrees and continue roasting for 1 hour, or until a meat thermometer reads 155 degrees. Remove to a carving board and let stand for 10 minutes before slicing. Reserve pan drippings.

4. To make red-wine sauce, heat ¼ cup pan drippings and whisk in remaining ¼ cup flour. Cook for 3 minutes, stirring constantly. Add chicken broth and water, whisking until sauce boils. Stir in wine and heat for 1 minute.

5. To serve, arrange pork on a serving platter, garnish with fresh sprigs of rosemary and pass red-wine sauce separately.

Analysis per serving: Calories: 525   Protein: 53g   Carbohydrate: 3g   Fat: 92g   Cholesterol: 200mg   Fiber: 0   Sodium: 169mg

SAUTÉED PORK TENDERLOIN IN TOMATILLO SALSA

Serves 8

Preparation: 50-60 minutes

2	**pork tenderloins (approximately 2 pounds total)**
4	**cloves garlic, minced**
3	**tablespoons butter**
3	**tablespoons oil**
	Tomatillo Salsa (below)
2	**tablespoons chopped fresh cilantro**
2	**tablespoons chopped tomatoes or red bell pepper**

1. Cut pork into ¼-inch slices, place between 2 sheets of waxed paper and flatten slightly with a meat mallet. Press garlic into pork slices.

2. In a large frying pan or skillet, heat 1½ tablespoons butter and 1½ tablespoons oil. When hot, add half the pork slices and quickly sauté until nicely browned. Transfer to a warmed plate. Add remaining butter and oil to pan and brown remaining pork. Transfer to plate.

3. Pour off any remaining oil and wipe pan with a paper towel. Return pork to pan and add tomatillo salsa. Simmer, covered, for 10 minutes. Remove cover and cook for 2 minutes more.

4. To serve, transfer meat to a platter, and garnish with cilantro and tomato or red pepper. Pass any extra salsa in a separate bowl.

TOMATILLO SALSA

Makes 2¼ cups

May be made a day ahead and refrigerated until ready to use.

10-12	**large tomatillos (approximately ¾ pound)**
1	**small onion, sliced**
2	**fresh California or other mild chiles, roasted, peeled and seeded**
1	**small jalapeño chile, seeded (optional)**
1	**clove garlic**
2	**tablespoons chopped fresh cilantro**
2	**tablespoons oil**
¾	**cup chicken broth**

1. Peel husks from tomatillos. Cut in half and remove stem ends.

2. In a food processor, mix together tomatillos, onion, chiles, garlic and cilantro. Process until finely chopped.

3. In a medium-sized saucepan, heat oil. When hot, add tomatillo mixture and chicken broth; simmer on low heat for 10-12 minutes. Cool, cover and refrigerate until ready to use.

Analysis per serving: Calories: 248   Protein: 25g   Carbohydrate: 2g   Fat: 15g   Cholesterol: 90mg   Fiber: 0   Sodium: 251mg

HAM, CHEESE AND SPINACH ROULADE

Serves 6

Whether served for an elegant lunch or a tailgate picnic, this recipe will be a winner! This do-ahead dish requires much less work than your guests will believe.

Preparation: 30 minutes
Bake: 45-55 minutes
Cool: 30 minutes

1	loaf frozen Bridgford bread dough, or other frozen bread dough
2	bunches spinach, washed, blanched, drained and chopped, or 1 package of frozen chopped spinach
1/4	cup Parmesan cheese
1	egg, separated
2	cloves garlic, minced
2	tablespoons chopped fresh basil
8	ounces cooked lean ham, thinly sliced
6	ounces mozzarella or provolone cheese, thinly sliced or grated
1	6-ounce jar marinated artichoke hearts, drained and sliced
1	2-ounce can sliced black olives, drained
	Poppy seeds or sesame seeds (optional)

1. Thaw bread according to instructions on package.

2. In a medium-sized bowl, combine spinach, Parmesan cheese, egg white, garlic and basil. Mix well and set aside.

3. On a floured surface roll out dough to a 10x14-inch rectangle. Top with ham, mozzarella, spinach mixture, artichoke hearts and olives in that order. From the long end, roll up dough in jelly roll fashion and seal all edges with a little water. Place loaf, seam down, on a baking sheet. Make 4 diagonal slits on top. Let dough rise in a warm place for at least 30 minutes.

4. Preheat oven to 375 degrees.

5. Mix egg yolk with 2 tablespoons water and brush dough with egg wash. Sprinkle with poppy or sesame seeds.

6. Bake 45-55 minutes. After 20 minutes, cover loaf with aluminum foil to prevent over-browning. Let loaf cool for 30 minutes before serving. Serve warm or at room temperature.

Analysis per serving: Calories: 410 Protein: 29g Carbohydrate: 44g Fat: 14g Cholesterol: 76 mg Fiber: 2g Sodium: 1240mg

SAUSAGE AND LEEK PIE

Serves 8

Culinary professional, and former director of The Perfect Pan Cooking School, Lois Stanton, teaches this recipe.

Preparation: 45 minutes
Bake: 35 minutes

PÂTE BRISÉE TART SHELL

1½	cups flour
	Pinch of salt
½	cup (4 ounces) frozen unsalted butter, cut into 8 pieces
2	teaspoons dry mustard
2	teaspoons caraway seeds
¼	cup iced water

1. Make a pâte brisée using the above ingredients. Roll out dough and line a 10-inch tart or flan ring, or 2-inch deep springform pan. Prick crust with fork. Fill with pie weights or dried beans; bake in a 400-degree oven for 15 minutes. Remove weights and cool.

FILLING

2	tablespoons dry breadcrumbs
2	tablespoons Parmesan cheese
12	ounces bulk sausage, sautéed, crumbled, drained and seasoned with thyme and sage
2	tablespoons unsalted butter
6	leeks, white parts only, washed and sliced
3	eggs
2	egg yolks
1½	teaspoons Dijon mustard
1	teaspoon salt
¼	teaspoon cayenne pepper
⅓	cup melted unsalted butter
⅓	cup grated imported Swiss cheese
2½	cups milk, scalded
¼	cup grated Parmesan cheese

1. Place baked tart shell on a baking sheet. In a small bowl, mix together breadcrumbs and Parmesan cheese. Sprinkle tart shell with crumb-cheese mixture, then add sausage.

2. Preheat oven to 350 degrees.

3. Melt butter in a saucepan. Add leeks and cook until soft.

4. Meanwhile, mix eggs and yolks with a whisk. Stir in mustard, salt, pepper, butter, Swiss cheese, scalded milk and cooked leeks. Spoon mixture into pastry shell, top with Parmesan cheese and bake for 20 minutes.

5. Serve hot or at room temperature.

Analysis per serving: Calories: 492 Protein: 16g Carbohydrate: 29g Fat: 35g Cholesterol: 207mg Fiber: 3g Sodium: 867mg

Tim Tulbert

The Old Lighthouse, overlooking the entrance to San Diego Bay, is now a museum. It is part of Cabrillo, National Monument, named for the Portuguese explorer, Juan Rodrigues Cabrillo, who, in 1542, sailing under the Spanish flag, was the first European to discover San Diego's natural harbor. The site offers panoramic views of the city and harbor; and in January and February, you may even see the gray whales migrating to the lagoons of Baja California for calving.

Greg Lawson © 1995

Mission Basilica San Diego de Alcala, founded by Father Junipero Serra in 1769, was the first of 21 Franciscan missions established in California, each a day's march apart. Still an active Catholic parish, it now includes a museum, archaeological excavation site and beautiful gardens. The restoration of the present church (the fifth on this site), with its beautiful painted interior, was completed in the 1970s, from the original designs of 1813.

The fountain at the entrance to the Bazaar del Mundo in Old Town San Diego State Historic Park.
Old Town was the site of the first mission, the location of the Spanish garrison and the hub of all commercial and civic activity until the founding of New Town in the 1860s.

The tortilla lady makes fresh tortillas daily for diners at the Casa de Pico Restaurant in the Bazaar del Mundo.

Greg Lawson © 1995

Ocotillo in bloom in the Anza-Borrego Desert State Park. Starting in February, depending on location and elevation, desert plants and wildflowers offer displays of spectacular color.

Greg Lawson ©1995

Photophile / M. Muckley

Citrus and avocados thrive in San Diego County. The climate provides ideal conditions for a rich and diverse agriculture with eye-pleasing vistas. Hillsides studded with avocado groves produce over half the avocados in the US.

Greg Lawson © 1995

The Flower Fields at Carlsbad Ranch. This display of ranunculus flowers can be seen every March and April. Millions of cut flowers, grown in San Diego, including carnations, roses and poinsettias, are shipped to destinations around the world.

San Diego Skyline
The second half of the 20th Century has seen the phenomenal growth of a glittering downtown cityscape overlooking San Diego Bay.

Robert Mosher, 1994

The California Tower, Balboa Park, housing the Museum of Man, was originally built for the Panama-California Exposition of 1915, celebrating the opening of the Panama Canal. Now the cultural heart of modern San Diego, Balboa Park, with its museums, theaters and world-famous zoo, owes much to horticulturist Kate Sessions. It was her vision and efforts, in 1892, that transformed the park's 1400 acres of barren land into the magnificent botanical setting of today.

The graceful curving blue span of the Coronado Bridge, two and a quarter miles long, links the city of San Diego to Coronado, and is a San Diego landmark. Before 1969, traffic relied on a ferry service and there is still a ferry service today for pedestrians and bicylists.

Sailing in San Diego Bay

San Diego is a paradise for year-round outdoor sports. Golfers enjoy a wealth of courses; but one of the most beautiful in the world - attracting world class competitors, is **Torrey Pines Golf Course** overlooking the Pacific.

The Culligan Holiday Bowl and the giant American flag featured in the pre-game show have been dazzling football fans for over two decades. Every December two top ranked collegiate teams meet at Qualcomm Stadium in what has become known as "America's Most Exciting Bowl Game."

Robert Mosher, 1994

Evoking the image of a sailing vessel, the **San Diego Convention Center**, designed by internationally-known architect, Arthur Erickson, makes a dramatic statement on San Diego's waterfront. A harborside pathway from the Convention Center to Shelter Island gives pedestrians and cyclists wonderful sights of both city and harbor.

Artists, as well as scientists and beach lovers have been attracted to **La Jolla Cove** since the1890s. The **Museum of Contemporary Art San Diego** in La Jolla enjoys a spectacular site overlooking the Pacilic.

The Geisel Library has become a symbol of the University of California, San Diego. The scientific strength of UCSD has served as a catalyst for developing San Diego into one of the leading scientific and bio-tech research communities in the country.

The Sun God by Niki de Saint Phalle has become an unofficial mascot of the University.

Photophile / James Blar

A trail in Torrey Pines State Reserve
The botanically rare Torrey pines, on the windswept cliffs near Del Mar, were an important landmark for early seafarers. Today the Reserve provides hiking trails, a museum, magnificent vistas and beach facilities.

SAVORING SAN DIEGO

A BOATING TRADITION

by Heather Stevenson and Lowell Lindsay
Sunbelt Publications

Casting off from the marina's bustling dock on a chilly December evening, it's difficult to imagine how serene and peaceful San Diego's quiet bay must have appeared to European explorer, Juan Cabrillo, as he sailed the *San Salvador* into this safe haven, long miles from Puerto de Navidad, in Mexico, over 450 years ago. Tonight, the salt-laden air is filled with the sound of carols and laughter. We are joining the many boats converging on the watery route to enjoy the bright spectacle of a favorite San Diego holiday tradition, the Parade of Lights.

Muffled in coats and hats, and wrapped in plaid blankets against a brisk breeze, the vigilant Sunbelt crew sips steaming hot chocolate and gives the captain timely warning of oncoming traffic. The ship's cook *du jour* braces herself carefully in the rolling galley, assembling colossal sandwiches of turkey and roast beef on sourdough and rye bread, with tomato, avocado and all the trimmings, which fly through the hatch to be consumed immediately, as if lost at sea.

We cruise the Bay amidst craft of all sizes and descriptions, on the lookout for each glowing anchor light that signals another prime viewing spot claimed. Settling into a near-perfect spot just before the parade begins, we refill our cups with hot chocolate or aromatic coffee. Then, making sure all small children are still on board, we haul out the hamper of goodies and sit back to enjoy the view.

It's a sight that would surely amaze the Bay's first navigators: a procession of vessels festooned with tiny white lights defining mast and rigging, or illuminated even more elaborately by colored bulbs blinking in time with the music booming from speakers on board. Munching on shortbread, tart lemon squares, chewy oatmeal cookies or chocolate-overdose brownies, we critique the passing "floats," with their synchronized light-portraits of Santas and angels and snowmen and Christmas trees. As they softly glide by and away, we can hear, faintly, over the distant hum of generators, the massed waterfront spectators cheering, and rival boat horns blaring, at each spectacular display.

The last entries blaze by, and the smallest members of our crew have long since drifted off to sleep belowdecks when we raise anchor to pursue our own private parade route. Past downtown's skyline traced in red and green, with messages of holiday cheer spelled out in many buildings' lighted windows, we are on our way to experience a "bridge eclipse" under the arching span connecting Coronado with the mainland. Most of the other revelers have already gone ashore by the time we tie up at our dock again, and the Bay is quiet once more.

Surprisingly, with San Diego's long history as a military base, only once has a naval engagement occurred within its waters. The American brig, *Lelia Byrd*, tried to smuggle out 500 confiscated otter skins in 1803. After the Spanish authorities placed them under arrest, the crew overwhelmed their guards and set sail, provoking first one warning shot from Ballast Point, and then another! Returning fire with a broadside from their own guns, the crew of the *Lelia Byrd* sailed away with no further incident.

The Sunbelt crew, however, associates danger and adventure at sea with the "exploding grill" episode. As in the *Lelia Byrd's* "Battle of San Diego," no lives were lost, no boats were sunk, and no heroes decorated. However, one memorable summer day, a novice barbecue cook rendered explosive results that were fatal to the meal.

On other sailing expeditions down to the Coronados and up to Catalina, we have enjoyed many delightful meals of sizzling seafood, cooked on a gas-fired charcoal grill, bolt-mounted to the boat's stern. There is, after all, no taste like "shrimp on the barbie," shared with good friends, while sprawled on the deck of a gently rocking boat, watching a San Diego sunset spangle the Pacific waters and gild the sails of passing ships.

We were indeed reminded, on that memorable occasion, of just how fortunate San Diegans are to be blessed with so many sail-in restaurants. Late that afternoon, we tied up at one such welcoming dock, to enjoy planked salmon, *sans* embedded charcoal flakes!

We recommend savoring San Diego's excellent seafood any time, at sea or ashore. Please, however, leave the fireworks to history and the memory of the *Lelia Byrd*.

MENU FOR A BEACH OR BOATING PICNIC

Pepper Wedges with Tomatoes and Basil, page 13

Scallop Ceviche, page 22

Chilled Spinach-Tarragon Soup, page 34

Picnic Steak with Ravigote Sauce, page 112

or

Grilled Whole Red Snapper with Oregano, page 153

Marinated Shrimp and Corn Salad, page 74

Salad of New Potatoes, Arugula and Mint, page 71

Green Beans with Walnut-Dill Sauce, page 187

Sweet Red Pepper and Fresh Fennel Salad, page 63

French Bread

Mocha Chocolate-Pecan Cake, page 232

Fresh Fruit

MUSSELS IN SHERRY-ORANGE VINAIGRETTE WITH PROSCIUTTO

Serves 4

Celebrity chef, Deborah MacDonald-Schneider, created this recipe for the Celebrities Cook for the UCSD Cancer Center. It makes a spectacular opening course and is not difficult.

Preparation: 30 minutes
Cook: 5 minutes
Marinate: 2 hours

½	**cup wine**
½	**cup water**
¼	**cup chopped shallots**
2	**pounds Maine mussels, scrubbed (use only those with tightly closed shells)**
	Sherry-Orange Vinaigrette (below)
1	**tablespoon chopped flat-leaf parsley**
¼	**cup finely chopped red onion**
4	**ounces prosciutto, julienne sliced**
¼	**cup finely diced tomato**
	Zest of 1 orange, cut into very thin julienne
	Lettuce leaves to line plates
1	**avocado, peeled and thinly sliced, for garnish (optional)**

1. Place wine, water and shallots in a large pan, and bring to a boil. Add mussels, cover and steam until shells open, approximately 5 minutes. Shake pan occasionally as mussels cook. Remove from heat and allow to cool.

2. Meanwhile, prepare Sherry-Orange Vinaigrette.

3. When mussels are cool, drain and discard any that have not opened. Remove mussels from their shells, reserving the best shells for serving. Cut off the fibrous "beard" and place mussels in a glass bowl with the Sherry-Orange Vinaigrette. Cover and marinate in refrigerator for at least 2 hours.

4. Just before serving, drain mussels, reserving vinaigrette. Fold parsley, onion, prosciutto and tomato into mussels. Spoon this mixture onto the reserved half-shells and garnish with orange zest and a little reserved vinaigrette.

5. To serve, arrange shells on lettuce-lined salad plates. If desired, garnish plate with a few slices of avocado, sprinkled with vinaigrette.

Variation: Mussels may also be served without shells. Place mixture directly on shredded greens with slices of avocado, hard-cooked egg slices and olives; top with a little extra vinaigrette.

Continued on next page

SHERRY-ORANGE VINAIGRETTE

2   tablespoons sherry vinegar (or 1 teaspoon sherry and 5 teaspoons red wine vinegar)
         Juice of $\frac{1}{2}$ lemon
         Juice of $\frac{1}{2}$ blood orange, reserving zest for garnish
$\frac{1}{2}$ teaspoon salt
$\frac{1}{4}$ teaspoon freshly ground pepper
1   clove garlic, minced
1   cup extra virgin olive oil

1. In a blender, combine vinegar, lemon juice, orange juice, salt, pepper and garlic. With blender running, slowly add oil and process until emulsified. Taste and add more salt, lemon or orange juice, as needed, to make a strong vinaigrette. Set aside in a glass bowl.

Analysis per serving: Calories: 129 Protein: 15g Carbohydrate: 4g Fat: 3g Cholesterol: 39mg Fiber: 1g Sodium: 618mg

LEMONY SEA SCALLOPS

Serves 6-8

Preparation: 15-20 minutes
Cook: 5-7 minutes

2   pounds fresh sea scallops
2   tablespoons water
2   tablespoons olive oil
3   cloves garlic, chopped
2   small zucchini, diced into $\frac{1}{4}$-inch pieces
1   large red bell pepper, seeded and diced into $\frac{1}{2}$-inch pieces
$\frac{1}{2}$ teaspoon freshly ground black pepper
1   lemon, peeled, and pulp diced into $\frac{1}{2}$-inch pieces ($\frac{1}{2}$ cup)
4   slices bread, diced into $\frac{1}{2}$-inch cubes and browned in oven, for garnish
3   tablespoons chopped chives, for garnish

1. In a large skillet, combine scallops and 2 tablespoons water; bring to a boil, cover and cook for 1 minute, or until firm but slightly raw in the center. Transfer to a bowl, cover and keep warm.

2. Return skillet to heat; add olive oil, and when hot, add garlic and sauté briefly. Add zucchini and red pepper and sauté, stirring, for 2-3 minutes. Drain scallops, add to skillet and season with pepper. Quickly toss vegetables and scallops together and add lemon. Remove from heat.

3. To serve, transfer to a shallow dish, top with croutons, sprinkle with chopped chives and serve immediately.

Analysis per serving: Calories: 187 Protein: 21g Carbohydrate: 15g Fat: 4g Cholesterol: 37mg Fiber: 1g Sodium: 262mg

SCALLOPS IN LEEK SAUCE

Serves 4

Serve as a starter with the smooth elegant sauce; or serve as the main course, accompanied by baby new potatoes.

Preparation: 5-10 minutes
Cook: 10-15 minutes

4	**leeks, medium to large size**
4	**tablespoons butter, divided**
¼	**cup dry white wine**
½	**cup cream**
	Freshly ground white pepper to taste
20	**large sea scallops**
	Fresh basil leaves, slivered

1. Cut leeks into small pieces and wash well. Drain and pat dry.

2. In a non-stick sauté pan, melt 3 tablespoons of the butter and sauté leeks over low heat until very soft. Add wine and cook until slightly evaporated. Add cream and continue cooking until it thickens slightly. Season to taste with pepper. Set aside and keep warm. If a smoother texture is desired, purée sauce in a blender, and gently reheat.

3. Rinse scallops and pat dry. In another non-stick skillet, melt remaining 1 tablespoon butter and sauté scallops quickly until golden brown.

4. To serve, spoon some of the leek sauce on each individual plate, and place scallops on top. Spoon remaining sauce over scallops and garnish with basil.

Analysis per serving: Calories: 332   Protein: 19g Carbohydrate: 10g Fat: 24g Cholesterol: 94mg Fiber: 2g Sodium: 282mg

SCALLOPS WITH TOMATO AND CORN SALSA

Serves 2-4

Preparation: 15-20 minutes
Microwave: 8 minutes

³/₄	**cup fresh corn (cut from 1 large ear of corn)**
³/₄	**pound tomatoes, peeled, seeded and chopped**
3	**tablespoons minced green onions**
2	**tablespoons shredded fresh basil leaves, divided**
2	**tablespoons olive oil, divided**
1	**tablespoon fresh lime juice**
	Freshly ground pepper to taste
¹/₂	**pound bay or sea scallops, rinsed, patted dry and, if large, cut in quarters**

1. Spread corn in a 9-inch glass pie plate, cover with plastic wrap, and microwave, on High for 1½ to 2½ minutes, until just tender.

2. Add tomatoes, green onions, 1 tablespoon of the basil, 1 tablespoon of the oil, lime juice and pepper.

3. Arrange scallops in one layer over salsa, sprinkle with remaining tablespoon basil and cover with plastic wrap, leaving an opening at one corner. Microwave, rotating dish 180 degrees every 2 minutes, until scallops just turn opaque, approximately 3-6 minutes, depending on size of scallops.

4. Correct seasoning with pepper to taste.

5. Arrange on individual serving plates and drizzle with remaining oil. Serve warm or at room temperature.

Analysis per serving: Calories: 380 Protein: 30g Carbohydrate: 33g Fat: 17g Cholesterol: 60mg Fiber: 5g Sodium: 331mg

SHRIMP AND SCALLOPS WITH LEMON-HONEY MUSTARD

Serves 4

Preparation: 25 minutes
Marinate: 30 minutes
Cook: 15 minutes

½	**pound large raw shrimp, shelled and deveined**
½	**pound fresh scallops**
	Grated zest and juice of 1 small lemon
2	**tablespoons Dijon mustard**
2	**tablespoons honey**
2	**cups water**
1	**cup rice**
1-2	**teaspoons cornstarch mixed with 1 tablespoon cold water**
2	**tablespoons olive oil**
8	**green onions, sliced**
8	**large mushrooms, sliced**
	Sprigs of cilantro, for garnish

1. Rinse shrimp, dry on paper towels and place in a medium-sized bowl. Drain scallops and combine with shrimp.

2. In a small bowl, mix together lemon zest and juice, mustard and honey. Pour over shrimp and scallops and mix gently with your hands. Marinate in the refrigerator for 30 minutes.

3. Meanwhile, bring 2 cups of water to a boil. Add rice and stir. Turn heat to low, cover and simmer until all water is absorbed, approximately 12-15 minutes. Keep warm.

4. Just before serving, heat wok over high heat; when very hot, add oil. When oil is hot, toss in green onions and mushrooms and sauté until mushrooms are tender. Add shrimp and scallops, including marinade. Stir-fry until shrimp are pink and scallops are opaque, approximately 1-2 minutes. Do not overcook. Move shrimp-mushroom mixture to sides of wok. Add cornstarch-water mixture in center; and cook, stirring continuously until thickened; then quickly combine with shrimp-mushroom mixture. Remove from heat.

5. To serve, place hot rice on a serving platter, attractively arrange shrimp and scallop mixture on top and garnish with sprigs of cilantro.

Analysis per serving: Calories: 230   Protein: 25g   Carbohydrate: 12g   Fat: 9g   Cholesterol: 141mg   Fiber: 0   Sodium: 467mg

THAI GARLIC SHRIMP

Serves 4

San Diego food writer and cooking teacher, Nancie McDermott, spent three years with the Peace Corps teaching English in Thailand. The expertise she gained there is contained in her informative cookbook, *Real Thai,* from which this quickly prepared recipe is adapted.

Preparation: 10 minutes
Cook: 3-5 minutes

2	**tablespoons Cilantro Pesto (below)**
3	**tablespoons vegetable oil, preferably canola**
½	**pound raw shrimp, peeled and deveined**
1	**tablespoon fish sauce (available at Asian markets)**
	Fresh cilantro leaves, for garnish

1. Prepare Cilantro Pesto.

2. Heat a wok or medium-sized skillet over medium-high heat. Add oil and swirl to coat the surface. When oil is very hot but not smoking, add shrimp and stir-fry until they begin to color on all sides, approximately 1 minute. Add Cilantro Pesto and stir-fry until it coats the shrimp and begins to cook, approximately 1 minute. Add fish sauce and toss for another 15 seconds, mixing well.

3. Transfer to a serving platter. Sprinkle with cilantro leaves and serve immediately with steamed rice.

CILANTRO PESTO

½	**teaspoon whole white or black peppercorns**
1	**tablespoon coarsely chopped cilantro roots (if available) or use cilantro leaves and stems**
1	**tablespoon coarsely chopped garlic**
	Canola or vegetable oil

1. Place pepper, cilantro and garlic in a food processor with a little oil to help process the mixture. Process to a paste. Alternatively, use a mortar and pestle, but eliminate the oil.

Adapted from *Real Thai* by Nancie McDermott; Copyright © 1992; Chronicle Books.

Analysis per serving: Calories: 147   Protein: 9g   Carbohydrate: 1g   Fat: 12g   Cholesterol: 81mg   Fiber: 0   Sodium: 263mg

SEAFOOD

GRILLED SAKE SHRIMP WITH TANGERINE VINAIGRETTE

Serves 6

This very special recipe was given to us by Chef James Cleffi, of San Diego's popular Cafe Japengo.

Preparation: 30 minutes
Grill: 5 minutes

18	**raw jumbo shrimp, peeled and deveined** **Spicy Sake-Shrimp Baste (below)**
1	**red bell pepper, seeded, veins removed and julienne sliced**
1	**yellow bell pepper, seeded, veins removed and julienne sliced**
1	**leek, white part only, rinsed and julienne sliced**
1	**small cucumber, skin only, julienne sliced**
2	**inches of fresh ginger, peeled and julienne sliced** **Tangerine Vinaigrette (below)**
18	**orange slices, for garnish** **Chopped cilantro, for garnish**

1. Preheat broiler, adjusting rack to top position.

2. Brush shrimp with Spicy Sake-Shrimp Baste and grill for 2-3 minutes or until pink, turning and basting as necessary.

3. Briefly steam vegetables over boiling water for about 20 seconds. Plunge into cold water to stop cooking. Drain.

4. To serve, arrange two-thirds of the vegetables on 6 plates. Place 3 shrimp on top and arrange remaining vegetables over shrimp. Spoon 2 tablespoons of the vinaigrette over each plate. Garnish with orange slices and chopped cilantro.

SPICY SAKE-SHRIMP BASTE

Makes 1¼ cups

May be made in advance and refrigerated.

2	**ounces bottled black-bean garlic sauce**
4	**cloves garlic**
¼	**cup minced fresh ginger**
2½	**tablespoons Vietnamese Chili Sauce (sweet)**
6	**tablespoons sake or rice wine**
¼	**cup sesame oil**
¼	**cup vegetable oil**
¼	**cup soy sauce**

1. Place all ingredients in a blender and process until smooth and emulsified.

Continued on next page

TANGERINE VINAIGRETTE

Makes 1 cup

May be made 2-3 days in advance.

½	**cup tangerine juice**
2	**tablespoons rice vinegar**
1	**small shallot, minced**
1	**clove garlic, minced**
2	**teaspoons mirin (sweet rice wine)**
½	**teaspoon soy sauce**
⅓	**cup vegetable oil (preferably canola)**
	White pepper to taste

1. In a medium-sized bowl, combine juice, vinegar, shallot, garlic, mirin and soy sauce. Whisk together until well-blended. While continuing to whisk, add oil in a steady stream and incorporate well. Season with pepper to taste.

2. Store in a covered container in refrigerator.

Analysis per serving: Calories: 274 Protein: 8g Carbohydrate: 10g Fat: 21g Cholesterol: 61mg Fiber: 1g Sodium: 596mg

SEAFOOD

BROILED SHRIMP WITH SOY-CITRUS MARINADE

Serves 4

Preparation: 10-15 minutes
Marinate: 8 hours
Grill: 2-5 minutes

2   pounds large raw shrimp, shelled and deveined

SOY-CITRUS MARINADE

⅓   cup freshly squeezed orange juice
2   tablespoons fresh lemon juice
2   tablespoons low-sodium soy sauce
1-2   tablespoons finely minced fresh ginger
1   tablespoon grated orange zest
1½   teaspoons canola or other vegetable oil
3   cloves garlic, crushed
     Freshly ground black pepper
     Orange slices, for garnish

1. Place shrimp in a rectangular glass baking dish.

2. In a small bowl, combine marinade ingredients. Pour mixture over shrimp, stirring to coat. Cover and marinate in refrigerator for 8 hours or overnight, turning occasionally.

3. Preheat broiler; setting rack 6 inches from heat source; or prepare a fire in a charcoal grill.

4. Drain shrimp, reserving marinade. Thread on skewers and broil or grill for 2-5 minutes total time, turning once. Baste occasionally with marinade.

5. To serve, arrange shrimp on individual plates (removing from skewers if preferred) and garnish with orange slices.

Analysis per serving: Calories: 262 Protein: 49g Carbohydrate: 5g Fat: 4g Cholesterol: 443mg Fiber: 0 Sodium: 773mg

SHRIMP IN LEMON CURRY

Serves 6

Preparation: 15 minutes
Cook: 15-20 minutes

¼	cup freshly squeezed lemon juice
⅓	cup cider vinegar
1	teaspoon cumin
1	teaspoon turmeric
¼	teaspoon cayenne pepper
¼	teaspoon black pepper
1½	pounds raw shrimp, shelled, deveined, tails attached
1	tablespoon vegetable oil
2	tablespoons finely minced fresh ginger
1	tablespoon finely minced garlic
1	cup finely chopped onion
6	medium tomatoes, seeded and coarsely chopped
2	teaspoons honey
2	teaspoons dark molasses
3	tablespoons finely chopped cilantro
1-3	tablespoons seeded and minced green chile

1. In a medium-sized bowl, combine lemon juice, vinegar, cumin, turmeric, cayenne and black peppers. Add shrimp and allow to marinate for 3 minutes.

2. In a large heavy skillet, heat oil over moderate heat. Quickly add ginger, garlic and onion. Stir-fry for 7-8 minutes.

3. Drain shrimp marinade into skillet, add tomatoes, and cook for 3 minutes. Stir in honey, molasses and cilantro. Add shrimp and stir. Sprinkle green chile on top; partially cover skillet and cook over medium heat until shrimp are just pink and firm, approximately 3-4 minutes.

4. Serve immediately accompanied by steamed rice and curry condiments.

Adapted, with permission, from *The UCSD Healthy Diet for Diabetes*, by Susan Algert, Barbara Grasse, Annie Durning; Copyright © 1990; Houghton Mifflin Co.

Analysis per serving: Calories: 204 Protein: 25g   Carbohydrate: 16g Fat: 5g Cholesterol: 175mg Fiber: 2g Sodium: 172mg

SPICY SHRIMP WITH CHICKEN CILANTRO

Serves 4

This fiery dish from Vista's La Paloma Restaurant, will appeal to those who like it hot. If preferred, the quantity of pepper may be reduced.

Preparation: 20 minutes
Cook: 5 minutes

2	teaspoons paprika
2	teaspoons onion powder
2	teaspoons garlic powder
1½	teaspoons cayenne pepper
1½	teaspoons white pepper
1½	teaspoons finely ground black pepper
1	teaspoon dried thyme, crumbled
1	teaspoon dried oregano, crumbled
	Salt to taste
4	tablespoons butter or margarine
2	cups ready-made salsa
1	pound boned chicken breast, sliced
1	pound raw shrimp (16-20), peeled and deveined
½	cup Monterey Jack cheese, grated
½	cup cheddar cheese, grated
	Sprigs of fresh cilantro, for garnish
1	avocado, sliced into 8 wedges, for garnish

1. In a small bowl, mix paprika, onion powder, garlic powder, cayenne, white and black peppers, thyme, oregano and salt.

2. In a medium-sized skillet, over medium-high heat, melt butter and add salsa. Add sliced chicken and cook until opaque, approximately 1-2 minutes.

3. Add shrimp and cook until just pink, approximately 1-2 minutes.

4. Sprinkle spices over shrimp and chicken and mix thoroughly.

5. Place in an oven-proof dish, sprinkle cheeses over the top and melt under the broiler.

6. To serve, divide between four plates, and garnish with cilantro sprigs and avocado wedges. Serve with black beans, rice and warmed tortillas.

Analysis per serving: Calories: 455 Protein: 46g Carbohydrate: 12g Fat: 26g Cholesterol: 228mg Fiber: 5g Sodium: 1254mg

SAN DIEGO SEAFOOD KEBABS

Serves 4

The secret to grilling these kebabs is to start with a very hot grill or broiler so that the pieces will be crisp on the outside and moist inside. Serve with rice.

Preparation: 30 minutes
Grill: 6 minutes

6	**tablespoons fresh lime juice**
10	**tablespoons olive oil**
1	**large clove garlic, crushed**
1	**teaspoon freshly ground black pepper**
2	**tablespoons chopped fresh dill**
¾	**pound swordfish steaks, boned, skinned and cut into 2-inch cubes**
2	**red bell peppers, seeded and cut into large pieces**
8	**raw jumbo shrimp, shelled, rinsed and deveined**
8	**large sea scallops, rinsed and patted dry**
2	**green bell peppers, seeded and cut into large pieces**
8	**skewers**

1. In a shallow bowl, prepare marinade by combining lime juice, oil, garlic, pepper and dill.

2. Add swordfish, bell peppers, shrimp and scallops to marinade. Stir to coat and set aside for at least 20 minutes, turning occasionally.

3. Heat a barbecue grill or preheat a gas grill.

4. Thread swordfish and bell peppers on 4 skewers. Thread shrimps and scallops, alternating, on remaining 4 skewers.

5. Grill over hot coals, allowing 2 minutes each side for shrimp-scallop skewers, and 3 minutes each side for swordfish-pepper skewers. Brush each side once with marinade.

6. Serve each person with one swordfish and one shrimp-scallop skewer. If serving with rice, mound the rice in the center of the plate, and arrange the skewers on top.

Analysis per serving: Calories: 292 Protein: 33g Carbohydrate: 6g Fat: 14g Cholesterol: 80mg Fiber: 1g Sodium: 311mg

THAI GRILLED FISH WITH LEMONGRASS AND BASIL

Serves 6

Carlsbad food writer and author, Nancie McDermott, tells us that, in Thailand, fish is traditionally grilled on a bed of dry fibrous coconut husks. She adapts that method for easy preparation in the United States.

Preparation: 25 minutes
Grill: 15 minutes

3	**stalks fresh lemongrass (available at Asian markets or at supermarkets on request)**
¼	**cup fish sauce (available in Asian markets and some supermarkets) or clam juice**
2	**tablespoons soy sauce**
2	**tablespoons finely minced garlic**
1	**teaspoon freshly ground pepper**
1	**teaspoon sugar**
2	**bunches lemon basil or other fresh basil (about 1½ cups of leaves), tough stems removed**
6	**meaty fish fillets, such as halibut, sea bass or shark (6-8 ounces each)**
6	**sheets aluminum foil (8x14 inches), for wrapping**
	Chili-Garlic Sauce (below), for accompaniment

1. Prepare a fire in a charcoal grill or preheat a gas grill.

2. Cut the grassy tops off the lemongrass, leaving about a 6-inch stalk. Peel off outer leaves and remove the woody root section at the base. Using the blunt edge of a heavy knife, bruise stalks by pounding at about 2-inch intervals, turning the stalk around to bruise on all sides. Slice diagonally into 2-inch lengths and set aside.

3. In a small bowl, combine fish sauce, soy sauce, garlic, pepper and sugar. Stir well and set aside.

4. Place each fish fillet on a piece of foil, and spoon fish sauce mixture on top to cover completely. Add pieces of lemongrass and basil. Double-fold foil to make a well-sealed package.

5. Arrange packages on prepared grill and cook over a hot fire for 8-10 minutes on each side.

6. Meanwhile, prepare Chili-Garlic Sauce.

7. To serve, transfer packages to individual plates, and serve immediately with a little Chili-Garlic Sauce on the side.

Lemongrass is an aromatic grass, native to India. It is a prized culinary herb used for its tangy lemon flavor. Introduced to us through Thai cooking, it is becoming increasingly familiar and accessible. If unable to find fresh lemongrass, use the grated zest of 3 limes, but do not use dry lemongrass as it lacks the flavor. If you like gardening, lemongrass is easy to grow and can be found in San Diego nurseries.

Analysis per serving: Calories: 349   Protein: 54g   Carbohydrate: 6g   Fat: 11g   Cholesterol: 86mg   Fiber: 1g   Sodium: 455mg

Continued on next page

CHILI-GARLIC SAUCE

Makes about ½ cup

Preparation: 5 minutes
Cook: 5 minutes

⅓	**cup fish sauce**
2	**tablespoons water**
2	**tablespoons brown sugar**
3	**tablespoons freshly squeezed lime juice**
1	**tablespoon finely minced garlic**
1	**tablespoon finely chopped green onion**
½	**teaspoon coarsely ground dried red chili**

1. In a small saucepan over medium heat, combine fish sauce, water and brown sugar. Cook gently, stirring occasionally, until sugar dissolves and sauce is smooth and slightly thickened.

2. Remove from heat and stir in lime juice, garlic, green onion and chili; mix well. Taste and adjust seasoning.

Adapted, with permission, from *Real Thai* by Nancie McDermott; Copyright © 1992; Chronicle Books.

Analysis per serving: Calories: 29   Protein: 1g   Carbohydrate: 6g   Fat: 0.1g   Cholesterol: 0   Fiber: 0.1g   Sodium: 454mg

HALIBUT IN HERBAL ZABAGLIONE SAUCE WITH RED PEPPER AIOLI

Serves 6

This recipe is from former Food Editor of *The San Diego Tribune*, Antonia Allegra. Two do-ahead sauces of contrasting color transform a simple fish into a spectacular dish.

Preparation: 40-60 minutes
Grill: 10 minutes

6	**fresh halibut steaks, ¾-inch thick (about 5 ounces each)**
	Herbal Zabaglione (below)
	Red Pepper Aioli (below)
	Vegetable oil
	Chives, for garnish

1. Prepare Red Pepper Aioli and Herbal Zabaglione Sauce several hours or a day ahead. Keep covered in refrigerator until ready to use.

2. Prepare a hot fire in a charcoal grill or preheat a gas grill. Brush grill and fish with vegetable oil, and grill halibut steaks for approximately 5 minutes on each side, or until thickest part of fish flakes easily when tested with a fork.

3. To serve, place halibut on individual plates and coat one half of steak with Herbal Zabaglione Sauce and the other half with Red Pepper Aioli. Garnish with a few chives.

HERBAL ZABAGLIONE

1	**cup fish fumet (or clam juice)**
½	**cup white wine**
1	**cup dry vermouth**
1	**teaspoon coarsely chopped shallots**
1	**carrot, cut in quarters**
3	**egg yolks**
1	**teaspoon fish fumet or Vietnamese fish sauce (available at Asian markets)**
1	**tablespoon freshly grated Parmesan cheese**
	Freshly ground pepper to taste
1	**tablespoon finely chopped chives**

1. In a medium saucepan, place 1 cup fish fumet, wine, vermouth, shallots and carrot, and boil until reduced by two-thirds (to approximately ¾ cup). Strain into a mixing bowl and set over a saucepan of hot water. Add egg yolks, 1 teaspoon fish fumet and cheese; whisk until thick. Add pepper and chives.

RED PEPPER AIOLI WITHOUT EGG

3	**red bell peppers**
2	**cloves garlic**
	Salt and white pepper
½	**cup olive oil**
	Lime juice to taste

1. Heat oven to 475 degrees. Roast bell peppers until blackened all over, approximately 20-25 minutes. Place in a plastic bag for 10 minutes, then remove skins, stalks and seeds.

Continued on next page

2.   In a blender or food processor, place peppers, garlic, salt and white pepper. Process to a purée, then, with the machine running, slowly add olive oil until sauce is emulsified. Add lime juice to taste.

Variation: This sauce is also delicious served as a vegetable dip or on steamed new potatoes.

Analysis per serving: Calories: 382   Protein: 30g   Carbohydrate: 5g   Fat: 22g   Cholesterol: 174mg   Fiber: 1g   Sodium: 277mg

BAKED HALIBUT WITH CILANTRO-CITRUS SAUCE

Serves 6

A perfect recipe for San Diego with our locally caught halibut and many citrus trees.

Preparation: 15 minutes
Bake: 20-25 minutes

2	pounds halibut steaks (about 4-6 ounces each)
1	tablespoon vegetable oil
¾	cup chopped onion
2	large cloves garlic, minced
3	tablespoons chopped fresh cilantro
⅛	teaspoon freshly ground black pepper
½	cup freshly squeezed orange juice
1	tablespoon freshly squeezed lemon juice
1	tablespoon grated lemon zest
1	tablespoon grated orange zest
	Lemon slices, for garnish
	Orange slices, for garnish
	Sprigs of cilantro, for garnish

1.   Preheat oven to 400 degrees.

2.   Arrange fish in a shallow baking dish.

3.   In a non-stick skillet, heat oil and sauté onion and garlic until soft and transparent. Add cilantro and pepper. Stir in orange juice, lemon juice and grated zest. Pour over fish.

4.   Cover and bake for 20-25 minutes or until fish flakes when tested with a fork.

5.   To serve, place on a serving platter and garnish with slices of lemon and orange and sprigs of cilantro. Serve sauce in a separate bowl.

Adapted, with permission, from *The UCSD Healthy Diet for Diabetes*, by Susan Algert, Barbara Grasse, Annie Durning; Copyright © 1990; Houghton Mifflin Co.

Analysis per serving: Calories: 198   Protein: 31g   Carbohydrate: 4g   Fat: 6g   Cholesterol: 46mg   Fiber: 3g   Sodium: 80mg

BAKED SEA BASS WITH FENNEL AND SPINACH

Serves 2

This dish is the creation of food writer and teacher, Judith Feinberg, who has generously shared her culinary expertise with many UCSD projects, and with this cookbook in particular.

Preparation: 25-30 minutes
Bake: 20 minutes

2	teaspoons olive oil
3	bunches spinach, stems trimmed, washed, drained and 1 bunch dried well
2	fillets Mexican sea bass or similar firm fish (approximately 1 pound)
	Freshly ground black pepper
4	sun-dried tomatoes, julienne sliced
1	clove garlic, very finely minced
4-5	large leaves fresh basil, julienne sliced
1	bulb fennel, leaves reserved and bulb thinly sliced horizontally
1	onion, thinly sliced
1	piece of parchment paper or aluminum foil large enough to enclose fish and ingredients comfortably
2	teaspoons olive oil

1. Preheat oven to 350 degrees.

2. Brush foil or parchment paper with a little of the olive oil, and spread the bunch of well-dried spinach over it.

3. Place fish on the bed of spinach; brush lightly with oil and season with pepper. Scatter sun-dried tomatoes, garlic, basil and fennel leaves over it. Top with onion and fennel slices and drizzle with remaining olive oil. Bring edges of foil or parchment paper together and double-fold to make a package (If using parchment, use paper clips to hold package firmly closed).

4. Place package on a cookie sheet with sides. Bake for 20 minutes, or until fish flakes easily when tested with a fork. (Before testing, carefully open one corner of package and let steam escape.)

5. While fish is cooking, toss the 2 remaining bunches of spinach in a sauté pan until wilted, allowing them to steam in the water clinging to their leaves. Season with pepper to taste.

6. To serve, spread a bed of sautéed spinach on each plate, top with contents of fish package. Serve with steamed rice.

Analysis per serving: Calories: 430 Protein: 61g Carbohydrate: 34g Fat: 9g Cholesterol: 122mg Fiber: 18g Sodium: 703mg

TAGINE OF MAHI MAHI AND VEGETABLES

Serves 4

San Diego author and food writer, Kitty Morse, grew up in Morocco, and we retain the Moroccan word "tagine" in her delicious seafood recipe, because the English word "stew" cannot do justice to the color and taste of this Mediterranian-inspired dish. Tagines are based on seasonal vegetables and fruit, and usually contain relatively small amounts of meat or seafood to add flavor to the sauce.

Preparation: 20 minutes
Bake: 45 minutes

4	thick slices mahi mahi, shark or monkfish (about 1½ pounds)
1	cup coarsely chopped parsley
½	cup coarsely chopped cilantro
3	cloves garlic, minced (or more to taste)
	Juice of ½ lemon
3	medium carrots, peeled and cut into sticks
1	green bell pepper, seeded and cut into rings
6	small tomatoes, peeled, seeded and sliced
1	small onion, thinly sliced
½	small lemon, thinly sliced
½	cup vegetable oil
½	teaspoon salt
1	teaspoon turmeric
8	Spanish saffron threads, crushed (see Note below)
1	teaspoon ground ginger
12	marinated Greek-style olives, pitted
	Extra chopped parsley, for garnish

1. Preheat oven to 350 degrees. In a large bowl, place the fish, parsley, cilantro, garlic and lemon juice. Stir to coat. Let stand for a few minutes.

2. In the meantime, place half the carrot sticks at the bottom of an oven-proof serving dish. Layer half the green pepper rings, half the tomatoes, half the onion, and half the lemon slices over carrots. Set fish on top of lemon slices, and top with remaining vegetables, ending with slices of lemon.

3. In a small bowl, mix vegetable oil with turmeric, saffron and ginger; pour over fish. Sprinkle with olives. Cover tightly with foil, and then a lid, and bake until fish flakes easily when tested with a fork, 45-50 minutes.

4. Before serving, taste sauce. For extra "tang", add more lemon juice. Sprinkle with chopped parsley. Serve immediately with warm, crusty bread, steamed couscous or white rice.

Note: Spanish saffron (not to be confused with safflower which is a food coloring) is available in small vials at gourmet speciality cooking stores and some oriental importers.

Analysis per serving: Calories: 508 Protein: 37g Carbohydrate: 20g Fat: 32g Cholesterol: 94mg Fiber: 5g Sodium: 503mg

SALMON WITH DILL OR TARRAGON SAUCE

Serves 4

Preparation: 10 minutes
Bake: 15 minutes

3	**tablespoons butter, divided**
1½	**pounds salmon fillet**
	Salt to taste
¼	**cup dry white wine**
½	**teaspoon fresh tarragon or dill**
4	**teaspoons Dijon mustard**
	Fresh dill or tarragon, for garnish

1. Heat oven to 400 degrees.

2. Melt 2 tablespoons butter in a roasting pan large enough to hold fish in one layer. Put fish in the butter and turn over to coat. Sprinkle with salt and pepper to taste.

3. Bake for 10-15 minutes, turning once. Test fish with a fork, and remove from heat just before flaky stage is reached.

4. Meanwhile, combine wine, dill or tarragon, and mustard in a small saucepan and simmer for 2 minutes. Remove sauce from heat, and set aside until fish is ready to serve.

5. Just before serving, gently reheat sauce and add remaining 1 tablespoon of butter, stirring until melted.

6. Cut fish into serving portions, top with sauce, and serve on warmed plates, garnished with fresh dill or tarragon.

Variation: Other white flaky fish fillet may be substituted for salmon.

Analysis per serving: Calories: 329   Protein: 47g   Carbohydrate: 0   Fat: 13g   Cholesterol: 83mg   Fiber: 0   Sodium: 166mg

BARBECUED SALMON WITH DILL-CUCUMBER BUTTER

Serves 6

With the dill butter prepared in advance, you can have a delicious barbecued meal in ten minutes. Serve with fresh vegetables and corn, grilled at the same time.

Preparation: 5 minutes
Grill: 6-8 minutes

6	**5-ounce salmon fillets**
2	**tablespoons lime juice**
	Dill-Cucumber Butter (below)
6	**sprigs of dill**

1. Lightly brush barbecue grill with oil and position it about 4-5 inches from the hot coals.

2. Brush salmon fillets with lime juice on both sides and grill approximately 3-4 minutes on each side or until fish flakes easily, when tested with a fork. Fish should still be a little moist.

3. To serve, cut Dill-Cucumber Butter into ½-inch slices and place one slice on each fillet. Garnish with sprigs of dill.

DILL-CUCUMBER BUTTER

Makes 1¼ cups

Preparation: 25 minutes
Chill: 3 hours

½	**cup white wine**
1	**large shallot, minced**
	Juice of 2 limes
2	**tablespoons chopped fresh dill weed**
1	**cup unsalted butter**
⅓	**cup seeded, coarsely chopped English cucumber**

1. In a small pan, combine white wine, shallot and lime juice. Cook over low heat until liquid is reduced to approximately 2 tablespoons of a syrupy consistency. Set aside to cool.

2. Combine cooled lime mixture, dill and butter in a food processor; blend well. Scrape mixture into a small bowl and stir in cucumber.

3. Place butter mixture on a 12-inch piece of waxed paper and roll to form a 1½-inch diameter log. Refrigerate for at least 3 hours until firm.

Analysis per serving: Calories: 139   Protein: 7g   Carbohydrate: 1g   Fat: 11g   Cholesterol: 39mg   Fiber: 0   Sodium: 18mg

BROILED SALMON WITH GINGER MARINADE

Serves 6

Culinary professional and cooking teacher, Edie Greenberg, sends us one of her favorite recipes for salmon. Be sure all bones, fat and skin are removed from the fillets.

Preparation: 15-20 minutes
Broil: 6-8 minutes

3	**pounds salmon fillets, cut into individual servings**
	Ginger Marinade (below)
	Lime wedges, for garnish
	Cilantro or parsley, for garnish

1. Preheat oven broiler.

2. Place salmon in a broiler pan and spoon over Ginger Marinade. Broil until browned, approximately 6-8 minutes. Fish should flake easily when tested with a fork, but still be moist. There is no need to turn fish over.

3. To serve, remove fish to a platter and garnish with lime wedges and cilantro or parsley.

GINGER MARINADE

2	**tablespoons canola oil**
3	**tablespoons finely chopped green onion**
2	**tablespoons finely grated fresh ginger**
¼	**cup low-sodium soy sauce**
1	**tablespoon sugar**
1	**teaspoon mirin (Japanese rice wine)**
1	**teaspoon sesame oil**
⅛	**teaspoon freshly ground black pepper**

1. In a medium-sized skillet, heat canola oil and sauté onion and ginger, stirring until slightly browned, approximately 3 minutes.

2. In a small bowl, combine soy sauce, sugar, mirin, sesame oil and pepper. Add to ginger mixture and mix well. If preparing in advance, refrigerate but bring to room temperature before cooking.

Note: marinade will store for several months in a tightly sealed jar in the refrigerator. It may also be used with sea bass, swordfish, shark or other flaky fish.

Analysis per serving: Calories: 54   Protein: 4g   Carbohydrate: 2g   Fat: 4g   Cholesterol: 10mg   Fiber: 0   Sodium: 210mg

GREEN ONION-BAKED SALMON

Serves 4-6

Preparation: 5-10 minutes
Bake: 15-20 minutes

2	**tablespoons dry sherry or any dry white wine**
1½	**pounds fresh salmon fillet**
2	**tablespoons olive oil**
4	**tablespoons chopped green onions, white and green parts**
	Freshly ground black pepper to taste
	Chopped parsley, green onions or a mixture of both, for garnish
	Lemon slices

1. Preheat oven to 450 degrees.

2. Place sherry in a wide shallow dish and dip fish to moisten both sides. Pat dry.

3. Place fish, skin side down, on a foil-lined shallow baking pan. Brush fish with oil and sprinkle with pepper and chopped onions.

4. Bake fish for 15 minutes per inch of thickness, measured at the thickest part. Fish should be just barely opaque when tested by slightly separating flakes with a fork.

5. Cut into serving pieces and garnish with parsley and chopped green onions. Serve with lemon slices.

Analysis per serving: Calories: 188   Protein: 21g   Carbohydrate: 1g   Fat: 10g   Cholesterol: 37mg   Fiber: 1g   Sodium: 45mg

GRILLED WHOLE RED SNAPPER WITH OREGANO

Serves 6-8

This is a delicious no-fuss dinner recipe and is especially good served with Papaya and Tomato Salsa.

Preparation: 5 minutes
Grill: 15-25 minutes (depending on thickness of fish)

1	**large whole Pacific red snapper, head and tail intact, (3-4 pounds or more)**
	Fresh lime juice
2-3	**large cloves garlic, crushed**
1	**bunch of fresh oregano**

1. Rub fish with lime juice and crushed garlic. Stuff cavity of fish with oregano.

2. Prepare a fire in a charcoal grill or preheat a gas grill. Grease the grill to prevent fish from sticking.

3. Carefully grill fish so that it stays intact and moist.

4. Transfer fish to a serving platter; and serve with tortillas or rice, and fresh salsa.

Analysis per serving: Calories: 292   Protein: 60g   Carbohydrate: 0   Fat: 4g   Cholesterol: 107mg   Fiber: 0   Sodium: 130mg

RED SNAPPER BAKED WITH VEGETABLES

Serves 6

Preparation: 35 minutes
Bake: 12 minutes

2	pounds skinless, boneless red snapper fillets, cut into 6 pieces
2	tablespoons olive oil
1½	cups thinly sliced onions
1	large green bell pepper, thinly sliced
1	tablespoon chopped garlic
1	cup finely sliced fennel bulb
2	cups seeded and chopped ripe tomatoes
¼	cup drained capers
¼	cup chopped fresh parsley leaves
¼	cup chopped fresh basil or dill
	Freshly ground black pepper (8 turns of the pepper mill)
¼	teaspoon hot pepper sauce
1	tablespoon butter
	Sprigs of parsley, for garnish

1. Preheat oven to 425 degrees.

2. In a medium-sized saucepan, heat olive oil and add onions, peppers, garlic and fennel. Cook, stirring occasionally, until vegetables are wilted, approximately 5 minutes. Add tomatoes, capers, parsley, basil, pepper, and hot pepper sauce. Cover and cook for 10 minutes.

3. Place fish in a baking dish. Spoon sauce over the fish and dot with butter. Bake in oven for 12 minutes.

4. Remove fish to a serving platter; spoon sauce on top, and garnish with parsley sprigs.

Analysis per serving: Calories: 246   Protein: 8g   Carbohydrate: 9g   Fat: 11g   Cholesterol: 91mg   Fiber: 2g   Sodium: 354mg

GRILLED THRESHER SHARK WITH TOMATO AND GREEN-ONION SALSA

Serves 8

Preparation: 15-20 minutes
Marinate: 2 hours
Grill: 10-15 minutes

8	thresher shark steaks, ½- to ¾-inch thick (about 6 ounces each), or other firm fish
⅓	cup lemon juice
¾	cup olive oil
2	large cloves garlic, minced
1	teaspoon freshly ground black pepper
	Tomato and Green-Onion Salsa (below)
	Flat-leaf parsley or fresh cilantro, for garnish

1. Rinse fish steaks and pat dry. Place in one layer in a shallow glass dish or pan.

2. In a small bowl, whisk together lemon juice, oil, garlic and pepper; pour over fish. Cover with plastic wrap and refrigerate for at least 2 hours, turning several times.

3. Prepare a hot grill or broiler. Oil the rack or pan to prevent sticking. Place fish on rack; grill for approximately 5 minutes on each side, until fish flakes. Do not overcook. Cooking time will depend on the thickness of the fish and the intensity of heat.

4. Arrange the fish on a serving platter and spoon on the Tomato and Green-Onion Salsa to cover half of each fish steak. Garnish with parsley or cilantro.

TOMATO AND GREEN-ONION SALSA

¼	cup olive oil
2	cups chopped green onions
¼	teaspoon sugar
2	large cloves garlic, finely chopped
1	heaping tablespoon finely chopped fresh ginger
4	cups tomatoes, peeled, seeded and chopped
¼	cup dry white wine
¼	teaspoon salt
¼	teaspoon freshly ground black pepper
	Sugar

1. In a large heavy skillet, heat olive oil over medium-high heat. Cook onions and sugar for 4-5 minutes, stirring occasionally. Add garlic and ginger; cook for 2-3 more minutes.

2. Add tomatoes, wine, salt and pepper; cook until liquid is reduced by half. Adjust seasoning, adding a pinch of sugar if taste is too acidic. Set aside. Reheat before serving.

Note: Relish can be made ahead. Cover and refrigerate. Bring to room temperature before reheating.

Analysis per serving: Calories: 577 Protein: 39g Carbohydrate: 8g Fat: 43g Cholesterol: 120mg Fiber: 2g Sodium: 173mg

SWORDFISH MEDITERRANEAN STYLE

Serves 6

Shark is a good substitute if swordfish is not available.

Preparation: 30-40 minutes
Cook: 25-30 minutes

3	swordfish steaks, 1-inch thick (about 1½-2 pounds total)
¼	cup flour
5	tablespoons olive oil, divided
1	large onion, thinly sliced
2	medium cloves garlic, peeled and minced
1	celery stalk, finely chopped
½	cup pitted and halved Mediterranean-style green olives
3	tablespoons pine nuts, toasted
1	tablespoon capers
2	tablespoons golden raisins, plumped in hot water until soft; drained
1	cup peeled, seeded and chopped tomatoes

1. Preheat oven to 400 degrees.

2. Lightly flour swordfish and shake off excess flour.

3. Heat 2 tablespoons of the olive oil in a large skillet over medium-high heat. Add fish and sauté until lightly browned, approximately 2-3 minutes per side. Remove from pan and set aside.

4. Reduce heat, add remaining 3 tablespoons olive oil to pan, add onions and sauté until soft. Add garlic, celery, olives, pine nuts, capers, drained raisins and tomatoes. Raise heat to medium-high and cook until sauce is thick, approximately 10 minutes. Remove from heat.

5. Place half the sauce in a shallow, oven-proof dish. Add fish and spoon remaining sauce on top. Bake until cooked, but still juicy, approximately 7-9 minutes. Be careful not to overcook.

6. To serve, cut steaks in half and serve hot. May also be served at room temperature.

Analysis per serving: Calories: 366 Protein: 33g Carbohydrate: 10g Fat: 22g Cholesterol: 60mg Fiber: 2g Sodium: 590mg

SAVORING SAN DIEGO

FLAVORS OF THE PACIFIC RIM

by Su-Mei Yu,
Chef and Owner of Saffron Restaurant

Recently, while walking through the university campus, an announcement caught my eye. Tagged casually to a wooden pole, a flyer said: "Pad Thai Night - All you can eat for $4.50". It would seem, by the lack of further explanation, that this Asian food is now as common as the hot dog or hamburger—at least among students.

San Diego has been home to an Asian community since migrations in the late 1800s and early 1900s. Chinese and Filipinos worked on the railroad, for the port, or crewed on fishing vessels based in San Diego. Early Japanese migrants here were attracted to the rich agricultural valleys and farming. Remnants of settlements downtown are evidenced in Chinese buildings on Island and J Streets. However, the Asian community was, for a long time, invisible to local San Diegans. Both markets and restaurants limited their offerings to the familiar stereotypical Asian food.

At the end of the Vietnam war, the dramatic exodus of Southeast Asians into America raised our consciousness of Asian life. Because Camp Pendleton was a major Vietnamese relocation center, many immigrants settled in San Diego. Their hunger for traditional menus and foods led to an explosion of Asian grocery stores. More than thirty markets now specialize in foods from Southeast Asian countries, Japan, the Philippines and Korea. Industrious entrepreneurs opened restaurants specializing in traditional or authentic Asian cuisines. Adventurous California chefs began to capitalize on this emerging dining market, and concocted unorthodox combinations and mixtures known as California and Pacific Rim cooking.

Today, more and more San Diegans are exploring the exotic tastes and health benefits of Asian foods. Nowhere is the exploration of Asian culture and foods more authentic and delightful than a visit to an Asian market. Before entering the door, a panorama of new adventures arouses the senses. You are greeted with the pungent aroma of spices, herbs, and fried garlic, mixed with smells of fresh baked breads and roast duck. Intense, strange languages pitched in bargaining tones, against a background of blaring Vietnamese music, assaults your ear. The glare of neon lighting, and the brightly packaged canned goods, stacked helter-skelter, without rhyme or reason in every available niche, challenge the eye. There are at least fifty types of noodles, fresh and dried, such as buckwheat, rice, spinach, egg, wheat, millet, potato and taro noodles. Varieties of rice include sweet, jasmine, gluten—in red, black and brown colors. Tofu can be purchased soft, firm, baked, seasoned or fried.

The seafood section is likely to take up a whole portion of the store, with several fish tanks filled with swimming carp, catfish, clams and crabs. Live fish are gutted and scaled on a cleaning board and washed with running water just behind the counter. Trays of fresh and frozen whole fish—mackerel, salmon, anchovies, sea bass and a dozen other varieties, plus shrimp and squid—are strewn about on ice packs. In the meat department, beautiful fresh kills of beef or pork are displayed in assorted cuts and parts. There are chickens, ducks and pigeons to be prepared a hundred ways.

The vegetable section of an Asian grocery is spectacular: greens—mustard, broccoli, baby bok choy—all flourish, placed neatly among chrysanthemums and garlic greens, along with swamp spinach, cilantro, mint, basil, lemongrass and piles of fresh red and green chiles. When the season allows, there are banana blossoms, green mangos, papayas, fresh turmeric, bamboo blossoms, baby eggplants and Lao ginger.

The growing appreciation of Asian food mirrors positive changes in the public attitude toward Asian settlers. As Asians rebuild their lives in a new country, Americans are gravitating toward the freshness and healthy aspects of Asian diets. A blend of East and West has begun to evidence itself through food, and is only the window to a vast new kaleidoscope of cultural amenities and benefits. Life is always such: when one frontier closes, another opens.

Su-Mei Yu was born to Chinese parents in Bangkok, and came to the US in 1961. Her culinary activities are only one part of a rich and diverse involvement in the community, which includes leadership on social issues, education and the arts.

MENU FOR A TASTE OF ASIA

Chicken Satay, page 26

Steamed Chicken and Shrimp Dim Sum, page 25

Spicy Shrimp Soup with Lemongrass and Lime, page 40

Tangerine Peel Chicken with Walnuts, page 160

Vietnamese Lemongrass Sautéed Beef, page 117

Mango Rice with Almonds, page 96

Asian Chilled Asparagus, page 184

Ginger-Lemon Broccoli, page 189

Sliced Bananas and Berries with Papaya Sauce, page 213

Light and Crisp Praline Cookies, page 242

TANGERINE PEEL CHICKEN WITH WALNUTS

Serves 4

This unique dish is taught by Jerrie Strom, cooking teacher, Charter Founding Member of the American Institute of Wine and Food, and former Food Editor of *San Diego Home/Garden*.

Preparation: 30-40 minutes
Cook: 10-15 minutes

1	pound boneless chicken breasts, cut into ¾-inch cubes
1	2-inch piece fresh ginger, peeled and minced
3-4	green onions, minced
½	teaspoon salt
½	teaspoon dark soy sauce
½	teaspoon dry sherry or Chinese Shao Hsing wine
2	teaspoons cornstarch
1	(2x½-inch) piece dried tangerine peel or mandarin (available at Asian markets)
1½	teaspoons sugar
½	teaspoon dark soy sauce
2	teaspoons light soy sauce
1	teaspoon Shao Hsing wine or dry sherry
2	teaspoons cider vinegar
½	teaspoon cornstarch
1	tablespoon water
	Canola oil
	A few drops sesame oil
½	cup walnut pieces
2	dried hot red chile peppers
	Salad greens, for garnish

1. In a large bowl, mix chicken, ginger and green onions thoroughly; then add salt, ½ teaspoon soy sauce, sherry and cornstarch. Blend well; marinate for 15 minutes.

2. Plunge dried tangerine peel into boiling water; when soft, chop finely; set aside.

3. In a small bowl, combine sugar, soy sauces, Shao Hsing wine and vinegar; set aside. In a separate bowl combine cornstarch and water; set aside.

4. Heat wok until smoking, then add canola oil to a depth of approximately 2-inches. Add a few drops of sesame oil. When very hot, deep-fry walnuts briefly, just until light brown and crisp. Remove and drain on paper towels.

5. Deep-fry chicken pieces until golden, approximately 1½ minutes. Drain on paper towels; and set aside. Pour off oil and discard.

6. Reheat wok, add 2 fresh tablespoons oil. Briefly stir-fry chile peppers until brown, for flavor. Remove from pan and discard. Stir in tangerine peel and chicken. Add soy and cornstarch mixtures; and stir until seasoning coats chicken. Mix in walnuts. Serve with a garnish of salad greens and Mango Rice with Almonds (page 96).

Analysis per serving: Calories: 249   Protein: 39   Carbohydrate: 4g   Fat: 8g   Cholesterol: 103mg   Fiber: 0   Sodium: 245mg

KIWI FRUIT CHICKEN

Serves 3-4

This recipe comes from California Project LEAN, an organization dedicated to educating consumers to make healthful food choices. If possible, use a pan with a non-stick finish, because it reduces the amount of oil or fat needed to stir-fry or sauté food by more than half.

Preparation: 10-15 minutes
Marinate: 30 minutes
Cook: 5-10 minutes

1	tablespoon low-sodium soy sauce
2	teaspoons dry sherry
1	teaspoon cornstarch
¾	pound boneless, skinless chicken, thinly sliced
2	teaspoons vegetable oil (more if using a pan with a regular finish)
½	red bell pepper, thinly sliced
¼	cup chicken broth, homemade or salt-free
½	teaspoon sesame oil
½	teaspoon sugar
¼	teaspoon salt
1	teaspoon cornstarch mixed with 2 teaspoons water
2	kiwi fruit, peeled and cut into thin strips
	Thinly sliced kiwi fruit, for garnish

1. In a large bowl, combine soy sauce, sherry and cornstarch. Add chicken and stir to coat. Set aside for 30 minutes.

2. Place a wok or skillet, preferably with a non-stick finish, over high heat until hot. Add vegetable oil, swirling to coat the sides. Add chicken and stir-fry for 2 minutes or until chicken turns opaque. Add bell pepper and stir-fry for 30 seconds. Add broth, sesame oil, sugar and salt. Cook for 1 minute or until bell pepper is tender-crisp. Add cornstarch-water mixture; stir and cook until sauce boils and thickens. Remove from heat.

3. Gently stir in kiwi strips. Garnish with sliced kiwi fruit and serve with rice.

Variation: For a spicier version, add any or all of the following: 2 cloves mashed garlic, 1 tablespoon grated fresh ginger, ½ teaspoon crushed red pepper.

Analysis per serving: Calories: 192 Protein: 24g Carbohydrate: 9g Fat: 6g Cholesterol: 63mg Fiber: 1g Sodium: 404mg

LIGHT AND EASY FRESH GINGER CHICKEN

Serves 4

Preparation: 10 minutes
Bake: 25 minutes

4   chicken breast halves, boned and skinned
2   teaspoons grated fresh ginger
1   teaspoon vegetable oil
4   green onions, finely chopped
2   cloves garlic, finely chopped
2   tablespoons low-sodium soy sauce
3   tablespoons oyster sauce
2   tablespoons water
2   tablespoons finely sliced green onions, for garnish

1.   Preheat oven to 350 degrees.

2.   Place chicken breasts in a shallow baking pan and bake for 10 minutes.

3.   In a small bowl, combine ginger, oil, onions, garlic, soy sauce, oyster sauce and water and pour over chicken breasts.

4.   Bake 15 minutes more or until juices run clear when chicken is pierced with a fork.

5.   To serve, place chicken on a platter, pour over pan juices and garnish with green onions.

Adapted, with permission, from *The UCSD Healthy Diet for Diabetes*, by Susan Algert, Barbara Grasse, Annie Durning; Copyright © 1990; Houghton Mifflin Company.

Analysis per serving: Calories: 178   Protein: 28g   Carbohydrate: 5g   Fat: 5g   Cholesterol: 66mg   Fiber:0   Sodium: 874mg

CHICKEN CHILI

Makes about 8 quarts (32 servings)

Here is a reduced-fat variation on traditional chili recipes. It can be prepared in advance and frozen.

Preparation: 30-40 minutes
Cook: 4-5 hours

1	pound dry pinto beans
6	cups chicken stock
3	28-ounce cans whole peeled tomatoes, drained and liquid reserved
1	12-ounce can tomato paste
1	teaspoon sugar
2	tablespoons olive oil
2	pounds green bell peppers, seeded and coarsely chopped
2	pounds onions, peeled and coarsely chopped
6	large cloves garlic, crushed
1	cup minced parsley
½	cup unsalted butter
3½	pounds boneless, skinless chicken breasts, cut into bite-sized pieces
¾	cup mild chili powder
2	tablespoons salt
1	tablespoon coarsely ground black pepper
1	tablespoon cumin seed
1	teaspoon ground cinnamon

1. Wash beans and place in a bowl with enough water to cover by 2 inches; soak overnight. (Alternatively, place beans in cold water and bring to a boil. Simmer for 1 minute; cover and allow to stand for 1 hour.)

2. Discard soaking water and place beans in a large kettle with chicken stock. Cover and simmer for 1½ - 2 hours, or until tender. Remove any chicken stock above the level of the beans and reserve. Add tomatoes, tomato paste and sugar to beans and simmer while preparing the next ingredients.

3. In a large skillet, heat oil and sauté green peppers for 5 minutes. Add onions and cook, stirring, until soft. Add garlic and parsley.

4. In another skillet, melt butter, and sauté chicken lightly. Add chicken to the onions and peppers . Add chili powder and cook for 10 minutes, stirring. Add chicken-onion-pepper mixture to the beans, then stir in cumin seed and cinnamon.

5. Cover and simmer chili for 2 hours. Use reserved chicken stock and/or reserved tomato liquid to increase liquid content of chili if desired or needed.

Note: You may wish to have a small bowl of crushed fried chili peppers on the table, so those who desire a spicier chili can add them, according to taste.

Analysis per serving: Calories: 223   Protein: 21g   Carbohydrate: 20g   Fat: 7g   Cholesterol: 50mg   Fiber: 3g Sodium: 819mg

CHICKEN BREASTS CHIPOTLE

Serves 6-8

Chipotle chiles may be found in small cans in the ethnic section of grocery stores.

Preparation: 5 minutes
Marinate: overnight
Grill: 8 minutes

8	**chicken breast halves, boned, skinned and trimmed of fat**
1	**large chipotle chile, chopped**
2	**cloves garlic, chopped**
¼	**cup fresh lime juice**
¼	**cup peanut oil**
	Freshly ground black pepper to taste
	Chopped fresh cilantro or parsley, for garnish

1. Arrange prepared chicken breasts in a glass or porcelain dish.

2. Put chile, garlic, lime juice, peanut oil and pepper in a blender or food processor and blend well. Pour over chicken breasts and marinate until cooking time, preferably overnight.

3. Remove chicken and reserve marinade.

4. To cook, either grill on a prepared barbecue, or sauté in 1 teaspoon of oil. Cook for approximately 3-4 minutes on each side, or until juices run clear when chicken is pierced with a fork. Remove from heat.

5. Heat reserved marinade and pour over cooked breasts. Serve immediately or keep warm in a 200-degree oven. Garnish with cilantro or parsley.

Analysis per serving: Calories: 226   Protein: 29g   Carbohydrate: 2g   Fat: 11g   Cholesterol: 78mg   Fiber: 0   Sodium: 69mg

PARCHMENT-BAKED CHICKEN WITH LEEKS

Serves 6

Preparation: 20 minutes
Bake: 12-15 minutes

6	**pieces of parchment paper or aluminum foil, 12x16 inches**
6	**chicken breast halves, boned and skinned**
3	**medium carrots, peeled and cut into 3-inch julienne**
3	**medium leeks, washed, trimmed and cut into 3-inch julienne**
6	**teaspoons Dijon mustard**
5	**teaspoons chopped fresh thyme or 1½ teaspoons dried thyme**
	Freshly ground pepper to taste

1. Preheat oven to 400 degrees.

2. Place chicken breasts in the center of each paper or foil; season to taste with pepper. Brush mustard over each chicken breast, and top with carrots, leeks and thyme. Bring edges of parchment or foil together and fold over several times to seal, forming neat packages, securely closed.

3. Place chicken packages on a baking sheet, and bake for approximately 12 minutes or until cooked. Packages will expand slightly and look puffed. To check if chicken is cooked, carefully open a small corner of one package to allow steam to escape first; then check to see that meat is no longer pink.

4. Serve packages on individual plates, allowing each person to open his or her own.

Analysis per serving: Calories: 307   Protein: 54g   Carbohydrate: 4g   Fat: 7g   Cholesterol: 146mg   Fiber: 1g   Sodium: 258mg

POULTRY

GRILLED CHICKEN WITH MELON RELISH

Serves 6

This has a Southwest zing to it, and makes a great al fresco meal in summer.

Preparation: 40 minutes
Marinate: 4 hours
Grill: 30-45 minutes

³⁄₄	**cup fresh orange juice**
3	**tablespoons honey**
3	**tablespoons teriyaki sauce**
6	**chicken breast halves, boned and skinned**
	Melon Relish (below)

1. In a shallow dish, place orange juice, honey and teriyaki sauce; add chicken and pierce with a fork to help it absorb the marinade. (If taking this dish to a picnic, place chicken and marinade in a ziplock bag for easy transportation and clean-up.) Marinate in the refrigerator for at least 4 hours.

2. Prepare a fire in a charcoal grill, or preheat a gas grill. Remove chicken from marinade and cook over a hot fire until juices run clear when pierced with a fork.

3. To serve, place chicken on a platter and top with Melon Relish. Serve extra relish separately.

MELON RELISH

3	**cups diced cantaloupe**
5	**cups diced watermelon, preferably seedless**
¹⁄₂	**jicama, peeled and finely diced**
¹⁄₂	**green bell pepper, stemmed, seeded and finely diced**
¹⁄₂	**red bell pepper, stemmed, seeded and finely diced**
1-2	**tablespoons chopped cilantro**
1-2	**serrano chiles, stemmed, seeded and finely diced**
	Juice of 1 lime
	Cayenne pepper or paprika (optional)

1. In a medium-sized bowl, combine chopped fruit and vegetables, adding as much serrano chile as desired for spiciness. Toss lightly with lime juice. Add cayenne pepper or paprika, to taste. Toss again.

Analysis per serving: Calories: 252 Protein: 28g Carbohydrate: 26g Fat: 4g Cholesterol: 72mg Fiber: 0 Sodium: 414mg

CHICKEN BREASTS IN TRIPLE MUSTARD SAUCE

Serves 6-8

This easy two-step stovetop dish is adapted from a recipe by Marlene Sorosky, cookbook author, syndicated food writer and cooking teacher. Both chicken and sauce may be prepared 1 hour ahead and kept covered, separately, at room temperature, for easy last minute preparation.

Preparation: 15-20 minutes
Cook: 15-20 minutes

8	large chicken breast halves, boned and skinned
	Freshly ground black pepper
	Paprika
1	tablespoon butter or margarine
2	tablespoons vegetable oil, divided
1	tablespoon whole-grain mustard
1	tablespoon Dijon mustard
1	teaspoon dry mustard
½	cup dry vermouth or dry white wine
1	cup heavy cream or lowfat sour cream, at room temperature

1. Sprinkle each chicken breast with pepper and paprika and rub into meat.

2. In a large skillet, heat butter or margarine and 1 tablespoon of the oil over medium-high heat. Cook half the chicken breasts top side down, until golden brown, approximately 4 minutes. Turn chicken and cook until springy to the touch and well browned, 4-5 minutes. Remove to a platter, cover loosely with foil and keep in a 200-degree oven. Repeat process with remaining breasts, using remaining 1 tablespoon of oil. When cooked, transfer chicken to a platter and reserve pan juices.

3. In a small bowl, stir the three mustards together.

4. Stir vermouth or wine into the skillet with drippings. Bring to a boil over medium-high heat, scraping up any brown bits sticking to the bottom of the pan. Stir in mustards and when incorporated, whisk in cream. Boil, whisking often, until it is thick enough to coat a spoon, approximately 3 minutes. If very thick, thin with some cream or wine. Season with pepper, pour sauce over chicken and serve.

Analysis per serving: Calories: 539 Protein: 71g Carbohydrate: 1g Fat: 24g Cholesterol: 233mg Fiber: 0 Sodium: 267mg

RANCHO CHICKEN WITH ORANGES

Serves 4-6

Preparation: 15-20 minutes
Bake: 40-50 minutes

¼	teaspoon ground cinnamon
¼	teaspoon ground cloves
2	cloves garlic
1	medium onion
	Olive oil
1	large frying chicken, cut into serving pieces and skinned
1	cup orange juice
4	Spanish saffron threads, crushed
2	tablespoons golden raisins
1	tablespoon capers, drained
1	cup water, or as needed
½	cup chopped or slivered almonds
1	large orange, peeled and sliced
	Chopped parsley, for garnish

1. Preheat broiler.

2. Place cinnamon, cloves, garlic and onion in a blender or food processor and add just enough oil to make a paste.

3. Rub chicken with this paste; place in a baking pan, and broil 4-6 inches from the grill, until just beginning to brown. Remove from oven. Turn off broiler and reduce temperature to 375 degrees.

4. In a small bowl, mix orange juice, saffron, raisins and capers and pour over browned chicken. Cover and bake for 35-40 minutes, or until juices run clear when chicken is pierced with a fork. Check during baking time and add water if dry.

5. Remove pan and turn oven up to Broil again.

6. Place almonds and orange slices over chicken and return pan to oven. Broil for 3-5 minutes until almonds are toasted and orange slices heated.

7. To serve, place chicken on warmed plates, spoon sauce, oranges and nuts on top, and sprinkle with chopped parsley.

Analysis per serving: Calories: 259 Protein: 25g Carbohydrate: 14g Fat: 12g Cholesterol: 68mg Fiber: 2g Sodium: 69mg

ROASTED CHICKEN BREAST WITH SWEET PEPPER SAUCE

Serves 6

Preparation: 45 minutes
Bake: 10 minutes

1	red bell pepper
1	green bell pepper
1	yellow bell pepper
3½	tablespoons olive oil, divided
1	medium onion, chopped
1	tablespoon red wine vinegar
1	cup chicken stock, defatted
6	chicken breast halves, boned
	Freshly ground pepper to taste
	Cherry tomatoes, for garnish
	Sliced zucchini, for garnish

1. In a 350-degree oven, roast peppers until blistered, turning at least once, approximately 30-45 minutes. Remove and place in a brown paper or plastic bag, and set aside. When cool enough to handle, peel, remove seeds and dice. Reserve ⅓ of each pepper for garnish and keep each color separate.

2. In a medium-sized saucepan, heat 2 tablespoons of the olive oil, and sauté onions until soft and transparent. Add remaining diced peppers (all colors), red wine vinegar and chicken stock; boil 15 minutes. Place mixture in a blender or food processor, and blend well into a smooth sauce.

3. Preheat oven to 450 degrees. Place chicken in a large baking pan and season to taste with pepper. Sprinkle with 1 tablespoon olive oil. Bake for 8-10 minutes, or until juices run clear when chicken is pierced with a fork.

4. In a small skillet, heat remaining ½ tablespoon oil and quickly sauté cherry tomatoes and zucchini. Set aside.

5. Remove skin from chicken. Cut each breast into slices; arrange in a circular shape on individual plates. Pour sauce around chicken. Top each chicken slice with alternating colors of reserved diced peppers. Garnish each plate with sautéed cherry tomatoes and sliced zucchini.

Analysis per serving: Calories: 422   Protein: 60g   Carbohydrate: 7g   Fat: 15g   Cholesterol: 157mg   Fiber: 1g   Sodium: 400mg

CHICKEN WITH RASPBERRY VINEGAR SAUCE

Serves 3-4

Preparation: 30 minutes
Cook: 1 hour

3	**tablespoons butter**
1	**tablespoon oil**
4	**chicken breast halves, boned and skinned**
¾	**cup raspberry vinegar**
	Salt and pepper to taste
1¼	**cups good quality chicken stock**
1¼	**cups whipping cream**
	Additional raspberry vinegar to taste
	Whole raspberries and watercress, for garnish

1. In a large skillet, heat butter and oil. Add chicken and sauté until golden brown. Remove from skillet, and set aside.

2. Drain off excess fat and return skillet to heat. Deglaze pan with raspberry vinegar, scraping the pan to incorporate all the flavoring from the chicken.

3. Return chicken to pan; add stock and simmer until juices run clear when chicken is pierced with a fork, approximately 30-40 minutes. Remove chicken and keep warm.

4. Bring liquid in pan to a boil, then reduce heat and cook until sauce is the consistency of light cream. Add cream and reduce again. Add additional vinegar and pepper, to taste, and any juices that have accumulated on chicken platter.

5. To serve, transfer chicken to a serving platter and pour on sauce. Garnish with whole raspberries and watercress. Serve immediately.

Analysis per serving: Calories: 665   Protein: 57g   Carbohydrate: 13g   Fat: 42g   Cholesterol: 252mg   Fiber: 0   Sodium: 755mg

CHICKEN STUFFED WITH CHILES AND CHEESE

Serves 8

Preparation: 30 minutes
Chill: 4 hours
Bake: 25 minutes

8	chicken breast halves, skinned and boned
1	7-ounce can diced green chiles
4	ounces Monterey Jack cheese, cut into 8 strips
½	cup fine, dry breadcrumbs
¼	cup grated Parmesan cheese
1	tablespoon chili powder
½	teaspoon salt
¼	teaspoon ground cumin
¼	teaspoon freshly ground black pepper
4	ounces butter, melted
	Tomato Sauce (below)

1. Flatten chicken pieces to a thickness of about ¼-inch, by placing between two pieces of plastic wrap or waxed paper and gently pounding with the flat side of a meat mallet. Place 1-2 tablespoons green chiles and 1 strip of Jack cheese in the center of each breast. Roll up, tucking under ends, to seal.

2. In a shallow bowl, combine breadcrumbs, Parmesan, chili powder, cumin and pepper. Brush each rolled breast with melted butter and then roll in crumb mixture.

3. Place rolls, seam side down, in an oiled baking dish and drizzle with a little melted butter. Cover and chill for 4 hours or overnight.

4. Heat oven to 375 degrees.

5. Bake rolled breasts uncovered for 25 minutes or until juices run clear when chicken is pierced with a fork. Serve hot with Tomato Sauce or other salsa, such as Papaya Salsa (see Index).

TOMATO SAUCE

Makes 2 cups

1	pound fresh tomatoes, peeled, seeded and chopped
½	teaspoon ground cumin
⅓	cup green onions, sliced
	Hot pepper sauce to taste
	Freshly ground black pepper to taste

1. In a small saucepan, combine tomatoes, cumin, green onions and pepper; bring just to the boil.

Analysis per serving: Calories: 405 Protein: 36g Carbohydrate: 14g Fat: 22g Cholesterol: 121mg Fiber: 2g Sodium: 860mg

CHICKEN BAKED IN YOGURT SAUCE

Serves 4

Preparation: 20 minutes
Marinate: 4 hours
Bake: 1 hour

YOGURT MARINADE

1	tablespoon minced garlic
1	tablespoon peeled and minced fresh ginger
1/8	teaspoon hot red pepper flakes, to taste
1½	teaspoons ground cumin
1½	teaspoons paprika
1½	teaspoons turmeric
1	tablespoon chopped shallots
2	teaspoons chopped fresh rosemary or 1 teaspoon dried
2	teaspoons freshly squeezed lemon juice
2	cups plain lowfat yogurt

4	chicken breast halves, boned, skinned and trimmed of all fat
1	tablespoon cornstarch, dissolved in 2 tablespoons cold water

1. In a medium-sized bowl, combine marinade ingredients and mix well.

2. Pour into a baking dish and add chicken breasts, turning them over to coat well. Cover and refrigerate for 4 hours or overnight.

3. Preheat oven to 350 degrees. Uncover chicken and bake in the marinade for 1 hour.

4. If sauce is watery, remove chicken and keep warm. Pour sauce into a saucepan and heat. Add cornstarch mixture, bring to a boil, then simmer for 2 minutes. Strain over chicken and serve.

TV food reporter, Burt Wolf, was the original source for this delicious light recipe for chicken.

Analysis per serving: Calories: 238 Protein: 33g Carbohydrate: 13g Fat: 5g Cholesterol: 79mg Fiber: 0 Sodium: 146mg

BAKED CHICKEN WITH RANCHERO SAUCE

Serves 4-6

Elena Cota, who gave us this old family recipe, is a local cooking teacher. Through her family, she represents a living link with San Diego's early ranching days.

Preparation 30 minutes
Bake: 35 minutes

1	**3-pound broiler-fryer chicken, cut up**
2 or 3	**Anaheim or California green chile peppers**
2	**tomatoes, chopped**
2	**green onions, sliced**
2	**cloves garlic, minced**
2	**teaspoons snipped cilantro**
½	**teaspoon salt**
⅛	**teaspoon freshly ground black pepper**

1. Preheat broiler.

2. Place chicken on a rack in an unheated broiler pan. Broil 3-4 inches from heat until browned, approximately 7 minutes per side. Transfer to a shallow baking dish.

3. Set oven to 375 degrees.

4. Remove stems from peppers, halve lengthwise, remove seeds and membranes, then chop peppers. Combine with tomatoes, onions, garlic, cilantro and black pepper. Pour over chicken.

5. Cover and bake for 35 minutes or until tender.

Hint: When preparing chile peppers, protect your skin by wearing plastic or rubber gloves.

Analysis per serving: Calories: 203   Protein: 23g   Carbohydrate: 4g   Fat: 10g   Cholesterol: 72 mg   Fiber: 1g   Sodium: 73mg

CHICKEN BAKED WITH ONIONS, APPLES AND DRIED FRUIT

Serves 4

This dish is best prepared in advance and baked about an hour before serving.

Preparation: 30-40 minutes
Bake: 1 hour 5 minutes

1½	tablespoons safflower oil, divided
1½	tablespoons unsalted butter or margarine, divided
2	medium onions, chopped
¼	cup flour
1¼	teaspoons ground sage
1¼	teaspoons ground coriander
	Freshly ground black pepper
1	4-pound chicken, cut into 8 pieces, skinned and trimmed of all fat
2	large Granny Smith apples, peeled and cut into thin slices
¾	cup golden raisins or dried apricots
1½	cups dry white wine
½	cup water
2	tablespoons minced parsley

1. In a 12-inch non-stick skillet, heat ¾ teaspoon of the oil and ¾ teaspoon of the butter over medium-high heat. Add onions and cook, stirring, until lightly browned, approximately 7 minutes. Set aside.

2. In a food processor or ziplock bag, blend flour with sage, coriander and pepper. Lightly dust chicken with flour mixture, or shake in a bag.

3. Heat remaining oil and butter in skillet over medium-high heat. Brown chicken on both sides, 4 pieces at a time, approximately 6 minutes each side.

4. In a large casserole, layer half the onions, apples and dried fruit; season well with pepper. Place chicken pieces on top. Cover with remaining onion and fruit; season again with pepper. May be prepared ahead to this point and refrigerated.

5. Preheat oven to 450 degrees. Add wine and water to chicken; cover casserole and bake in center of oven for 50 minutes, turning pieces and basting once. Remove cover and bake for an additional 15 minutes, allowing mixture to thicken. If too thick, add some water. Adjust seasonings and serve, garnished with parsley.

Analysis per serving: Calories: 428   Protein: 20g   Carbohydrate: 48g   Fat: 12g   Cholesterol: 48mg   Fiber: 3g   Sodium: 54mg

BAKED FIVE-SPICE CHICKEN

Serves 4-6

Preparation: 10-15 minutes
Marinate: 2-3 hours
Bake: 1 hour

5	**large garlic cloves, finely chopped**
3	**tablespoons finely minced onion**
1	**teaspoon Chinese five-spice powder**
¹⁄₃	**cup soy sauce**
1	**tablespoon sugar**
1	**teaspoon salt**
1	**teaspoon sesame oil**
1	**tablespoon canola oil**
1	**4-5-pound whole chicken**
	Sprigs of cilantro, for garnish

1. In a small bowl, mix garlic, onion, five-spice powder, soy sauce, sugar, and sesame and canola oils. Put 2-3 tablespoons of this mixture into the cavity of the chicken. Place chicken in a plastic bag and pour the remaining mixture into the bag. Place bag with chicken in a large bowl and let marinate in refrigerator for at least 2-3 hours, turning occasionally.

2. Preheat oven to 475 degrees. Line a 3-inch high roasting pan with foil.

3. Remove chicken from bag; place in prepared pan and bake for approximately 1 hour, turning the chicken every 20 minutes and basting generously with the marinade.

4. To serve, cut into serving pieces, place on a serving platter and garnish with sprigs of cilantro.

Note: Chinese five-spice powder is a combination of fennel, anise, ginger, licorice root, cinnamon and cloves. It can be found in the Asian or spice sections of your supermarket.

Analysis per serving: Calories: 182   Protein: 25g   Carbohydrate: 5g   Fat: 7g   Cholesterol: 68mg   Fiber: 0   Sodium: 1324mg

CHICKEN STEW PROVENÇAL WITH LIGHT AIOLI

Serves 8

This delicious chicken dish was devised by La Jollan, Jeanne Jones, syndicated columnist and food consultant.

Preparation: 30 minutes
Cook: 1½ hours

3	medium onions, coarsely chopped (6 cups)
3	fennel bulbs, including feathery tops, coarsely chopped (9 cups)
4	large tomatoes, peeled and coarsely chopped (4 cups)
6	cloves garlic, pressed or minced
3	bay leaves
1½	tablespoons dried thyme, crushed with a mortar and pestle
1	teaspoon salt (omit if using salted stock)
¾	teaspoon freshly ground black pepper
¼	teaspoon cayenne pepper
½	cup Pernod, divided (Anisette or Ouzo could be substituted)
8	whole chicken legs, thighs attached (3 pounds), skinned and thigh bones removed
16	small new potatoes (2 pounds), or 4 medium potatoes, scrubbed and cubed
2	cups defatted chicken stock

1. In a large pot or soup kettle, combine onion, fennel, tomatoes, garlic, bay leaves, thyme, salt, cayenne and black pepper; mix well. Add ¼ cup of the Pernod; cover and slowly bring to a boil. Reduce heat and simmer for 30 minutes.

2. Add chicken legs to the pot, burying them in the mixture so they will absorb the flavors as they cook. Continue to simmer, covered, for 30 minutes.

3. Meanwhile, combine potatoes and chicken stock in another pan; cook until potatoes can be pierced with a fork. Add to stew. Add remaining ¼ cup Pernod; simmer, covered, for 30 more minutes.

4. To serve, spoon approximately 2 cups of the stew and a chicken leg into large individual bowls. Serve with Light Aioli (below).

Analysis per serving: Calories: 332 Protein: 24g Carbohydrate: 37g Fat: 11g Cholesterol: 64mg Fiber: 7g Sodium: 365mg

LIGHT AIOLI

Makes 1 cup

1	cup (8 ounces) silken firm tofu
2	tablespoons freshly squeezed lemon juice
2	tablespoons extra virgin olive oil
1	tablespoon minced garlic
½	teaspoon salt
⅛	teaspoon freshly ground black pepper

1. In a blender or food processor, combine and blend all ingredients until very smooth.

Analysis per serving: Calories: 78 Protein: 5g Carbohydrate: 2g Fat: 6g Cholesterol: 0 Fiber: 0.2g Sodium: 138mg

TAGINE OF CHICKEN WITH DATES

Serves 4

Food writer Kitty Morse's sumptuous tagine—a Moroccan classic—makes good use of one of Southern California's exotic specialties: plump, honey-tasting dates. The readily available Medjools, grown in the area around Palm Springs, are the largest and plumpest of all. Have plenty of crusty bread on hand to mop up this sauce!

Preparation: 20-30 minutes
Cook: 1 hour 10 minutes

2	**tablespoons vegetable oil**
1	**frying chicken (about 3 pounds), cut into pieces**
¼	**cup chopped parsley**
2	**tablespoons chopped cilantro**
1	**clove garlic, minced**
1	**teaspoon ground cinnamon**
1	**teaspoon turmeric**
1	**teaspoon ground ginger**
8	**Spanish saffron threads, crushed**
	Freshly ground black pepper to taste
1	**cup water**
½	**cup honey**
½	**pound pitted dates (Medjool are best)**

1. In a Dutch oven, heat oil over medium heat. Brown chicken pieces on all sides. Add parsley, cilantro, garlic, cinnamon, turmeric, ginger, saffron, pepper to taste and water. Cover and simmer until chicken is tender and juices run clear, approximately 1 hour. Transfer chicken to a serving platter and keep warm in the oven. Leave juices in the saucepan.

2. Strain off the fat from the sauce. Heat sauce to a simmer and add honey, stirring until sauce thickens somewhat. Add dates, mashing them down slightly, and cook for 10 minutes. Return chicken to the sauce, and heat through.

3. To serve, return chicken to serving platter; spoon sauce and dates over the top. Serve with crusty bread or couscous.

Analysis per serving: Calories: 681   Protein: 51g   Carbohydrate: 77g   Fat: 20g   Cholesterol: 154mg   Fiber: 5g   Sodium: 155mg

CORNISH HENS WITH ALMOND-HONEY-MUSTARD GLAZE

Serves 4-6

Preparation: 10 minutes
Bake: 40-45 minutes

4	**Cornish hens**
1	**onion, quartered**
	Sprigs of fresh thyme
4-5	**tablespoons English or Dijon mustard**
4	**tablespoons canola oil**
¾	**cup sliced almonds**
3	**tablespoons honey**
2	**tablespoons mustard seeds**
	Watercress, for garnish

1. Preheat oven to 450 degrees.

2. Stuff each hen with ¼ onion and several sprigs of thyme. Dry hens with paper towels and spread mustard evenly over each hen.

3. Place hens on a rack in a roasting pan. Pour oil over and roast for 20 minutes on the top rack of the oven.

4. In a small bowl, combine almonds, honey and mustard seeds. Remove hens from oven; spread mixture over breasts and return hens to middle rack of oven. Reduce heat to 400 degrees and roast for 20-25 minutes, or until nuts are browned and juices run clear when birds are pierced with a fork.

5. To serve, split each hen in half down the breast bone and place on a serving platter. Garnish with watercress.

Variation: Boned chicken breasts may also be used.

Analysis per serving: Calories: 899   Protein: 80g   Carbohydrate: 20g   Fat: 55g   Cholesterol: 227mg   Fiber: 3g   Sodium: 437mg

CORNISH HENS WITH PLUM-RICE STUFFING

Serves 4-8

Preparation: 30 minutes
Bake: 1¼ hours

1	16-ounce can or jar purple plums
2	tablespoons butter
½	cup chopped onion
½	cup diced celery
2	tablespoons low-sodium soy sauce
½	teaspoon ground ginger
1	teaspoon grated lemon zest
1	5-ounce can water chestnuts, drained and sliced
2	cups cooked long-grain white rice
4	Cornish hens, rinsed and patted dry
	Plum Glaze (below)
	Watercress, for garnish

1. Preheat oven to 375 degrees.

2. Drain plums, reserving ½ cup of the syrup for glaze. Pit and coarsely chop.

3. In a medium-sized skillet, melt butter on low-to-medium heat. Add onions and celery; cook for 10 minutes, stirring often. Stir in soy sauce, ginger, lemon zest and water chestnuts.

4. In a medium-sized bowl, gently fold together the cooked rice, onion-celery mixture and plums.

5. Fill the cavity of the hens with plum-rice stuffing and tie legs together to hold in place. Remaining stuffing may be put into a casserole with a tight-fitting lid and baked with hens.

6. Place hens, breast side up, in a shallow roasting pan. Bake until tender, approximately 1 hour, basting often with Plum Glaze.

7. To serve, place hens on a platter, remove strings and garnish with watercress. Serve extra stuffing separately.

PLUM GLAZE

Ingredients may be doubled for serving 8.

½	cup reserved plum syrup
2	tablespoons lemon juice
1	teaspoon low-sodium soy sauce
2	tablespoons butter

1. In a small saucepan, combine all ingredients; bring to a boil. Turn heat to low; simmer for 5 minutes.

Note: Analysis is based on 1 hen per person. For those with less robust appetites, the hens may be halved. Cut them lengthwise down the breast bone, and serve, cut side down, on a mound of stuffing.

Analysis per serving: Calories: 877   Protein: 79g   Carbohydrate: 74g   Fat: 28g   Cholesterol: 238mg   Fiber:5g   Sodium: 1238mg

ASIAN HONEY DUCK

Serves 2-3

Preparation: 15 minutes
Marinate: 8 hours
Bake: 1½ hours

1	**5-pound duck**
	Honey Marinade (below)
6	**green onions, finely chopped, for garnish**
	Hoisin sauce, for garnish

1. Prepare Honey Marinade (below).

2. Place duck in a deep dish, pour over Honey Marinade and turn to coat well. Cover dish and marinate in refrigerator for a minimum of 8 hours, or overnight. Turn and baste occasionally.

3. Preheat oven to 325 degrees.

4. Set duck on a rack in a roasting pan. Prick all over breast skin with a fork and roast, uncovered, for 35 minutes.

5. Cover with foil and roast for an additional 45 minutes. Raise oven heat to 425 degrees, remove foil and roast for 15 minutes longer, or until tender.

6. To serve, cut duck into serving pieces and place on a platter; garnish with chopped green onions and hoisin sauce.

HONEY MARINADE

4	**tablespoons honey**
2	**tablespoons soy sauce**
1	**tablespoon sugar**
2	**tablespoons sake or dry sherry**
2	**tablespoons hoisin sauce (available in the Asian food section)**

1. In a small bowl, mix all ingredients until well blended.

Analysis per serving: Calories: 821   Protein: 41g   Carbohydrate: 22g   Fat: 61g   Cholesterol: 181mg   Fiber: 0   Sodium: 644mg

VEGETABLES

SAVORING SAN DIEGO

HEALTH IN PERSPECTIVE

by Pam Wischkaemper
Food Editor, *San Diego Home/Garden Lifestyles*

Although trained in classical French cooking, I realized several years ago that some changes in my own and my family's diets were necessary. None of us has high cholesterol, heart disease, or any kind of cancer; but we were getting older and more sedentary, and our children were visiting the fast-food restaurants too often. Then I was offered a job developing a program of heart-healthy cooking for a local hospital.

"Health" is the new buzzword in food circles. Americans are looking for a healthier lifestyle, but unfortunately, the media and the medical community seem to have made being healthy a project demanding a college degree in jargon. My students weren't interested in that. Like the rest of us, they wanted simple instructions for some lifestyle changes, especially in the kitchen. Basically, this amounts to care in selection, and moderation in consumption of food—less saturated fat, less salt, fewer calories and smaller portions. The following simple strategies help achieve this.

The first step is to understand the difference between saturated and unsaturated fat. If you simply remember that saturated fat remains solid at room temperature—like butter, lard, and the fat found in many cuts of red meat—you can begin to cut back on its consumption. The recipes in this book have been adapted, where possible, to use olive oil or canola oil instead of saturated fats.

The next step is to choose lean cuts of red meat, and limit the number of times you serve it per week. Make one night a week seafood night, and explore other possibilities offered in this book - main dish salads, soups, hearty vegetable and rice dishes, or pastas.

Use herbs or Asian spices for seasoning rather than salt. Often we don't realize that as we grow older, our taste buds are not as acute as they used to be. So, instead of decreasing salt, we tend to add more to compensate.

Limit calorie-laden sweets and snack foods; change to skim and low-fat dairy products; try less dressing on your salad; and eat lots of vegetables. It's fun to take a family outing to a farmers' market to see what is available, and integrate the fresh produce into your meal planning. Even supermarkets now provide more variety and more local produce—when it tastes good, people buy it. Explore this book's vegetable recipes for variety and new ways to use vegetables.

While our book doesn't attempt to address specific health problems, it does allow people to enjoy the flavors of San Diego to their fullest. The nutritional analyses provided are just guidelines to help you balance your diet. Balance, not deprivation, is the philosophy of this book. Don't be afraid to substitute ingredients, reduce salt if you prefer, or serve smaller portions. But most importantly, make meals a time for the family to enjoy good food and conversation. It's a natural stress reducer, which results not only in healthier hearts and bodies, but in healthier psyches too.

VEGETARIAN MENU

Spiced Vegetarian Pâté, page 20

Winter Squash Spread with Garlic and Cilantro, page 18

Assorted Crackers

Carrot and Potato Soup with Chervil, page 46

or

French Country Soup, page 47

Spinach, Eggplant and Red Pepper Lasagna, page 94

or

Polenta with Sun-Dried Tomatoes and Mushrooms, page 103

Elegant Baked Onions, page 196

Watercress and Belgian Endive Salad, page 58

Red Fruit Summer Pudding, page 218

Lemon Pavlova, page 220

VEGETABLES

ASIAN CHILLED ASPARAGUS

Serves 2-3

Preparation: 15-20 minutes
Cook: 1-2 minutes

½	pound medium-sized asparagus
1½	quarts water
½	teaspoon salt
1	tablespoon sugar
1	teaspoon sesame oil

1. Break off tough ends of asparagus and discard. Cut spears diagonally into 1½-inch pieces.

2. In a wok, bring water to a boil; add asparagus and blanch for 1½ minutes. Remove promptly; immerse in ice water to stop further cooking. Cool asparagus completely. Drain and pat dry. Refrigerate covered.

3. To serve, arrange on plates and sprinkle with salt, sugar and sesame oil.

Analysis per serving: Calories: 47   Protein: 2g   Carbohydrate: 7g   Fat: 2g   Cholesterol: 0   Fiber: 0.9g   Sodium: 473mg

COLLAGE OF SUMMER VEGETABLES WITH BLACK BEANS

Serves 6

Preparation: 30 minutes
Cook: 10 minutes

1	tablespoon canola oil
1	red onion, chopped
2	cups cubed zucchini (or half zucchini and half summer squash)
1	red bell pepper, seeded and cut in ¼-inch cubes
1	yellow or purple bell pepper, seeded and cut in ¼-inch cubes
4	ears fresh corn, kernels removed from cob
1	cup cooked black beans (see Note)
¼	cup chopped cilantro
1	tablespoon chopped flat-leaf parsley

1. In a large skillet, heat oil and sauté onions over high heat, adding 2 tablespoons of water to prevent burning. Add zucchini and peppers and continue to sauté, stirring constantly.

2. When vegetables begin to soften, add corn and beans and cook for another 2 minutes. Stir in herbs and remove from heat.

3. Serve warm, garnished with cilantro or flat-leaf parsley.

Note: To cook beans, place in a heavy-bottomed saucepan, cover with water and add half an onion, cut into pieces. Do not salt. Cook gently, adding extra water if necessary, for approximately 1 hour, until beans are barely tender. If salt is desired, add it after cooking to avoid toughening beans.

Analysis per serving: Calories: 137   Protein: 5g   Carbohydrate: 25g   Fat: 3g   Cholesterol: 0   Fiber: 7.2g   Sodium: 13mg

BLACK BEANS WITH CUMIN AND VEGETABLES

Serves 4-6

Preparation: 10-15 minutes
Stand: overnight
Cook: 1½ hours

2	cups black beans
4	cups chicken stock
½	cup chopped carrots
½	cup chopped onions
½	cup chopped celery
½	cup chopped red bell pepper
½	teaspoon dried thyme
2	teaspoons cumin seed, toasted
	Bouquet garni of 4 whole cloves and 2 bay leaves tied together in a small square of cheese cloth
3	tablespoons chopped cilantro, for garnish

1. Soak beans overnight in enough cold water to cover by 2 inches.

2. Drain beans and place in a large saucepan. Add stock, carrots, onions, celery, peppers, thyme, cumin and bouquet garni; bring to a boil. Skim scum off top, reduce heat, partially cover and simmer for 1½ hours or until beans are tender. Do not overcook or beans will be mushy. Remove bouquet garni.

3. Serve as a side dish, garnished with cilantro.

Note: To toast cumin seeds, spread on a cookie sheet and roast in a 350-degree oven until browned; or place in an ungreased frying pan and stir for approximately 5 minutes until brown.

Analysis per serving: Calories: 265 Protein: 17.5g Carbohydrate: 45g Fat: 2g Cholesterol: 0 Fiber: 12g Sodium: 533mg

GREEN BEANS WITH RED PEPPER AND HONEY-ROASTED PECANS

Serves 6

Chef Harris Golden, who created this recipe, is spa cuisine consultant at San Diego's Triangles Restaurant, and a noted cookbook author.

Preparation: 20-25 minutes

½	**cup pecan halves**
1	**teaspoon honey**
1¼	**pounds green beans**
½	**cup chicken stock or canned chicken consommé**
1	**teaspoon peanut oil**
¼	**cup julienne sliced red bell pepper**

1. Preheat oven to 400 degrees.

2. Mix pecans with honey; place on a lightly oiled baking pan, and bake for 10 minutes, or until lightly toasted. Set aside.

3. In a skillet with a tight-fitting cover, add beans, stock and oil. Cover and cook over high heat for a few minutes. Uncover, and continue to cook until all the stock has evaporated and beans are tender but still crunchy.

4. To serve, top with strips of bell pepper and a few honey-roasted pecan halves.

Adapted, with permission, from *Pleasures of the Palate* by Harris Golden; Copyright © 1989; Golden's Kitchen.

Analysis per serving: Calories: 108   Protein: 3g   Carbohydrate: 10g   Fat: 7g   Cholesterol: 0   Fiber: 2.3g   Sodium: 68mg

GREEN BEANS WITH WALNUT-DILL SAUCE

Serves 6-8

Preparation: 30 minutes
Cook: 5-8 minutes
Chill: 1 hour minimum, or overnight

1½	**pounds very fresh green beans, ends removed**
¾	**cup minced green onions (green and white parts)**
3	**tablespoons minced parsley**
4	**tablespoons minced fresh dill**
3	**tablespoons cider vinegar**
⅓	**cup coarsely chopped walnuts**
¼-½	**cup extra virgin olive oil**
	Freshly ground black pepper to taste
	Sprigs of dill, for garnish

1. Steam beans for 5-8 minutes or until just tender; do not overcook. Cool quickly in ice-cold water. Drain well and pat dry with paper towels. Place in a serving dish.

2. In a blender or food processor, combine onions, parsley, dill, vinegar, nuts and ¼ cup oil and process until smooth. Season with pepper.

3. Pour sauce over beans, and refrigerate for at least 1 hour or, preferably, overnight.

4. To serve, bring to room temperature and garnish with sprigs of dill.

Analysis per serving: Calories: 118   Protein: 2.6g   Carbohydrate: 8g   Fat: 10gm   Cholesterol: 0   Fiber: 2g   Sodium: 46mg

WHITE BEANS WITH TOMATOES AND HERBS

Serves 6-8

This recipe, from Celebrity Chef Giovanni Caprioglio, was prepared for the Celebrities Cook for the UCSD Cancer Center benefit. He suggests serving the beans with sausages of your choice which have been sautéed in dry white wine.

Soak: 24 hours
Preparation: 20-25 minutes
Bake: 1 hour

1	pound cannellini beans or Great Northern white beans
2	tablespoons extra virgin olive oil or other high quality oil
2	medium yellow onions, finely chopped
1	large red onion, finely chopped
2-3	cloves garlic, minced
	Sage
10	plum tomatoes, peeled, drained, and cut in pieces
1	tablespoon tomato paste
	Salt and pepper
	Parsley, chopped

1. Soak beans overnight in enough cold water to cover by 2 inches. Do not salt.

2. Preheat oven to 325 degrees.

3. Drain beans, rinse and put into a flameproof casserole with cold water to cover by 2 inches. Do not salt. Cover and bring to a boil on top of the stove, then place in the oven, and bake for approximately 45-60 minutes, or until tender. Leave in the liquid until ready to use.

4. In a non-stick skillet, heat ½ tablespoon oil and sauté onions, garlic and sage until tender but not brown. Add tomatoes and tomato paste and stir for several minutes until incorporated.

5. Drain beans and add to mixture. Cook for approximately 15 minutes. Add salt and pepper to taste, remove sage leaves, add parsley and remaining olive oil.

Analysis per serving: Calories: 250 Protein: 15g Carbohydrate: 45g Fat: 2g Cholesterol: 0 Fiber: 10g Sodium: 36mg

GINGER-LEMON BROCCOLI

Serves 6

This recipe, from UCSD dieticians, is nutritious, healthy and delicious.

Preparation: 5 minutes
Cook: 5-8 minutes

1	**bunch broccoli (about 1¼ pounds)**
1	**tablespoon canola or other vegetable oil**
2	**teaspoons minced fresh ginger**
1	**teaspoon minced garlic**
2	**tablespoons fresh lemon juice**
	Freshly ground black pepper

1. Cut broccoli into ½-inch thick pieces, and steam for 3-4 minutes, or until tender.

2. Meanwhile, heat oil in a skillet over medium-low heat. Add ginger and garlic and cook for 2 minutes. Stir in lemon juice.

3. Pour lemon juice mixture over broccoli and sprinkle with ground pepper to taste.

Adapted, with permission, from *The UCSD Healthy Diet for Diabetes*, by Susan Algert, Barbara Grasse, Annie Durning; Copyright © 1990; Houghton Mifflin Co.

Analysis per serving: Calories: 27 Protein: 1g Carbohydrate: 2g Fat: 2g Cholesterol: 0 Fiber: 0.6g Sodium: 5mg

LEMONY CAULIFLOWER

Serves 6-8

Preparation: 5-10 minutes
Cook: 5-8 minutes

1	**large head cauliflower, about 2 pounds, rinsed and trimmed**
½	**cup plain, nonfat yogurt, at room temperature**
½	**teaspoon grated lemon zest**
2	**tablespoons fresh lemon juice**
2	**teaspoons Dijon mustard**
2	**tablespoons low-calorie mayonnaise**
1	**tablespoon chopped chives, for garnish**

1. Break cauliflower into florets and steam until tender but crisp, approximately 4-5 minutes.

2. In a bowl, whisk remaining ingredients together, to make a sauce.

3. To serve, arrange hot cauliflower on a serving dish, pour over sauce, and garnish with chopped chives.

Note: Cauliflower may be microwaved. Do not overcook.

Analysis per serving: Calories: 48 Protein: 3g Carbohydrate: 7g Fat: 1g Cholesterol: 1.5mg Fiber: 2.5g Sodium: 49mg

THAI-FLAVORED CABBAGE

Serves 6

Have all the ingredients ready and cook this dish quickly to retain the crispness and flavor of each vegetable.

Preparation: 20-30 minutes
Cook: 10 minutes

1	**tablespoon peanut oil**
3	**large cloves garlic, minced**
1½	**tablespoons minced fresh ginger**
1	**sweet onion, chopped**
2	**large carrots, peeled and chopped**
½	**large head cabbage, coarsely chopped**
1-2	**teaspoons lime juice**
2	**tablespoons fish sauce (available at Asian markets)**
1	**teaspoon sugar**
½	**medium-sized Chinese cabbage, stems and leaves separated and thinly sliced**
8-10	**green onions, thinly sliced**
⅓	**cup dry-roasted peanuts**
4	**tablespoons chopped cilantro**
3	**tablespoons chopped mint, for garnish**

1. Heat oil in a wok over medium-high heat. When very hot, add garlic, ginger and onion and stir-fry for 30 seconds. Add carrots, cabbage, 1 teaspoon lime juice, fish sauce and sugar; combine well. Cook for 2 minutes, stirring occasionally.

2. Toss in stems of Chinese cabbage and cook for 1 minute. Add cabbage leaves, green onions, peanuts and cilantro, tossing to combine and heat through.

3. Serve at once, garnished with mint.

Analysis per serving: Calories: 149   Protein: 6g   Carbohydrate: 20g   Fat: 6.5g   Cholesterol: 0   Fiber: 6.3g   Sodium: 330mg

PURÉED CELERY ROOT WITH APPLES

Serves 4-6

Internationally known cooking teacher and author, Paula Wolfert, taught this recipe at the Perfect Pan School of Cooking, San Diego. It may be prepared ahead, and kept covered in the refrigerator. Reheat gently before serving.

Preparation: 15-20 minutes
Cook: 25-30 minutes

1	**pound celery root**
1	**quart milk**
¾	**pound Delicious apples**
2-3	**tablespoons heavy cream**
	Freshly ground black pepper to taste

1. Using a stainless steel knife, peel the celery root; cut into chunks and place in a 3-quart stainless or enamel saucepan.

2. Pour in the milk to cover; bring to a simmer and cook for 10 minutes.

3. Meanwhile, peel, core and quarter apples. Add to celery root and cook together for 10 minutes or until celery root is tender. Drain.

4. In a processor or blender, purée celery root and apples in batches, until smooth. (For a perfectly textured purée, push the blended mixture through a fine wire sieve.) Add cream, if necessary, to thin mixture slightly. Season with salt and pepper and serve.

Note: In this recipe, apples replace the more traditionally used potatoes, resulting in a silkier purée. The flavor of the apples is hardly noticeable, yet it heightens the flavor of the celery root. The moist quality of the apples also eliminates the need for the traditional quantities of butter and cream.

Analysis per serving: Calories: 119   Protein: 6g   Carbohydrate: 19g   Fat: 3g   Cholesterol: 8.5mg   Fiber: 2g   Sodium: 328mg

VEGETABLES

MUSHROOM-STUFFED GREEN CHILES WITH GOAT CHEESE SAUCE

Serves 6

Preparation: 30-35 minutes
Cook: 5 minutes

¾	pound mushrooms (white, brown or shiitake), chopped
1¼	cups heavy cream, divided
6	poblano or other mild chiles, or green bell peppers
½	teaspoon finely minced garlic
3	ounces fresh goat cheese
1-2	tablespoons finely chopped cilantro, for garnish

1. Purée mushrooms in a food processor or blender. Remove to a bowl and mix in ½ cup of the cream. Set aside.

2. Carefully slit chiles and cut out seeds and white membranes. Roast chiles in a hot oven until blackened. Place in a plastic bag and allow to steam for 15 minutes. When cool enough to handle, carefully remove skins.

3. Stuff chiles with mushroom purée, being careful not to fill them so full that filling oozes out. Wrap each chile in foil or plastic wrap.

4. Place chiles on a steamer rack in a large pan over simmering water, cover and steam for 5-6 minutes. Remove to a serving platter, or individual plates, and keep warm until ready to serve.

5. While chiles are steaming, place remaining ¾ cup cream and garlic in a medium-sized pan, and bring to a simmer. Using a whisk, mix in cheese until very smooth.

6. To serve, unwrap chiles, place on a platter or individual plates and top each with 2 tablespoons of sauce. Garnish with cilantro.

Analysis per serving: Calories: 231   Protein: 6g   Carbohydrate: 9g   Fat: 20g   Cholesterol: 68mg   Fiber: 2g   Sodium: 100mg

BAKED ESCAROLE WITH GARLIC AND ANCHOVIES

Serves 6

This unusual tasting vegetable goes well with fish, chicken or beef. Escarole has a mildly bitter taste when raw, yet calms its personality to assume an almost nutty flavor when cooked. It is abundant in markets during the cooler months.

Preparation: 10-15 minutes
Bake: 35-40 minutes

1	**large head escarole or curly chicory**
3	**tablespoons olive oil**
3	**cloves garlic, crushed**
3	**anchovy fillets, finely chopped**
	Freshly ground black pepper to taste
	Parsley, finely chopped, for garnish

1. Preheat oven to 350 degrees.

2. Trim and discard the wilted outer leaves and any hard core of escarole. Cut into 6 wedges and wash well.

3. In a shallow baking dish, combine olive oil, garlic and anchovies. Add escarole wedges and turn so they are thoroughly coated with oil-anchovy mixture. Season to taste with pepper. Cover dish with foil.

4. Bake for 35-45 minutes, basting occasionally, until escarole is very tender.

5. To serve, fold escarole wedges to form neat packages and transfer to serving dish or individual plates. Lightly sprinkle with parsley.

Analysis per serving: Calories: 80 Protein: 2g Carbohydrate: 3g Fat: 7g Cholesterol: 2mg Fiber: 1.4g Sodium: 101mg

VEGETABLES

FENNEL GRATIN

Serves 6-8

Antonia Allegra, who contributed this recipe, was formerly Food Editor of *The San Diego Tribune*.

Preparation: 15 minutes
Bake: 15 minutes

4	**medium fennel bulbs**
3	**tablespoons olive oil**
2	**medium onions, sliced**
2	**ounces Parmesan cheese, grated**
	Chopped parsley, chives or fennel tops, for garnish

1. Prepare fennel by slicing off dark root and tough stems. Cut into thin (⅛-inch) slices across the bulb. Set aside.

2. Preheat oven to 400 degrees.

3. In a skillet, heat olive oil and sauté onion until transparent. Remove from pan. Adding more oil if necessary, sauté fennel slices, for approximately 2 minutes. Toss onion with fennel.

4. Place fennel and onion mixture in a gratin dish. Sprinkle with cheese. Bake for 12-15 minutes.

5. To serve, garnish with chopped fresh parsley, chives or fennel tops. Serve immediately.

Analysis per serving: Calories: 95   Protein: 3.5g   Carbohydrate: 4g   Fat: 7g   Cholesterol: 5.6mg   Fiber: 1g   Sodium: 217mg

LEEKS AND ZUCCHINI IN WINE-CREAM SAUCE

Serves 4

Preparation: 10 minutes
Cook: 8-10 minutes

3	**medium leeks**
1	**tablespoon butter**
2	**tablespoons finely chopped shallots**
½	**cup dry white wine**
3	**zucchini, thinly sliced and patted dry**
⅛	**teaspoon freshly grated nutmeg**
½	**cup heavy cream**
	Freshly ground black pepper to taste
	Chopped parsley, for garnish

1. Trim leeks to remove ends and tough green stalks. Cut leeks in half lengthwise. Keeping shape intact, wash well to remove any dirt. Pat dry and slice crosswise into ½-inch pieces.

2. In a non-stick skillet, melt butter over medium heat until it bubbles, but does not brown. Add

Continued on next page

shallots and sauté for 2 minutes. Stir in leeks and cook for 3-4 minutes, stirring. They will remain crisp.

3. Add wine and cook down until mostly evaporated. Add zucchini and stir briefly. Raise heat; add nutmeg and cream; boil for 3-4 minutes to thicken sauce. Add pepper to taste, and garnish with parsley.

Analysis per serving: Calories: 206   Protein: 3g   Carbohydrate: 16g   Fat: 14g   Cholesterol: 49mg   Fiber: 3g   Sodium: 63mg

BLACK FOREST MUSHROOMS

Serves 4

This is a light dish that doesn't compromise on taste.

Preparation: 10-15 minutes
Cook: 15 minutes

2	teaspoons olive oil
1	cup chopped onion
3	cups sliced fresh mushrooms (preferably several varieties)
½	cup chopped red bell pepper
2	tablespoons Dijon mustard
2	tablespoons Worcestershire sauce
1	teaspoon molasses
2	tablespoons sherry
	Freshly ground black pepper to taste

1. In a saucepan, heat oil; add onions and cook over medium heat until transparent. Add mushrooms and red pepper. Cook for 5 minutes, stirring often.

2. In a small bowl, combine mustard, Worcestershire sauce, molasses, sherry and pepper. Stir into vegetables and cook over medium-high heat, stirring, until sauce thickens.

Adapted, with permission, from *The UCSD Healthy Diet for Diabetes*, by Susan Algert, Barbara Grasse, Annie Durning; Copyright © 1990; Houghton Mifflin Company.

Analysis per serving: Calories: 78   Protein: 2g   Carbohydrate: 10g   Fat: 3g   Cholesterol: 0   Fiber: 1.5g   Sodium: 181mg

VEGETABLES

ELEGANT BAKED ONIONS

Serves 6

A dish for spring, when sweet onions are typically available.

Preparation: 10-15 minutes
Cook: 45-50 minutes

2	**tablespoons butter**
1½	**tablespoons flour**
	Salt and pepper to taste
5	**cups sliced sweet onions**
1½	**cups half-and-half**
½	**cup chopped parsley, for garnish**

1. Preheat oven to 350 degrees, and generously butter a baking dish.

2. Put flour, salt and pepper in a plastic bag; add onions and toss.

3. Spread onions in prepared baking dish; pour half-and-half over them. Bake until onions are very tender, approximately 45-50 minutes.

4. Garnish with chopped parsley and serve immediately.

Analysis per serving: Calories: 171   Protein: 4g   Carbohydrate: 16g   Fat: 11g   Cholesterol: 32mg   Fiber: 2g   Sodium: 69mg

ROSEMARY-ROASTED ONIONS

Serves 6

These onions are a great accompaniment to barbecued turkey. For the adventurous San Diegans who celebrate Thanksgiving al fresco, this may be prepared in advance and taken to the picnic site for roasting.

Preparation: 30 minutes
Grill: 45 minutes

6	**medium to large yellow onions**
6	**teaspoons butter or margarine**
	Freshly ground black pepper to taste
6	**sprigs of fresh rosemary**
	Aluminum foil

1. Peel onions and cut out the centers. Place a teaspoon of butter and pepper to taste in each onion cavity.

2. Individually wrap each onion with a sprig of rosemary in a piece of foil.

3. Place onions over a low, steady wood or charcoal fire. Roast, turning frequently, until cooked, approximately 45 minutes. Onions should be soft enough to be pricked easily with a fork and should have a lovely roasted aroma.

Analysis per serving: Calories: 100   Protein: 2g   Carbohydrate: 15g   Fat: 4g   Cholesterol: 0   Fiber: 2.6g   Sodium: 50mg

NEW POTATOES IN LEMON-HERB SAUCE

Serves 6-8

Preparation: 20-30 minutes
Cook: 20 minutes

2	pounds small new potatoes or small red potatoes
¼	cup butter
1	tablespoon extra virgin olive oil
	Grated zest of 1 lemon
¼	cup chopped fresh parsley
2	tablespoons chopped fresh chives
⅛	teaspoon freshly grated nutmeg
¼	teaspoon flour
	Salt and freshly ground pepper to taste
3	tablespoons fresh lemon juice

1. In a large saucepan, cover unpeeled potatoes with water and bring to a boil. Boil gently until tender, approximately 15-20 minutes. Drain and immediately peel while hot. Place in a serving dish, cover and keep warm.

2. In a small saucepan, melt butter with olive oil over low heat. Stir in lemon zest, parsley, chives, nutmeg and flour. Blend well and add salt and pepper to taste. Cook, stirring constantly until mixture thickens slightly. Do not allow to boil.

3. Just before serving, stir lemon juice into the hot butter mixture and pour over warm potatoes. Using a wooden spoon, gently toss, coating each potato evenly with the sauce.

Analysis per serving: Calories: 167 Protein: 2g Carbohydrate: 24g Fat:8g Cholesterol: 15mg Fiber: 2g Sodium: 197mg

HERBED ROASTED POTATOES WITH GARLIC

Serves 8

Preparation: 5 minutes
Bake: 1 hour

3	pounds small red potatoes, quartered, skins left on
3	tablespoons olive oil
¼	teaspoon salt
½	teaspoon freshly ground black pepper
3	large cloves garlic, thinly sliced
¼	cup minced flat-leaf parsley

1. Preheat oven to 350 degrees.

2. In a large roasting pan, toss together potatoes, oil, salt, pepper and garlic. Roast uncovered, for 1 hour, or until tender and golden, turning occasionally.

3. Toss with parsley and serve.

Analysis per serving: Calories: 195 Protein: 3g Carbohydrate: 35g Fat: 5g Cholesterol: 0 Fiber: 2.7g Sodium: 69mg

WILTED SPINACH WITH ORANGES

Serves 4-6

This Asian-flavored spinach may be served as a side dish at room temperature, or as a salad.

Preparation: 20-30 minutes
Cook: 5 minutes

1½	pounds spinach, washed and stems removed
¼	cup chicken broth
½	teaspoon sugar
1	tablespoon soy sauce
2	oranges
	Freshly ground pepper to taste
1	tablespoon sesame seeds, toasted

1. In a saucepan, steam wet spinach just until wilted. Drain and refresh in cold water, then drain again. Using your hands, squeeze as dry as possible. Place on a cutting board and cut into approximately 1-inch slices; set aside in a bowl.

2. In a small saucepan, combine chicken broth, sugar and soy sauce; bring to a boil. Remove from heat and cool to room temperature.

3. Peel oranges, removing any white outer membrane. Cut in half and then into quarters and slice into ⅛-inch slices. Add to spinach.

4. Pour sauce over spinach and oranges. Toss to mix, and season to taste with pepper.

5. Serve in individual bowls and top with sesame seeds.

Analysis per serving: Calories: 60 Protein: 4.5g Carbohydrate: 10g Fat: 1g Cholesterol: 0   Fiber: 4g Sodium: 327mg

SPINACH WITH PINE NUTS

Serves 6

We love the simplicity of this recipe from Antonia Allegra, formerly Food Editor of *The San Diego Tribune*.

Preparation: 10 minutes
Cook: 5 minutes

2	tablespoons olive oil
2	large cloves garlic, minced
4	bunches of spinach, washed and stemmed
2	ounces pine nuts, toasted
	Freshly ground pepper to taste

1. In a large skillet, over medium-low heat, add oil and cook garlic for about 2 minutes. Increase heat, add spinach, and cook, stirring well, until leaves are limp.

2. Add pine nuts, season with pepper, and serve.

Analysis per serving: Calories: 97 Protein: 3g Carbohydrate: 3g Fat: 9g Cholesterol: 0 Fiber: 1g Sodium: 29.8mg

FOIL-BAKED JULIENNE OF SUMMER SQUASH

Serves 10

Preparation: 25 minutes
Bake: 15-20 minutes

	Aluminum foil
	Non-stick vegetable spray
6	**summer squashes (a combination such as zucchini, yellow crooked neck or other varieties), cut into 2-3-inch fine julienne**
1	**carrot, peeled and cut into 2-3-inch fine julienne**
	Salt and white pepper
2	**tablespoons fresh herbs (rosemary and/or dill)**
3	**tablespoons butter or margarine, cubed**

1. Preheat oven to 450 degrees.

2. Lightly coat two large pieces of aluminum foil with non-stick vegetable spray. Place vegetables in a bowl; add salt, pepper and fresh herbs; toss to blend. Divide and place in mounds on each sheet of foil; add 1½ tablespoons butter to each mound; then wrap securely.

3. Bake vegetables for 20 minutes, or until tender.

Variation: These same ingredients may be transformed into a cold summer salad, ideal for picnics. Blanch julienned vegetables for 1 minute and drain. Toss lightly in a bowl with oil and vinegar or a favorite Italian dressing.

Analysis per serving: Calories: 52   Protein: 2g   Carbohydrate: 5g   Fat: 3.6g   Cholesterol: 9mg   Fiber: 2.3g   Sodium: 255mg

BAKED YAMS WITH APPLES AND NUTS

Serves 16

This dish may be prepared ahead, refrigerated and reheated prior to serving.

Preparation: 30 minutes
Bake: 1 hour

8	**medium yams**
4	**tablespoons butter, melted**
¼	**cup nonfat milk, heated**
2	**tablespoons bourbon or brandy**
½	**cup nonfat plain yogurt**
	Grated zest of 1 orange
½	**teaspoon cinnamon**
2	**green apples, grated**
½	**cup walnuts, coarsely chopped**
½	**cup dates, coarsely chopped**

1. Preheat oven to 425 degrees.

2. Bake yams until just softened, approximately 30-40 minutes. Remove skin, and place in a large bowl. Add butter, milk, liquor and yogurt; beat until smooth and well-blended. Fold in orange zest, cinnamon, apple, nuts and dates.

3. Re-set oven to 350 degrees.

4. Place yam mixture in a large oven-proof dish or baking pan. Cover and bake until heated through.

Analysis per serving: Calories: 142   Protein: 2 g   Carbohydrate: 22g   Fat: 5g   Cholesterol: 8 mg   Fiber: 2g   Sodium: 33mg

ROASTED TOMATO SLICES WITH BASIL CRUMBS

Serves 4

Preparation: 15 minutes
Bake: 20-25 minutes

1	clove garlic, peeled and cut in half lengthwise
1	cup coarse breadcrumbs from day-old Italian bread
2	tablespoons extra virgin olive oil, divided
1	teaspoon chopped fresh oregano, or ¼ teaspoon dried
1	tablespoon minced garlic
3	large tomatoes, cut into ¾-inch slices
	Freshly ground black pepper
8	large basil leaves, coarsely chopped

1. Preheat oven to 375 degrees. Rub the bottom of a shallow 2-quart glass baking dish with the cut side of the garlic halves.

2. In a food processor, combine breadcrumbs, 1 tablespoon of the oil, oregano and the minced garlic. Pulse just to mix.

3. Arrange tomato slices in a single layer in baking dish; sprinkle with pepper; top with basil leaves; drizzle on remaining 1 tablespoon olive oil. Scatter crumb mixture evenly .

4. Bake until crumbs are golden brown, approximately 20-25 minutes. Serve warm or at room temperature.

Analysis per serving: Calories: 165   Protein: 4g   Carbohydrate: 23g   Fat: 6.6g   Cholesterol: 0   Fiber: 2.1g   Sodium: 193mg

ZUCCHINI WITH FRESH CILANTRO

Serves 4

Preparation: 10 minutes
Cook: 5-10 minutes

1	pound zucchini, thinly sliced
	Fresh ginger, grated
	Freshly ground black pepper to taste
1	tablespoon butter
2	tablespoons coarsely chopped cilantro
4	ounces plain yogurt
	Sprigs of cilantro, for garnish

1. Sprinkle zucchini with grated ginger and steam for approximately 5 minutes, until cooked but not mushy. Turn into a hot serving dish; season with pepper and keep warm.

2. In a small saucepan, melt butter; add cilantro and yogurt; stir for 2 minutes until hot; do not boil. Pour over zucchini; serve immediately, garnished with a few sprigs of cilantro.

Analysis per serving: Calories: 63   Protein: 2 g   Carbohydrate: 7g   Fat: 3g   Cholesterol: 9mg   Fiber: 1.5g   Sodium: 53mg

MEXICAN SAUTÉED ZUCCHINI WITH CORN

Serves 6

This recipe, from Elena Cota, reflects the historic rancho cooking which she has been teaching for over 15 years in San Diego community colleges.

Preparation: 10-15 minutes
Cook: 15-25 minutes

3	green onions, minced
1	clove garlic, minced
¼	cup defatted chicken broth
3-4	zucchini, diced
2	ears fresh corn, kernels removed from cob
2	fresh tomatoes, diced
	Oregano to taste
	Salt and freshly ground pepper to taste
1	cup grated lowfat Monterey Jack cheese

1. Heat a non-stick skillet; add onion and garlic and sauté without fat, adding just enough chicken broth to keep vegetables moist and avoid burning. Stirring continuously, cook until onion is soft and tender. It is essential to have them cooked through before adding the rest of the ingredients.

2. Combine zucchini, corn, tomatoes, oregano and seasoning. Add to onion and garlic mixture. Cover and cook gently until vegetables are tender. Add grated cheese and mix thoroughly.

Analysis per serving: Calories: 118   Protein: 10g   Carbohydrate: 11g   Fat: 5g   Cholesterol: 19mg   Fiber: 4g   Sodium: 121mg

GREEN-ONION QUICHE

Serves 4-6

This makes a tasty vegetarian main dish.

Preparation: 30 minutes
Bake: 45-50 minutes

2	**tablespoons butter**
4	**cups sliced green onions, both white and green parts**
1	**medium yellow onion, diced**
3	**ounces egg substitute or 3 eggs**
1	**cup lowfat cottage cheese (1%)**
1½	**cups nonfat milk**
¼	**teaspoon hot pepper sauce**
¼	**teaspoon salt**
⅛	**teaspoon white pepper**
1	**9-inch unbaked pie shell**
1	**tablespoon freshly grated Parmesan cheese**

1. Preheat oven to 400 degrees.

2. In a non-stick skillet, melt butter and sauté onions until soft and transparent, approximately 6 minutes.

3. In a medium-sized bowl, beat eggs, then add cottage cheese, milk, hot pepper sauce, salt and pepper; mix well. Gently stir in onions until well mixed. Pour into pie shell and sprinkle with Parmesan cheese.

4. Bake until set, approximately 10 minutes. Then lower oven temperature to 325 degrees and bake until filling is firm, approximately 35-45 minutes. Serve hot or at room temperature.

Analysis per serving (with egg substitute): Calories: 325   Protein: 14g   Carbohydrate: 27g   Fat: 19g   Cholesterol: 14mg   Fiber: 3g   Sodium: 568mg

ALMOND-CRUSTED BROCCOLI AND SPINACH CASSEROLE

Serves 10

This casserole may be made ahead and reheated.

Preparation: 30-40 minutes
Bake: 30 minutes

4	**tablespoons olive oil, divided**
1	**large onion, coarsely chopped**
2	**pounds broccoli, (florets and peeled stems), coarsely chopped**
1	**pound fresh spinach, Swiss chard or beet greens, washed in three changes of water, drained and stems removed**
3	**tablespoons ground almonds**
2½	**cups nonfat milk, heated**
⅔	**cup uncooked rice, parboiled 5 minutes and drained**
⅔	**cup grated Parmesan cheese, divided into ⅓ cup portions**
	Freshly ground black pepper to taste
	Ground nutmeg to taste (optional)
¼	**cup sliced almonds, lightly toasted**

1. Preheat oven to 375 degrees.

2. In a large oven-proof skillet, preferably non-stick, heat 2 tablespoons of the oil over medium heat; sauté onions until golden and tender, but not brown. Add chopped broccoli and toss for a few minutes. Add spinach and toss until wilted. Stir in ground almonds and add milk, stirring. Add parboiled rice, ⅓ cup of the Parmesan cheese, pepper and, if desired, nutmeg. Stir to mix well.

3. Sprinkle sliced almonds and remaining ⅓ cup Parmesan cheese on top. Drizzle with remaining 2 tablespoons olive oil; and heat on stove top until bubbling.

4. Transfer to middle rack of oven and bake for 30 minutes or until top is golden brown and all liquid is absorbed. Serve hot or at room temperature.

Analysis per serving: Calories: 185   Protein: 11g   Carbohydrate: 23g   Fat: 7g   Cholesterol: 6mg   Fiber: 5g   Sodium: 217mg

CALIFORNIA AVOCADO TACOS WITH FRESH TOMATO SALSA

Makes 12 tacos

San Diego County is the country's major producer of avocados. In this vegetarian taco recipe from the California Avocado Commission, avocado is used as a nutritious alternative to sour cream and cheese.

Preparation: 30 minutes
Chill: 2 hours

1½	cups Fresh Tomato Salsa (below)
12	flour tortillas, warmed in oven
	Non-stick vegetable spray
1	medium onion, julienne sliced
2	large green bell peppers, julienne sliced
2	large red bell peppers, julienne sliced
1	cup cilantro, minced
1	large avocado

1. Prepare Fresh Tomato Salsa, and chill.

2. Wrap tortillas in foil and warm in oven.

3. Just before serving, heat a large, preferably non-stick, skillet, and coat with vegetable spray. Add onion and bell peppers and sauté until softened.

4. Peel, seed and cut avocado into 12 slices. Fill each warmed tortilla with sautéed vegetables, cilantro to taste, a slice of avocado, and a topping of salsa. Fold tortillas over and serve.

FRESH TOMATO SALSA

1	cup fresh tomatoes, seeded and diced
⅓	cup diced onions
½-1	clove garlic, minced
⅓	tablespoon minced jalapeño chile
2	tablespoons minced cilantro
	Pinch of cumin
1½	tablespoons fresh lime juice

1. In a medium-sized bowl, combine all ingredients, mixing well. Chill.

Note on avocados: Our dietician tells us that avocados are a good source of potassium, folic acid, fiber and B-vitamins; and although their fat content is high, It consists of the "good" mono-unsaturated fat.

Analysis per taco: Calories: 182   Protein: 5g   Carbohydrate: 30g   Fat: 5g   Cholesterol: 0   Fiber: 3g   Sodium: 337mg

VEGETABLES

OLD TOWN VEGETABLE FAJITAS

Serves 4

A favorite recipe from the popular Casa de Pico restaurant in Old Town.

Preparation: 20-30 minutes
Cook: 5-10 minutes

2	**large zucchini, julienne sliced**
2	**large yellow squash, julienne sliced**
2	**large green bell peppers, julienne sliced**
2	**large red bell peppers, julienne sliced**
½	**jumbo red onion, julienne sliced**
2	**large carrots**
¼	**head of cabbage**
1	**tablespoon soybean oil**
2	**tablespoons Worcestershire sauce**
¼	**cup Achiote Salsa (below)**

1. In a large bowl, combine zucchini, yellow squash, green bell pepper, red bell pepper and onions. Cut carrots in half lengthwise and then into thin slices, approximately ⅛-inch thick to resemble small half moons. Add carrots to other vegetables and mix thoroughly.

2. Chop cabbage into 1-inch chunks; keep separate from other vegetables.

3. Heat oil in a large skillet and add all vegetables except cabbage. Sauté for approximately 2 minutes or until half done. Add cabbage, Worcestershire sauce and achiote sauce, and sauté until all vegetables are softened.

4. Serve with fresh, hot corn or flour tortillas.

ACHIOTE SALSA

Makes about 1¼ cups

3	**tablespoons achiote spice paste (available in the Mexican section of most supermarkets, or in gourmet groceries)**
1¼	**cups orange juice**
¼	**teaspoon minced garlic**

1. In a blender, combine all ingredients and blend at medium speed until a rich, smooth, red sauce forms.

Note: If achiote paste is unavailable, use ½ tablespoon chili powder and ¼ cup tomato paste.

Analysis per serving: Calories: 123   Protein: 4g   Carbohydrate: 20g   Fat: 4g   Cholesterol: 0   Fiber: 6g   Sodium: 231mg

DESSERTS AND SWEETS

SAVORING SAN DIEGO

ACADEMIC TREASURES

by Pat Johnson JaCoby
University of California, San Diego

Cruising south at dusk on Interstate 5 near the Genesee off-ramp, you may be amazed by what appears to be a lighted spaceship about to lift off. The sight definitely deserves investigating. Leaving the freeway at La Jolla Village Drive, a short drive west will bring you to the four-flag entrance to the University of California, San Diego. What you have spotted is the architecturally distinctive University Library—a massive, central concrete pedestal from which there seems to soar and float the six glass-enclosed floors of book stacks, widening and then narrowing as the structure rises. Designed by William L.Pereira in the late 1960s, this powerful architectural statement has become a familiar symbol of UCSD, and a focal point of the campus.

Twenty years later, the Library needed to be enlarged. The problem was to double its size without marring its image and architectural integrity. The inspired solution of noted architect, Gunnar Birkerts, added 200,000 square feet—the equivalent of a five-story building—entirely underground, and surrounding the Central Library on three sides. This addition created an engaging quality of its own—an atmosphere that is surprisingly light and airy. Atrium gardens at the foot of the light wells symbolically bring the outside vegetation inside, and areas of the building which front on the canyons seem to be open to the natural world, through the glass walls.

Among the library's special collections are hundreds of rare books on food, wine and agriculture that formed part of the world-famous Simon-Lowenstein Collection of Gastronomic Literature. This collection was donated by the San Diego Chapter of the American Institute of Wine and Food, with the blessing of AIWF founder, Julia Child. Experts say it probably is unmatched in its representation of English, French and American gastronomical works from the 16th through the 19th centuries. Included in its treasures are a 1559 Latin discourse on wine drinking, a 1623 guidebook on the duties of an English housewife, a 1703 list of dessert recipes for French royalty, and what is generally thought to be the first book about American cuisine, published in 1808. The UCSD library is available to the public, whether scholar or cook, for research and reference. Plans call for building on the AIWF collection, with emphasis on Latin America, the Pacific Basin, the American Southwest and the Hispanic tradition—areas in which other libraries have not specialized.

While UCSD is renowned for its eclectic architecture, high-tech science programs, and Nobel Laureates, it is also known and lauded nationally for its Stuart Collection of outdoor sculptures, with their brilliant integration of art into the intellectual and physical fabric of the campus. Over the past thirteen years, forty artists of international esteem, from Vito Acconci to Alexis Smith, have been invited to wander through the campus, soak up the stimuli, and create proposals for permanent outdoor works of art. So far, twelve works have been installed, including Niki de Saint Phalle's "Sun God" (1983) and Jenny Holzer's "Green Table" (1993). Visitors are welcomed on guided and self-guided tours.

The University has further enriched the area with its prize-winning theaters, art galleries, music programs, and many speakers of international repute. It is not surprising that historian-columnist, Neil Morgan, cites the arrival of the UCSD campus in San Diego as the single most important event in the recent history of the city. From its establishment in the '60s, he notes, modern San Diego evolved.

MENU FOR A CELEBRATION DINNER

Wild Mushroom and Hazelnut Pâté, page 19

Mussels in Sherry-Orange Vinaigrette with Prosciutto, page 132

Roast Fillet of Beef with Cornichon-Tarragon Sauce, page 111

or

Chicken Breasts in Triple Mustard Sauce, page 167

New Potatoes in Lemon Herb Sauce, page 197

Roasted Tomato Slices with Basil Crumbs, page 201

Green Beans with Red Pepper and Honey-Roasted Pecans, page 186

Spinach and Salad Greens with Macadamia Nuts, page 56

Cantaloupe Sherbet, page 210

Rich Chocolate Cherry Torte, page 234

Strawberries with Strawberry Sauce, page 212

DESSERTS and SWEETS

CANTALOUPE SHERBET

Serves 4-6

This refreshing fruit sherbet comes from the renowned spa, The Golden Door, in Escondido. It may also be made with fresh peaches, apricots or berries. When using berries, reduce orange juice to half a cup and add one additional tablespoon of honey.

Preparation: 15-20 minutes
Freeze: 3-4 hours

1	**cantaloupe (about 1¾ pound)**
1	**cup fresh orange juice**
2	**tablespoons honey**
2	**ice cubes**
	Fresh fruit for garnish

1. Cut cantaloupe in half and discard seeds. Scoop out pulp—there should be about 3 cups.

2. In a blender or food processor, purée cantaloupe, orange juice, honey and ice cubes until smooth. Pour into a mixing bowl, and freeze for 3-4 hours, stirring occasionally with a wire whisk. Do not store in freezer for more than 12 hours, or it will become too hard.

3. To serve, scoop sherbet into individual dessert dishes and garnish with fresh fruit.

Note: If using an ice-cream maker, purée cantaloupe, orange juice and honey until smooth, omitting ice cubes. Put into ice-cream maker and process according to the manufacturer's instructions.

Analysis per serving: Calories: 102   Protein: 1g   Carbohydrate: 25g   Fat: 0.5g   Cholesterol: 0   Fiber: 1.5g   Sodium: 12mg

FRESH RASPBERRY SORBET

Makes 3 cups; Serves 4

Preparation: 20-25 minutes
Freeze: 30 minutes or 3-6 hours (depending on method)

3	**boxes fresh raspberries (about 4½ loosely filled cups)**
½	**cup sugar**
2	**tablespoons freshly squeezed lemon juice**
5	**tablespoons heavy or whipping cream**
3	**tablespoons Grand Marnier**

1. Rinse raspberries and drain on paper. Process briefly in food processor. Sieve part or all of raspberries to remove some or all of the seeds, according to preference. There should be 2 cups of raspberry purée.

2. Return raspberries to food processor and add remaining ingredients. Process briefly until smooth; chill.

3. Freeze in an ice-cream maker, following manufacturer's instructions, until soft-frozen. It may also be frozen in the freezer in a tray or metal bowl. Allow at least 3 hours.

Analysis per serving: Calories: 260   Protein: 2g   Carbohydrate: 45g   Fat: 8g   Cholesterol: 25mg   Fiber: 6g   Sodium: 8mg

APRICOT-ORANGE ICE

Serves 4-6

This recipe, adapted from the American Heart Association, makes a refreshing end to a rich meal. It may also be made in an ice-cream maker. Follow the manufacturer's instructions, and process until frozen but still soft.

Preparation: 30 minutes
Freeze: 2 hours

1½	**cups chopped dried apricots**
¾	**cup orange juice**
2	**tablespoons lemon juice**
¼	**cup sugar**

1. Place apricots in a saucepan with enough water to cover, and bring to a boil over medium heat. Reduce heat, cover and simmer until fruit is soft, approximately 20 minutes. Drain apricots and cool.

2. In a blender or food processor, purée apricots with orange juice until smooth. Add lemon juice and sugar; process for an additional 30 seconds.

3. Pour into an 8-inch square pan, place in freezer and stir every 15 minutes until creamy. Cover and freeze until soft frozen.

Adapted, with permission, from *The American Heart Association Cookbook*, 5th edition; Copyright ©1991; Random House Inc.

Analysis per serving: Calories: 109 Protein: 1g Carbohydrate: 29g Fat: 0 Cholesterol: 0 Fiber: 2.5g Sodium: 3mg

LEMON ICE CREAM

Serves 6-8

For a special presentation, serve in scooped-out lemon shells.

Preparation: 5 minutes
Freeze: 10-12 hours

1	**cup sugar**
1⅓	**cup whipping cream**
⅔	**cup half-and-half**
1	**lemon, zest and juice**
	Berries and sprigs of mint, for garnish

1. In a medium-sized bowl, combine sugar, whipping cream and half-and-half. Stir to mix.

2. Grate zest of lemon into cream mixture, then pour in strained juice, and blend together. Cream will appear to curdle slightly.

3. Pour into small individual serving dishes or lemon cases, and freeze 10-12 hours at coldest temperature. Serve directly from the freezer, garnished with berries and mint.

Analysis per serving: Calories: 253 Protein: 1g Carbohydrate: 27g Fat: 17g Cholesterol: 61mg Fiber: 0 Sodium: 23mg

DESSERTS and SWEETS

FROZEN COFFEE-PECAN DESSERT WITH CARAMEL SAUCE

Serves 8

Preparation: 15 minutes
Freeze: 24 hours

4	**tablespoons butter, divided**
1	**cup dark brown sugar, packed**
½	**cup light corn syrup**
½	**cup heavy cream**
½	**teaspoon vanilla extract**
1	**cup coarsely chopped pecans**
1	**quart good quality coffee ice cream**

1. In a small saucepan, melt 3 tablespoons butter and brown very slowly. Add brown sugar, corn syrup and cream; heat until melted and sauce thickens slightly. Remove from heat, add vanilla and cool.

2. In a small skillet, melt remaining tablespoon butter and sauté pecans until slightly browned. Remove from heat and cool.

3. To assemble, place 1 tablespoon of the pecans in the bottom of small individual dessert bowls or ramekins. Top with 1 tablespoon of sauce; add a scoop of ice cream, add another tablespoon of sauce and finish with a spoonful of pecans.

4. Cover dishes with plastic wrap or foil and freeze for 24 hours. Twenty minutes before serving, remove from freezer to allow dessert to soften.

Analysis per serving: Calories: 426   Protein: 3g   Carbohydrate: 54g   Fat: 24g   Cholesterol: 47mg   Fiber: 1g   Sodium: 112mg

STRAWBERRIES WITH STRAWBERRY SAUCE

Serves 6

Preparation: 10 minutes
Chill: 2 hours

3	**pints ripe strawberries (about 2½ pounds)**
⅓	**cup sugar**
	Fresh mint, for garnish

1. Separate the best unblemished strawberries from any that are bruised. Wash and hull; dry on paper towels, and place in a glass bowl. Set aside.

2. To prepare sauce, trim and clean bruised berries, adding enough good berries to make up 2 cups. Place in a food processor or blender. Add sugar and blend until smooth.

3. Pour sauce over whole strawberries and toss carefully to coat all the fruit. Refrigerate for at least 2 hours before serving.

4. Spoon strawberries into wide champagne glasses or individual glass bowls and garnish with fresh mint. Serve with shortbread or other rich cookies, cake or ice cream.

Analysis per serving: Calories: 96   Protein: 1g   Carbohydrate: 24g   Fat: 0.69g   Cholesterol: 0   Fiber: 4.9g   Sodium: 2mg

SLICED BANANAS AND BERRIES WITH PAPAYA SAUCE

Serves 4-6

Preparation: 15 minutes
Cook: 10 minutes
Cool: 30 minutes

	Papaya Sauce (below)
4	**small bananas, sliced**
1	**cup fresh ripe berries (blackberries, raspberries or a mixture)**
	Sprigs of mint, for garnish

1. Place banana slices in individual dessert bowls; top with berries and spoon Papaya Sauce around the edges. Garnish with a sprig of mint, if desired.

PAPAYA SAUCE

1-2	**teaspoons grated fresh ginger**
¼	**cup sugar**
¼	**cup water**
¼	**cup fresh lime juice or lemon juice**
3	**tablespoons light rum or Grand Marnier**
¼	**cup butter**
2	**ripe papayas, seeded, peeled and cut into ½-inch chunks**

1. In a small saucepan, combine ginger, sugar and water; stir over medium heat until sugar dissolves and water is hot. Add lime juice and rum; set aside to cool.

2. Melt butter in a skillet, add papaya chunks and sauté until slightly softened, approximately 5 minutes. Remove from heat and stir into ginger mixture; set aside to cool.

Note: The sauce is also good with other fruit, ices or pound cake.

Analysis per serving: Calories: 223   Protein: 2g   Carbohydrate: 36g   Fat: 8g   Cholesterol: 20mg   Fiber: 3g   Sodium: 80mg

DESSERTS and SWEETS

POACHED GREEN FIGS WITH MASCARPONE CHEESE

Serves 8

White Genoa or Kadota fig trees grow in many water-conscious San Diego gardens, producing two prolific crops of green-skinned fruit a year in early and late summer. This delightful recipe is an excellent way to prepare this fragile fruit. The dish will keep for several days in the refrigerator.

Preparation: 10 minutes
Cook: 15 minutes
Chill: 1 hour

1	**cup sugar**
6	**cups water**
2	**vanilla beans**
16	**green figs with stems, gently washed**
	Mascarpone cream or crème fraîche, for topping

1. In a medium-sized saucepan, mix sugar and water; stir over low heat until sugar has dissolved. Bring to a boil and simmer for 2 minutes to form a syrup. Remove from heat.

2. Pour syrup into a wide shallow pan; add vanilla beans; bring to a simmer. Carefully add figs; poach approximately 5 minutes. Remove with a slotted spoon and set aside to cool.

3. Bring the syrup back to a boil and reduce by a quarter. Set aside to cool.

4. Serve in individual deep plates or small bowls. Place 2 figs on each plate; spoon over some of the syrup, and add a generous spoonful of mascarpone or crème fraîche.

Analysis per serving: Calories: 200 Protein: 0.9g Carbohydrate: 41g Fat: 4.9g Cholesterol: 16mg Fiber: 3.3g Sodium: 6mg

GERANIUM CREAM WITH FRESH BLACKBERRIES

Serves 6

The delicate perfumed flavor of geranium is exquisite with fresh blackberries. A unique dessert from the garden.

Preparation: 10 minutes
Cook: 10 minutes
Chill: 2-12 hours

1	cup whipping cream
4	tablespoons sugar
2	sweet-scented geranium leaves
4	ounces cream cheese
5	cups fresh blackberries

1. Pour cream into the top of a double boiler over simmering water; add sugar and 2 whole geranium leaves. Cook over low heat, gently, letting cream get thoroughly hot without boiling. Set aside to cool.

2. Without removing geranium leaves, gently combine infused cream with cream cheese, mixing until thick and smooth. Cover and chill in refrigerator for 12 hours, if possible.

3. To serve, discard geranium leaves and place blackberries in individual glass bowls. Spoon cream on top.

Analysis per serving: Calories: 151   Protein: 3g   Carbohydrate: 9 g   Fat: 12g   Cholesterol: 38mg   Fiber: 0   Sodium: 67mg

LIME CHIFFON MOUSSE

Serves 4

Preparation: 15 minutes
Cook: 5-10 minutes
Chill: 2 hours

1	egg yolk
5	egg whites
1	tablespoon grated lime zest
½	cup sugar
1	cup fresh lime juice (9 small limes)

1. In the top of a double boiler, place yolk, whites, zest, sugar and lime juice. Set over simmering water and cook, stirring continuously, for 4-5 minutes or until mixture thickens.

2. Spoon mousse into wine glasses and chill in refrigerator for at least 2 hours. Serve with cookies or fresh berries.

Adapted, with permission, from *Santa Fe Lite and Spicy*, by Joan Stromquist; Copyright © 1992; Tierra Publications.

Analysis per serving: Calories: 143   Protein: 5g   Carbohydrate: 30g   Fat: 1g   Cholesterol: 53mg   Fiber: 0   Sodium: 71mg

DOUBLE-BAKED CARAMEL PEARS WITH ICE CREAM

Serves 4-6

Preparation: 25-35 minutes
Bake: 45-60 minutes

3	large, ripe but firm Bartlett pears, peeled, halved lengthwise and cored
2	tablespoons light brown sugar
2	tablespoons dark rum
1/2	teaspoon lemon juice
1	tablespoon unsalted butter
13	3/4-inch square caramels (2 ounces)
1	teaspoon dark rum
	Cooking juices from pears
	Vanilla ice cream (1/2 cup per person)
6	sprigs of mint, for garnish

1. Preheat oven to 400 degrees.

2. In a 9-inch pie plate, arrange pears, cut side down, with narrow tips pointing toward the center.

3. In a microwaveable dish, combine brown sugar, rum, lemon juice and butter. Microwave on High until butter is melted, approximately 30 seconds (or heat in a saucepan, stirring). Brush mixture over pears.

4. Place, uncovered, in preheated oven. Baste pears with pan juices every 5-10 minutes, until just tender, approximately 20-25 minutes (depending on their ripeness).

5. Remove from oven; drain and reserve pear juice for use in Caramel Sauce. Recipe may be prepared a day ahead to this point. Cover and refrigerate pears; return to room temperature before reheating.

6. Place caramels with rum and reserved pear juices in a deep microwaveable dish. Microwave on Medium for approximately 1-1 1/2 minutes until melted, stirring twice (or melt on stove top). Watch carefully to avoid scorching. Do not boil. Stir caramel until smooth.

7. Adjust oven temperature to 300 degrees. Cut pears lengthwise again, and pour sauce over evenly. Bake, uncovered for 6 minutes; baste with caramel sauce and continue baking just until heated through, approximately 12 minutes in all.

8. To serve, arrange pear quarters in a shallow soup dish. Top with ice cream, spoon caramel sauce on top and tuck a sprig of mint in the side. Serve immediately.

Analysis per serving: Calories: 311 Protein: 3g Carbohydrate: 40g Fat: 15g Cholesterol: 50mg Fiber: 2g Sodium: 77mg

SUMMER BERRIES IN CARAMELIZED MASCARPONE SAUCE

Serves 4

Preparation: 20 minutes
Chill: 2-3 hours
Grill: 2 minutes

1	**large egg**
1	**large egg yolk**
1	**tablespoon flour**
1	**teaspoon cornstarch**
¼	**cup plus 1 tablespoon sugar**
1	**cup lowfat milk**
½	**teaspoon vanilla extract**
2	**tablespoons unsalted butter, cut into small pieces**
⅓	**cup mascarpone cheese (Italian cream cheese)**
1	**pint, or more if desired, mixed berries (such as raspberries, blackberries or blueberries)**
	Brown sugar for topping
	Sprigs of mint and extra berries, for garnish

1. In a medium-sized bowl, beat egg and egg yolk until lemon-colored and fluffy.

2. In a small bowl, sift flour, cornstarch and sugar together; then gradually beat into eggs, until mixture is light and fluffy, approximately 2 minutes.

3. In a small saucepan, heat milk to scalding. Gradually, pour half of the hot milk into the egg mixture, beating constantly. When blended, pour mixture back into the saucepan and return to low heat. Beat constantly until custard begins to boil and thicken. Remove promptly from heat and beat for 1 minute.

4. Stir in vanilla, add butter and mix until fully incorporated. Pour into a bowl and chill. The custard may be stored in the refrigerator for up to two days.

5. Adjust rack to top position, and preheat broiler for at least 10 minutes.

6. While oven is heating, mix berries and divide among 4 individual 4-inch gratin dishes. If you do not have gratin dishes, use a 1-quart shallow baking dish. Do not use ramekins.

7. Gently fold mascarpone into cold custard and spoon over berries in the gratin dishes. Sprinkle a thin even layer of sugar over each dish and place on a baking sheet.

8. Broil until evenly browned, approximately 2 minutes or less, watching carefully to avoid burning. Remove immediately and cool for 1 minute. To serve, garnish with a few more berries or tiny sprigs of mint.

Analysis per serving: Calories: 290 Protein: 7g Carbohydrate: 29g Fat: 17g Cholesterol: 150mg Fiber: 4g Sodium: 113mg

DESSERTS and SWEETS

RED FRUIT SUMMER PUDDING

Serves 6

A delicious dessert that uses the sweet red fruits of summer. The juice-soaked bread provides a surprisingly delightful contrast to the mixed fruits, without the richness of pastry. For a quick and easy version, frozen mixed berries combined with frozen cherries may be used.

Preparation: 30 minutes
Cook: 10 minutes
Chill: overnight

1 ½	**pounds mixed fruit, using a combination of at least 3 of the following: raspberries, pitted cherries or chopped plums, blueberries, blackberries, but not strawberries.**
½-¾	**cup sugar, depending on sweetness of berries**
8	**slices very thin white bread**
	Whipped cream or crème fraîche

1. Place fruit and sugar in a medium-sized stainless steel saucepan over very low heat; stir to mix. Cover and cook gently, stirring occasionally, until fruits are soft and release their juices, approximately 10 minutes. Do not allow juices to evaporate, as the more juice there is, the better it will be. Adjust sugar to taste and set aside.

2. Remove crusts from bread. Line bottom and sides of a 1-quart rounded bowl, (*bombe* shape, not straight-sided), fitting bread pieces to cover completely. Reserve enough slices for center layer and top.

3. Spoon fruit mixture into bread-lined bowl. When fruit half fills the bowl, cover with a layer of bread. Add remaining fruit to fill the bowl, and cover top with a final layer of bread.

4. Place a plate (small enough to fit just inside the bowl) directly on top. Weight down with a heavy object (such as a 5-pound package of sugar), so that the bread will be pressed into the juice and become red. Refrigerate overnight.

5. Just before serving, gently loosen sides with a knife and invert "pudding" onto a serving plate. Decorate the unmolded bombe with a few fresh berries placed on top and around the base. Serve with a dollop of whipped cream or crème fraîche.

Note: To make crème fraîche, combine 1 cup whipping cream and 2 tablespoons buttermilk in a glass or ceramic container. Cover and let stand for 8-24 hours at room temperature, or until very thick. Stir well, cover tightly and refrigerate for up to 10 days.

Analysis per serving: Calories: 207   Protein: 4g   Carbohydrate: 47g   Fat: 2g   Cholesterol: 0   Fiber: 5.1g   Sodium: 174mg

MEXICAN BREAD PUDDING WITH MAPLE-PECAN SAUCE

Serves 8-10

This recipe is adapted from Project LEAN, an organization educating consumers to make healthful food choices. This sauce may also be used with ice cream or yogurt.

Preparation: 20-30 minutes
Bake: 45 minutes

2	egg whites
1	6-ounce can evaporated skim milk
½	cup lowfat or nonfat milk
½	cup sugar
½	teaspoon ground cinnamon
½	teaspoon ground anise
½	cup hot water
1	teaspoon vanilla extract
½	pound whole-wheat bread, cubed
1	ripe banana, sliced
¼	cup raisins
1	apple, grated
	Maple-Pecan Sauce (below), optional

1. Preheat oven to 375 degrees. Grease an 8-inch square baking pan, or use a non-stick pan.

2. In a medium-sized bowl, beat egg whites until frothy; add both evaporated and fresh milk and mix well.

3. In another bowl, mix sugar, cinnamon, anise, hot water and vanilla. Stir into milk-egg mixture.

4. Place half the bread on the bottom of prepared baking pan. Then layer half each of the banana, raisins and apple on top of bread. Pour half the liquid over this layer.

5. Repeat layering with remaining ingredients.

6. Bake for 45 minutes. Serve warm with Maple-Pecan Sauce.

MAPLE-PECAN SAUCE

1	cup maple syrup
1	teaspoon lemon zest
½	teaspoon nutmeg
2	tablespoons margarine, cut into small pieces
½	cup pecans, toasted

1. In a medium-sized saucepan, combine syrup, lemon zest and nutmeg. Heat until hot, but do not boil. Allow to cool slightly and whisk in margarine and pecans.

Analysis per serving: Calories: 289   Protein: 5g   Carbohydrate: 55g   Fat:7g   Cholesterol: 0.8mg   Fiber: 4g   Sodium: 241mg

LEMON PAVLOVA

Serves 12

This lemon dessert melts in the mouth. It must be made a day before serving; but it may also be made well ahead of time and frozen. If frozen, allow to defrost in refrigerator for 8 hours before serving.

Preparation: 1 hour
Bake: 1 hour
Chill: overnight

MERINGUE

1	cup superfine sugar (or use granulated sugar, ground in a food processor for 5 seconds)
2	teaspoons cornstarch
4	large egg whites
¼	teaspoon cream of tartar
1	teaspoon vanilla extract

LEMON FILLING

½	cup sugar
4	egg yolks
3	tablespoons lemon juice
2	tablespoons grated lemon zest
1	cup whipping cream
	Lemon slices and mint, for garnish

1. Preheat oven to 300 degrees. Spray two 8-inch round pans with vegetable oil. Line bottom with foil and spray again.

2. In a small bowl, mix sugar and cornstarch together; set aside.

3. In a large bowl, slowly whisk egg whites with cream of tartar. Gradually increase speed and whisk until standing in stiff peaks. Add sugar-cornstarch mixture, one tablespoon at a time, beating until stiff after each addition. Whisk in vanilla.

4. Divide meringue mixture between prepared pans and spread evenly. Place on the middle rack of oven; turn heat down immediately to 275 degrees. Bake until meringue top feels firm and crisp to the touch, at least 1 hour.

5. Remove from oven. Carefully lift meringues from pans (they should come out easily). Place on wire racks to cool, and remove foil.

6. In a small heavy saucepan, combine yolks and sugar, beating with a wooden spoon until creamy and light in color. Stir in lemon juice and zest. Cook over gentle heat, stirring constantly, until mixture just thickens. Do not boil. Immediately take pan off heat and continue stirring for 1-2 minutes as the mixture will continue to thicken with heat from the pan. Allow to cool. Whip cream and fold into lemon mixture.

7. Place one meringue layer on a serving plate and spread with ¾ of the lemon filling. Cover with second meringue and spread with remaining lemon filling. Refrigerate overnight. To serve, decorate with halved lemon slices and mint leaves.

Analysis per serving: Calories: 178   Protein: 3g   Carbohydrate: 26g   Fat: 8g   Cholesterol: 93mg   Fiber: 0   Sodium: 28mg

CARAMELIZED MERINGUE RING WITH MANGOS

Serves 8-10

In this very light dessert, a ring of soft meringue is topped with golden caramelized sugar, which forms both a thin brittle film and a smooth syrup. Fill center with slices of any fresh fruit in season—peaches, nectarines, melons, poached pears, sautéed apples or others. This dessert is best if made a day ahead.

Preparation: 20-25 minutes
Bake: 1½ hours
Chill: 3-24 hours

2½	cups superfine sugar, divided
1	cup egg whites (about 7 whites)
1	teaspoon white vinegar
1-2	teaspoons vanilla extract
4	ripe mangos, peeled, pitted and sliced
	Berries and mint sprigs, for garnish

1. Adjust oven racks to lower half of oven. Preheat oven to 500 degrees. Assemble a 1½-quart ring mold and a larger pan, inside which the mold can sit.

2. Place 1 cup of the sugar in a heavy saucepan over medium heat. Swirl pan constantly until sugar melts and caramelizes to a golden brown. Pour into ring mold, and quickly tilt to cover bottom and sides with caramelized sugar. Set aside.

3. In a large bowl, beat egg whites to froth stage. Add vinegar and vanilla. Continue to beat, and add remaining 1½ cups sugar, beating until sugar is completely incorporated and whites are stiff.

4. Transfer to prepared mold with a spatula. Set ring mold inside the larger pan; pour in enough hot water to reach halfway up the sides of the ring mold.

5. Watching carefully, bake at 500 degrees until meringue puffs and turns golden brown, approximately 10 minutes. Then lower temperature to 250 degrees and bake for 40 minutes. Next, turn off oven and open door slightly but slowly so meringue does not collapse. Leave meringue in oven with door partially open for 40 minutes more, so meringue cools gradually. (If oven door is designed to be fully open or closed without an intermediate position, place a hot pad between door and frame to hold it open about half an inch). Remove from oven and let cool to room temperature, then refrigerate for a least 3 hours, preferably overnight.

6. Well before serving, unmold meringue: run a knife around the edges and invert onto a large platter. To remove syrup remaining in the mold, pour in 2-3 tablespoons of water, place over moderate heat, swirling occasionally, and melt caramel. Pour over meringue, as desired. Refrigerate until ready to serve.

7. Arrange mangos decoratively around platter and in center of meringue, and garnish with berries and a few sprigs of mint. To serve, slice meringue into wedges, spoon on fruit and caramel syrup.

Note: Instead of superfine sugar, you may use granulated sugar processed in a food processor until finely ground.

Analysis per serving: Calories: 354 Protein: 6g Carbohydrate: 78g Fat: 3g Cholesterol: 89mg Fiber: 2g Sodium: 69mg

DESSERTS and SWEETS

UPSIDE-DOWN LEMON DELIGHT

Serves 6-8

In San Diego, the chances are you will have lemon trees in your garden or on your patio, offering year-round fruit. This American classic dessert is a wonderful way to use that abundance. However, you do not need to have your own tree to enjoy it!

Preparation: 25 minutes
Bake: 40-45 minutes

1	cup sugar
1/3	cup all-purpose flour
1/8	teaspoon salt
3	tablespoons butter or margarine
1 1/2-2	tablespoons grated lemon zest
1/3	cup lemon juice (2-3 medium lemons)
3	eggs
1 1/2	cups nonfat milk
1/8	teaspoon vanilla extract
	Lemon zest, julienne sliced, for garnish
	Fresh berries (optional)

1. Preheat oven to 325 degrees. Arrange an ungreased 9-inch deep pie plate or 8 custard cups, inside a large deep baking pan.

2. In a medium-sized bowl, blend sugar, flour and salt. With a pastry blender or 2 knives, cut in butter until light and crumbly. Stir in lemon zest and juice, blending well.

3. Separate eggs, placing whites in a second medium-sized bowl, and yolks in a small bowl. Beat whites until stiff but not dry. Set aside.

4. With the same beater, beat yolks until thick and lemon-colored; stir in milk and vanilla. Blend yolk mixture into lemon mixture; then gently fold in beaten egg whites.

5. Pour batter into pre-arranged pie plate (or custard cups), and add enough boiling water to larger pan to reach halfway up the sides of the pie plate or cups.

6. Bake for 40-45 minutes, until the top is browned and firm, but underneath is soft and creamy. To serve, invert onto a serving plate or, if using custard cups, onto individual dessert plates. Spoon over sauce from pan. Decorate with lemon zest. Serve warm, or at room temperature; accompany with fresh berries, if desired.

Analysis per serving: Calories: 194 Protein: 4.5g Carbohydrate: 32g Fat: 6g Cholesterol: 92mg Fiber: 0.2 g Sodium: 125mg

PUMPKIN ICE CREAM PIE IN OATMEAL-NUT CRUST

Serves 8

Preparation: 35 minutes
Freeze: 24 hours

	Oatmeal Nut Crust (below)
1/4	**cup brown sugar**
3/4	**cup canned pumpkin**
1/2	**teaspoon cinnamon**
1/3	**teaspoon ground ginger**
	Dash of grated nutmeg
	Dash of ground cloves
1/4	**teaspoon salt**
1	**quart vanilla ice cream**
1/2	**cup pecan pieces**

1. Prepare Oatmeal-Nut Crust and refrigerate.

2. In a medium-sized saucepan, bring sugar, pumpkin, spices and salt to a boil; transfer to a large bowl and cool slightly.

3. Add ice cream to pumpkin mixture; mix well until dissolved. Stir in pecans and pour into chilled oatmeal crust. Freeze for at least 24 hours.

OATMEAL-NUT CRUST

1	**cup uncooked rolled oats**
3	**tablespoons brown sugar**
2/3	**cup minced walnuts**
1/3	**cup of melted butter**

1. Preheat oven to 350 degrees.

2. Spread oats in a large shallow pan. Bake for approximately 15 minutes, until nicely toasted.

3. Toss with sugar, nuts and melted butter. Press evenly into the bottom and sides of a 9-inch pie plate. Refrigerate until ready to use.

Analysis per serving: Calories: 378 Protein: 6.5g Carbohydrate: 38g Fat: 24g Cholesterol: 50mg Fiber: 1.9g Sodium: 207mg

DESSERTS and SWEETS

FRESH PINK GRAPEFRUIT CHIFFON PIE

Serves 8

Grapefruit gives this dessert a delicate and intriguing flavor. It is also delightful served in individual glass bowls or stemmed glasses, without the crust.

Preparation: 20-30 minutes
Chill: 4 hours

1	**envelope unflavored gelatin**
¾	**cup sugar**
⅓	**teaspoon salt**
1-1½	**cups fresh pink grapefruit juice**
1	**tablespoons grated grapefruit zest**
2	**large eggs, separated**
2	**tablespoons lemon juice**
½	**cup heavy cream, whipped**
	Vanilla wafer crumb crust or baked pie crust
	Grapefruit segments, for garnish

1. In a medium-sized saucepan, combine gelatin, sugar, salt, grapefruit juice and grated zest. Stir over medium heat until almost boiling. Remove from heat and set aside.

2. In a small bowl, lightly beat egg yolks. Stir in a small amount of hot gelatin mixture to heat eggs gently; then whisk them carefully and completely into the hot mixture.

3. Return pan to low heat and stir for 1 minute; mix in lemon juice, then remove from heat. Transfer to a large bowl and chill until mixture mounds when dropped from a spoon, approximately 1 hour.

4. In a medium-sized bowl, beat egg whites until stiff. In another bowl, beat cream until stiff. Fold egg whites and cream into gelatin mixture.

5. Pour into prepared crust and chill for at least 3 hours.

6. Garnish with grapefruit segments and serve.

Analysis per serving: Calories: 253 Protein: 4g Carbohydrate: 32g Fat: 13g Cholesterol: 74mg Fiber: 1g Sodium: 273mg

APRICOT-HAZELNUT TART

Serves 8-12

Preparation: 30 minutes
Bake: 1 hour

PASTRY

⅔	**cup butter or margarine**
2	**cups flour**
5-7	**tablespoons iced water**

FILLING

¾	**cup butter, softened**
1	**cup sugar**
2	**eggs**
1½	**cups ground hazelnuts (see Note)**
1½	**tablespoons flour**
¾	**teaspoon vanilla extract**
2	**ounces light rum, or hazelnut or apricot brandy**
8-10	**fresh apricots, pitted and halved, or canned apricots, drained**

1. In a large bowl, cut butter into flour, using a pastry blender or two knives. Adding only as much of the iced water as needed, mix dough until it just forms a ball.

2. Roll out dough and line an 11-inch tart pan; refrigerate for 30 minutes. If preferred, pastry may be prepared a day ahead and refrigerated.

3. Preheat oven to 350 degrees.

4. In a medium-sized bowl, cream butter and sugar together. Stir in eggs, hazelnuts, flour and vanilla. Gradually pour rum into mixture, blending well. Pour into pastry-lined pan.

5. Arrange apricots, cut-side down, in tight circles over filling.

6. Bake for approximately 1 hour, covering tart with foil for the last 10 minutes. Let cool to room temperature on a wire rack, and serve the same day.

Note: To remove skins from hazelnuts, brown them in a hot oven for 5-6 minutes; then rub briskly in a rough cloth or tea towel to remove the dry skins.

Analysis per serving: Calories: 511 Protein: 7g Carbohydrate: 36g Fat: 40g Cholesterol: 93mg Fiber: 4g Sodium: 230mg

DESSERTS and SWEETS

APPLE AND CRANBERRY PIE WITH NUT TOPPING

Serves 10-12

This pie may be prepared ahead. At room temperature, it will hold for up to 6 hours; alternatively, refrigerate but return to room temperature before serving.

Preparation: 45 minutes
Bake: 1½ hours

¾	**cup loosely packed light brown sugar**
5	**tablespoons cornstarch**
½	**teaspoon nutmeg**
1	**teaspoon ground cinnamon**
	Pinch of salt
2	**pounds Granny Smith or Newton-Pippin apples, peeled, cored and sliced ¼-inch thick**
1¾	**cups fresh cranberries**
2	**tablespoons fresh lemon juice**
1	**tablespoon grated lemon zest**
1	**9-inch deep dish pastry crust, chilled**
	Nut Topping (below)

1. Preheat oven to 350 degrees.

2. In a large bowl, mix brown sugar, cornstarch, nutmeg, cinnamon and salt. Add apples, cranberries, lemon juice and zest; toss well. Transfer mixture to pastry crust, mounding in center.

3. Bake for 1¼ hours. Cover with foil and bake for another 15 minutes. Transfer to a wire rack, uncover and cool.

4. Prepare Nut Topping.

5. Spoon topping over pie, covering completely. Let stand for about 30 minutes until topping sets.

NUT TOPPING

½	**cup unsalted butter**
¾	**cup loosely packed light brown sugar**
2	**tablespoons evaporated milk**
1	**teaspoon vanilla extract**
1	**cup chopped walnuts**

1. In a heavy saucepan, over low heat, melt butter with sugar and milk, stirring frequently.

2. Bring to a simmer over medium heat, stirring constantly. Mix in vanilla, then walnuts. Pour mixture into a bowl. Let stand for approximately 10 minutes, stirring occasionally, until cool and slightly thickened.

Variation: This topping would also go well on quick breads, pound cake or angel food cake.

Analysis per serving: Calories: 323   Protein: 3g   Carbohydrate: 47g   Fat: 15g   Cholesterol: 24mg   Fiber: 3g   Sodium: 52mg

THE ULTIMATE CHOCOLATE DESSERT

Serves 8

Preparation: 15 minutes
Chill: 3 hours

6	ounces unsweetened chocolate, chopped into bits (1 cup)
1	cup semi-sweet chocolate bits (6 ounces)
3	large eggs
¼	cup sugar
1	teaspoon vanilla
2-3	tablespoons orange, peppermint or coffee liqueur, or dark rum
1	cup whole milk
	Whipped cream, for garnish (optional)
	Mint leaves, for garnish

1. In a blender (not a food processor), chop chocolate, and blend with eggs, sugar, vanilla and liquor until very finely chopped. Leave in the blender.

2. In a saucepan, bring milk just to a boil. Immediately turn on blender and begin pouring hot milk into chocolate mixture. Blend until smooth.

3. Pour into small individual bowls, ramekins or *pots de crème*, to about ⅔ full. Chill at least 3 hours. Serve very cold, topped with a dab of whipped cream, if desired, and garnished with 1 or 2 mint leaves.

Variation: If you prefer to use a non-alcoholic flavoring, substitute one of the following: orange or peppermint extract, instant coffee granules or rum flavoring. Use ½-1 teaspoon.

Analysis per serving: Calories: 232   Protein: 4g   Carbohydrate: 33g   Fat: 10g   Cholesterol: 67mg   Fiber: 0   Sodium: 55mg

CHOCOLATE DECADENCE

Serves 12

Antonia Allegra, food writer, editor and teacher, tempts us with this fabulous chocolate dessert. Serve following a light meal and enjoy its richness.

Preparation: 30-40 minutes
Bake: 1¼ hours

14	ounces semi-sweet chocolate
2	ounces unsweetened chocolate
¼	cup strong brewed coffee
6	large eggs
½	cup sugar
1	cup whipping cream
1	teaspoon vanilla extract
	Extra whipped cream, for decoration (optional)
	Chocolate coffee beans, for decoration

1. Preheat oven to 350 degrees. Butter a 9-inch springform pan. Place a small bowl in freezer to chill.

2. Combine both types of chocolate with coffee in the top of a double boiler, and set above simmering water. Leave until melted, stirring occasionally. Cool slightly, then beat until shiny.

3. In a large mixing bowl, beat eggs until frothy. Slowly add sugar and beat until light, thick and lemon-colored, approximately 5 minutes. Beat in chocolate and combine well.

4. In the small chilled bowl, whip cream until stiff, add vanilla, and fold into chocolate mixture until well combined.

5. Pour mixture into prepared springform pan. Set pan inside a larger pan containing enough hot water to reach halfway up the sides of the cake pan. Bake for 1 hour. Turn off oven and allow to stand for 15 more minutes. Remove from oven and cool on a wire rack for 30 minutes.

6. Serve cake warm, or at room temperature, with vanilla ice cream or frozen vanilla yogurt. If you wish, pipe rosettes of whipped cream around the top of the cake, using a pastry bag and a medium star tip. Decorate with chocolate coffee beans.

Note: Cake may be prepared up to 6 hours in advance and kept at room temperature, without the cream decoration. Alternatively, cake with whipped cream may be refrigerated up to 8 hours, although this changes the texture slightly. Remove from refrigerator at least 1 hour before serving.

Analysis per serving (cake only): Calories: 308   Protein: 6g   Carbohydrate: 30g   Fat: 22g   Cholesterol: 129mg   Fiber: 0
Sodium: 39mg

GUILTLESS CHOCOLATE CAKE WITH ORANGE LIQUEUR FROSTING

Serves 8-10

This recipe allows chocolate lovers to enjoy a truly guilt-free dessert.

Preparation: 30-45 minutes
Bake: 25-30 minutes

	Vegetable oil
1/3	**cup unsweetened cocoa powder**
1	**cup plus 1 tablespoon flour**
1	**teaspoon baking powder**
1	**teaspoon baking soda**
6	**large egg whites**
1 1/3	**cups dark brown sugar, packed down**
1	**cup nonfat vanilla yogurt**
1	**teaspoon vanilla extract**
1	**tablespoon Amaretto or hazelnut liqueur**
	Orange Liqueur Frosting (below)

1. Preheat oven to 350 degrees. Oil and flour an 8-inch springform pan.

2. In a medium-sized bowl, combine cocoa powder, flour, baking powder and baking soda; set aside.

3. In a large bowl, combine egg whites, sugar, yogurt, vanilla and liqueur. Beat for 1-2 minutes at medium speed or until well-blended.

4. Fold in dry ingredients until fully incorporated.

5. Pour into prepared pan and bake for 25-30 minutes or until center is slightly firm to the touch. Cool to room temperature on a wire rack before frosting.

ORANGE LIQUEUR FROSTING

3	**egg whites**
3/4	**cup granulated sugar**
1/8	**teaspoon salt**
3	**tablespoons water**
1	**teaspoon orange liqueur**

1. In the top of a double boiler, combine egg whites, sugar, salt and water; mix well. Set over simmering water, and beat until the mixture is honey-like in consistency, approximately 3-4 minutes. Carefully stir in liqueur.

Adapted, with permission, from *Santa Fe Lite and Spicy* by Joan Stromquist; Copyright © 1992; Tierra Publications.

Analysis per serving: Calories: 326   Protein: 8g   Carbohydrate: 74g   Fat: 1g   Cholesterol: 1mg   Fiber: 0   Sodium: 276mg

DESSERTS and SWEETS

DEVILISH COCOA CAKE WITH RASPBERRY SAUCE

Serves 12

A prize-winning cake from cooking teacher, Tulie Trejo.

Preparation: 20 minutes
Bake: 35-40 minutes

1	**cup whole-wheat flour or unbleached flour**
1	**cup unbleached flour**
3/4	**cup packed light brown sugar**
1/2	**cup unsweetened cocoa powder**
1	**teaspoon baking powder**
1	**teaspoon baking soda**
1 1/4	**cups nonfat plain or vanilla yogurt**
1/2	**cup canola oil**
1/2	**cup fat-free egg substitute**
1	**teaspoon vanilla extract**
	Raspberry Sauce (below)

1. Preheat oven to 350 degrees. Coat a 9-inch springform pan with non-stick vegetable spray, and line the bottom with waxed paper and spray again.

2. In a large bowl, blend flours, brown sugar, cocoa, baking powder and baking soda.

3. In another large bowl, place yogurt, oil, egg and vanilla. With electric mixer on low speed, beat for about 30 seconds to combine. Add dry ingredients and beat on low speed until just combined; then increase speed to high; beat for approximately 3 minutes.

4. Pour batter into prepared pan; bake for 35-45 minutes, or until a toothpick inserted in center comes out clean.

5. Cool on a wire rack for 10 minutes. Unmold, peel off paper, and cool completely.

6. To serve, pour a circle of sauce on each plate and place a slice of cocoa cake in the center; or if preferred, pass sauce separately.

RASPBERRY SAUCE

3	**cups raspberries**
1/3	**cup all-fruit raspberry preserves**
1	**teaspoon lemon juice**

1. In a food processor or blender, purée 1 cup of the raspberries; pass through a sieve to remove seeds; set aside.

2. In a 2-quart saucepan over medium-low heat, melt preserves. Stir in lemon juice and puréed raspberries. Heat for 1 minute. Add remaining 2 cups of raspberries and stir well to coat with glaze; set aside to cool.

Analysis per serving: Calories: 255 Protein: 6g Carbohydrate: 39g Fat: 10g Cholesterol: 0 Fiber: 3g Sodium: 142mg

CAPPUCCINO NUT TORTE

8-10 servings

Graham cracker crumbs and pecans replace flour in this easy-to-make, chocolate-flecked extravaganza from cookbook author and teacher, Marlene Sorosky.

Preparation: 30 minutes
Bake: 40 minutes
Cool: 2-3 hours

1¾	cups graham cracker crumbs
1½	cups very finely chopped pecans (about 6 ounces)
6	ounces semi-sweet chocolate chips
2	teaspoons baking powder
5	egg whites, at room temperature
1-2	tablespoons instant coffee granules
1	cup sugar
2	teaspoons vanilla extract
	Chocolate Cappuccino Frosting (below)

1.   Preheat oven to 350 degrees. Grease and flour a 9-inch springform pan.

2.   In a medium-sized bowl, stir together crumbs, pecans, chocolate chips and baking powder; set aside.

3.   In a large bowl, using an electric mixer, beat egg whites and instant coffee until soft peaks form. Gradually add sugar, beating constantly, until mixture is stiff and creamy, but not dry. Mix in vanilla and fold in dry ingredients. Spoon into prepared pan, smoothing top.

4.   Bake for 40 minutes or until top is crusty and feels firm to the touch. Remove from oven and run a knife around the edge. Remove sides of pan, but leave cake on springform bottom. Cool to room temperature on a wire rack.

5.   Prepare Chocolate Cappuccino Frosting.

6.   Place a sheet of waxed paper under the wire rack. Spoon hot frosting over top of cake, and spread around sides. Allow to sit several hours for frosting to set. Serve at room temperature.

CHOCOLATE CAPPUCCINO FROSTING

½	cup heavy cream
¾	teaspoon instant coffee granules
6	ounces semi-sweet chocolate chips

1.   In a medium-sized saucepan over moderate heat, bring cream and instant coffee just to a boil. Remove from heat and whisk in chocolate chips until melted and smooth.

Note: The torte may be held, uncovered, at room temperature overnight, or frozen. Freeze, uncovered, until frosting is solid; cover tightly. Defrost, uncovered, at room temperature.

Analysis per serving: Calories: 476   Protein: 6g   Carbohydrate: 62g   Fat: 25g   Cholesterol: 16mg   Fiber: 2g   Sodium: 214mg

MOCHA CHOCOLATE-PECAN CAKE

Serves 14-16

Serve this rich and flourless chocolate cake in thin slices. It may be made ahead of time and kept in the refrigerator for several days.

Preparation: 20 minutes
Bake: 45-50 minutes
Chill: overnight

½	cup unsalted butter
8	ounces semi-sweet chocolate
1	cup sugar
1	cup unsweetened cocoa powder
6	eggs or 1½ cups egg substitute
2	cups chopped toasted pecans, divided
3	tablespoons coffee liqueur

GLAZE

4	ounces semi-sweet chocolate
¼	cup unsalted butter

1. Preheat oven to 350 degrees. Butter a 9-inch round cake pan, and line with a circle of waxed or parchment paper, cut to fit. Butter the paper.

2. Heat butter and chocolate in the top of a double boiler over simmering water, stirring frequently, until melted and smooth. Set aside to cool.

3. In a medium-sized bowl, combine sugar, cocoa powder and eggs. Stir in melted chocolate and blend well. Add 1½ cups of the pecans; stir in liqueur.

4. Pour batter into prepared cake pan. Set this pan inside a larger pan, containing enough hot water to reach halfway up the sides of the cake pan. Bake for 45 minutes or until cake is firm to the touch; the surface may crack slightly. Cool on a wire rack.

5. Remove cake from pan, leaving waxed paper in place. Wrap in plastic wrap and refrigerate overnight.

6. To prepare glaze, melt butter and chocolate in the top of a double boiler over simmering water, and stir until smooth; cool.

7. Meanwhile, unwrap the cake and place upside down on a wire rack; remove circle of waxed paper. Placing a sheet of paper underneath the rack to catch any drips, drizzle the glaze down the sides until completely covered; then pour the remainder on top, and spread with a spatula until smooth.

8. Transfer to a serving plate. Press the remaining ½ cup of pecans against the sides of the cake and return to refrigerator. Remove from refrigerator a half hour before serving.

Analysis per serving: Calories: 356   Protein: 6g   Carbohydrate: 31g   Fat: 27g   Cholesterol: 91mg   Fiber: 1g   Sodium: 107mg

Analysis per serving, with egg substitute: Calories: 348   Protein: 6g   Carbohydrate: 31g   Fat: 26g   Cholesterol: 11mg   Fiber: 0.9g   Sodium: 125mg

ORANGE AND ALMOND FLOURLESS CAKE

Serves 12

This very moist cake has its origins in the Sephardic Jewish tradition. It is made with ground almonds instead of flour. At the first UCSD Medical Center Auxiliary Cooking Series, James Beard demonstrated how simple it is to prepare, using a food processor.

Preparation: 30-45 minutes
Cook: 1 hour

2	large navel oranges
2	cups whole almonds
1	cup sugar
6	eggs
1	teaspoon baking powder
	Pinch of salt
	Sweetened Whipped Cream (below), optional
	Fresh berries or orange slices, for garnish

1. Preheat oven to 400 degrees. Butter and flour a 9-inch springform cake pan.

2. Wash oranges and boil, unpeeled, in water until very soft. Remove from water, pat dry, cut open and let cool briefly.

3. Meanwhile, coarsely chop almonds in a food processor. To prevent almonds becoming too oily, add 2 tablespoons of the sugar, and continue processing until finely ground. Transfer to a large bowl.

4. Add eggs to processor and beat. Transfer to bowl with nuts and stir in remaining sugar, baking powder and salt.

5. Cut oranges into about eight sections each, remove any seeds and add to processor, process to a pulp. Mix with other ingredients. Pour into prepared cake pan and bake for 1 hour. Let cool in the pan, then turn out onto a serving platter.

6. Garnish with fresh berries, or slices of orange, with all peel and pith removed. If desired, serve with Sweetened Whipped Cream, passed separately, or piped on top of cake, using a pastry bag fitted with a star tip.

Analysis per serving: Calories: 204 Protein: 6.6g Carbohydrate: 22.5g Fat: 11g Cholesterol: 107mg Fiber: 2g Sodium: 61mg

SWEETENED WHIPPED CREAM

1	cup whipping cream
2	tablespoons sugar
1	teaspoon Grand Marnier

1. In a food processor, whip cream until thick. Add sugar and Grand Marnier and blend.

Analysis per serving: Calories: 77 Protein: 0.4g Carbohydrate: 3g Fat: 7g Cholesterol: 27mg Fiber: 0 Sodium: 7mg

RICH CHOCOLATE CHERRY TORTE

Serves 12-15

This delicious torte was the grand finale to a successful UCSD Medical Center Auxiliary fund-raising dinner. It is well worth the extra effort, especially as it is prepared a day or two ahead.

Preparation: 1 hour
Bake: 20 minutes
Cool: 45 minutes

FOR CAKE

8	ounces semi-sweet chocolate bits
1	tablespoon instant coffee granules
1/4	cup plus 2 tablespoons kirsch
4	eggs, separated
6	ounces unsalted butter, at room temperature
1/3	cup all-purpose flour
	Pinch of salt
2/3	cup sugar, divided
1	1-pound can pitted sour cherries in water, drained (or 1 pound fresh)

FOR GLAZE

6	ounces semi-sweet chocolate bits
1	tablespoon instant coffee granules
3	tablespoons water
2	tablespoons kirsch
	Fresh cherries for garnish (optional)

1. Preheat oven to 375 degrees. Line the bottom of a 9-inch round cake pan with buttered waxed paper, and butter the sides.

2. In a double boiler over simmering water, melt chocolate with coffee granules and 1/4 cup kirsch, stirring frequently until smooth. Add egg yolks, one at a time, stirring continuously, until yolks are warmed and have thickened the chocolate slightly. Beat in butter by tablespoons, stirring until smooth. Stir in flour.

3. In a separate bowl, beat egg whites with a pinch of salt until they form soft peaks. Sprinkle on 1/3 cup of the sugar and continue beating until whites form fairly stiff and shiny peaks. Fold warm chocolate mixture delicately into the whites and turn into prepared pan. Bake for 20-25 minutes, until cake has puffed and a knife inserted in the center comes out with only a slightly creamy layer. Do not overcook. Set on a wire rack to cool for at least 45 minutes before unmolding. Cake will sink and surface will crack slightly.

4. While cake is baking and cooling, prepare cherries. Put pitted fruit into a saucepan with remaining 1/3 cup sugar and 2 tablespoons of kirsch. Cook over medium-low heat, partially covered, for 20-25 minutes (or 10 minutes longer if using fresh cherries); stir occasionally. Uncover pan for the last 10 minutes. Cherries should reduce to a thick compote. Remove from heat and chop cherries roughly. Set aside.

Continued on next page

5. Invert cake onto a serving platter and remove paper. Using a large spoon, trace about a 5-inch circle in the center of the cake, scoop out the top part of the circle, leaving at least half of the cake at the bottom. Add the scooped-out cake to the cherries and mix well. Spoon the cherry-chocolate mixture back into cake, smoothing top with a spatula.

6. To prepare glaze, melt chocolate with coffee granules, water and kirsch in a heavy-bottomed sauce pan, stirring occasionally, until smooth. Allow to cool slightly, then spread evenly over top and sides of cake. Remove any smudges from the platter with a towel dipped in hot water.

7. Chill in refrigerator. The glaze will lose a bit of its shine when chilled, but the cake is better served slightly below room temperature. Remove from refrigerator 30 minutes before serving. Garnish with fresh cherries, if desired.

Adapted from *New Menus from Simca's Cuisine* by Simone Beck, in collaboration with Michael James, published 1979 by Harcourt Brace Jovanovich Inc.

Analysis per serving: Calories: 396   Protein: 6g   Carbohydrate: 28g   Fat: 32g   Cholesterol: 102mg   Fiber: 6g   Sodium: 50mg

DELICIOUSLY SIMPLE APPLE CAKE

Serves 12

This cake is moist and freezes well. Use as a coffee cake or serve as a dessert with ice cream, rum sauce, frozen yogurt or fresh berries.

Preparation: 20-25 minutes
Bake: 50-60 minutes

2	**cups flour**
1	**teaspoon baking soda**
2	**teaspoons cinnamon**
1	**teaspoon salt**
5	**cups peeled, cored and chopped apples**
1½	**cups sugar**
½	**cup cooking oil**
2	**eggs**
2	**teaspoons vanilla extract**
1	**cup chopped walnuts**

1. Preheat oven to 350 degrees. Grease a 9x13-inch pan.

2. In a medium-sized bowl, sift together flour, baking soda, cinnamon and salt; set aside.

3. In a separate bowl, combine apples with sugar; set aside.

4. In a large bowl, beat together oil, eggs and vanilla. Add walnuts and mix well. Add flour mixture and blend well. Stir in apples and sugar.

5. Pour mixture into prepared pan. Bake for 50-60 minutes. Cool on a wire rack.

Analysis per serving: Calories: 359   Protein: 6g   Carbohydrate: 49g   Fat: 16g   Cholesterol: 36mg   Fiber: 2g   Sodium: 258mg

ALMOND CAKE WITH BERRY SAUCE

Serves 8

Preparation: 20-30 minutes
Bake: 40-50 minutes

¾	**cup sugar**
½	**cup (4 ounces) unsalted butter, at room temperature**
8	**ounces almond paste, preferably canned**
3	**eggs**
1	**tablespoon kirsch or Triple Sec**
¼	**teaspoon almond extract**
¼	**cup flour**
⅓	**teaspoon baking powder**
	Powdered sugar
2	**10-ounce packages frozen raspberries, or 2 boxes fresh strawberries with ½ cup sugar**

1. Preheat oven to 350 degrees. Butter and flour an 8-inch round cake pan.

2. In a medium-sized bowl, combine sugar, butter and almond paste. Blend well. Beat in eggs, liquor and almond extract. Add flour and baking powder; beat until just mixed. Do not overbeat.

3. Pour into prepared cake pan and bake for approximately 40-50 minutes, or until a toothpick inserted in the center comes out clean. Cool on a wire rack.

4. In a food processor or blender, purée berries; then pass through a sieve to remove seeds. Add sugar to taste.

5. Transfer cake to a serving plate and dust with powdered sugar; surround with raspberry purée.

Analysis per serving: Calories: 373   Protein: 6g   Carbohydrate: 43g   Fat: 21g   Cholesterol: 101mg   Fiber: 2g   Sodium: 40mg

ORANGE CAKE WITH RAISINS AND PECANS

Serves 8-10

Preparation: 15-20 minutes
Bake: 35-45 minutes

1	orange
1	cup raisins
1/3	cup walnuts or pecans
2	cups all-purpose flour
1	cup sugar
1	teaspoon baking soda
1	teaspoon salt
2	eggs, beaten
1	cup lowfat milk
1/2	cup corn oil
1/3	cup orange juice (reserved from orange)
1/3	cup sugar
1	teaspoon cinnamon
1/4	cup chopped pecans

1. Heat oven to 350 degrees. Grease and flour a 9x13-inch pan.

2. Squeeze orange, reserving 1/3 cup juice for topping. In a food processor, grind together orange peel and pulp with raisins and nuts.

3. In a large mixing bowl, blend flour, sugar, baking soda and salt. Add eggs, milk and oil. Beat well, then add orange mixture.

4. Pour into prepared pan, and bake for 35-40 minutes or until a toothpick inserted in the center comes out clean.

5. Drizzle reserved orange juice over warm cake. Combine sugar, cinnamon and pecans, and sprinkle on top.

Analysis per serving: Calories: 424   Protein: 6g   Carbohydrate: 62g   Fat: 19g   Cholesterol: 44mg   Fiber: 2g   Sodium: 323mg

FRESH PLUM CAKE

Serves 10-14

This cake is deliciously moist and is also good served with sweetened whipped cream, frozen vanilla yogurt or vanilla ice cream.

Preparation: 20 minutes
Bake: 50 minutes

2	**cups flour**
1	**teaspoon baking soda**
1	**teaspoon salt**
1	**teaspoon cinnamon**
3	**eggs**
1¾	**cups sugar**
1	**cup canola oil**
2	**heaping cups chopped blue or Italian plums (cut into eighths, if large, and quarters if small)**
1	**cup chopped nuts (optional)**

1. Preheat oven to 350 degrees. Grease a 9x13-inch baking dish with ½ teaspoon of oil.

2. Sift together flour, baking soda, salt and cinnamon; set aside.

3. In a large mixing bowl, combine eggs, sugar and oil and beat well. Add flour mixture to egg mixture and fold together. Fold in plums and nuts. Pour into baking dish and gently spread to distribute fruit and nuts evenly.

4. Bake until cake is golden and edges are pulling away from the sides, approximately 50 minutes.

5. When cool, dust with powdered sugar and serve.

Variation: In October, during the apple season in Julian, try substituting good firm apples instead of plums.

Analysis per serving: Calories: 369   Protein: 5g   Carbohydrate: 41g   Fat: 22g   Cholesterol: 46mg   Fiber:1g   Sodium: 225mg

LEMON HERB TEA BREAD

Makes 1 loaf

Lemon balm and lemon thyme, which are useful small plants to grow in garden borders, give an unusual, delicate lemon flavor to this attractive tea bread.

Preparation: 20-30 minutes
Bake: 50-60 minutes

¾	**cup milk**
1	**tablespoon finely chopped lemon balm**
1	**tablespoon finely chopped lemon thyme**
2	**cups flour**
1½	**teaspoons baking powder**
¼	**teaspoon salt**
6	**tablespoons butter, at room temperature**
1	**cup sugar**
2	**eggs, beaten**
1	**tablespoon grated lemon zest**
	Lemon Glaze (below)
	Sprigs of lemon thyme (preferably with flowers), for garnish

1. Preheat oven to 325 degrees. Butter a 9x5-inch loaf pan.

2. Place milk and herbs in a small saucepan; heat gently until almost simmering. Remove from heat and set aside to cool, allowing herb flavors to infuse milk.

3. In a small bowl, combine flour, baking powder and salt. Set aside.

4. In a large bowl, using an electric mixer, cream butter with sugar, beating until light and fluffy. Beat in eggs one at a time. Stir in lemon zest. Gradually add flour mixture and infused milk, alternating until just blended.

5. Pour into prepared loaf pan and bake for approximately 50 minutes, or until a toothpick inserted in the center comes out clean. Remove from pan to a wire rack.

6. Meanwhile, prepare Lemon Glaze.

7. While cake is hot, slowly pour over the Lemon Glaze (a sheet of waxed paper under the rack will catch the drips). Decorate the top with sprigs of flowering lemon thyme.

LEMON GLAZE

Juice of 2 lemons
Powdered sugar

1. In a medium-sized bowl, gradually combine lemon juice and sugar, whisking until the glaze is thick but pourable.

This recipe is from the beautiful book, *Herbs - Gardens, Decorations, and Recipes* by Emelie Tolley and Chris Mead. Text Copyright © 1985 by Emelie Tolley; Crown Publishers Inc.

Analysis per serving: Calories: 248   Protein: 5g   Carbohydrate: 40g   Fat: 8g   Cholesterol: 62mg   Fiber: 1g   Sodium: 195mg

AVOCADO BREAD

Makes 1 loaf; Serves 12

Preparation: 30 minutes
Bake: 1 hour 10 minutes

½	**cup butter, softened**
1	**cup sugar**
1	**cup mashed avocado mixed with 2 teaspoons lemon juice**
½	**cup egg substitute (equivalent to 2 eggs)**
2	**cups all-purpose flour**
½	**teaspoon salt**
1½	**teaspoon baking powder**
¼	**teaspoon ground cloves**
¼	**teaspoon ground cinnamon**
⅔	**cup chopped pecans**

1. Preheat oven to 375 degrees. Grease a 9x5-inch loaf pan.

2. In a medium-sized bowl, combine flour, salt, baking powder, cloves and cinnamon; set aside.

3. In a large bowl, cream butter and sugar together. Add avocado, egg and the flour mixture. Blend well to form a batter. Stir in pecans.

4. Pour into prepared loaf pan and bake for 15 minutes. Lower oven temperature to 350 degrees and bake for 55 minutes, or until done. Cool on a wire rack before slicing.

Analysis per serving: Calories: 260 Protein: 4g Carbohydrate: 34g Fat: 13g Cholesterol: 20mg Fiber: 1g Sodium: 195mg

ORANGE PECAN BREAD

Makes 1 loaf; Serves 10

Preparation: 20 minutes
Bake: 50-60 minutes

2¾	**cups sifted all-purpose flour**
2½	**teaspoons baking powder**
½	**teaspoon baking soda**
½	**teaspoon salt**
2	**tablespoons butter or margarine**
1	**cup honey**
1	**egg**
¾	**cup fresh orange juice (about 2 oranges)**
	Grated zest of 1 orange
2	**cups broken pecans**

1. Preheat oven to 325 degrees. Spray a 9x5-inch loaf pan with non-stick vegetable spray.

2. In a medium-sized bowl, sift flour with baking powder, soda and salt. Set aside.

3. In a large bowl, beat butter until creamy. Stir in honey, unbeaten egg and orange zest. Add flour mixture and orange juice, a little at a time, alternating. Mix well after each addition. Stir in pecans.

4. Pour into prepared pan. Bake for 50-60 minutes, or until golden brown. Cool in the pan on a wire rack.

Analysis per serving: Calories: 400 Protein: 6g Carbohydrate: 58g Fat: 18g Cholesterol: 21mg Fiber: 2.5g Sodium: 265mg

DESSERTS and SWEETS

LIGHT AND CRISP PRALINE COOKIES

Makes 2½ dozen

Store these easy-to-make cookies in an air-tight container or keep in the freezer.

Preparation: 10 minutes
Bake: 10 minutes

3	**tablespoons butter, melted**
¾	**cup dark brown sugar**
1	**large egg, beaten**
3	**tablespoons flour**
1	**cup pecan halves**
1	**teaspoon vanilla extract**
	Pinch of salt (optional)

1. Preheat oven to 350 degrees. Grease a cookie sheet and dust with flour.

2. In a medium-sized bowl, cream butter and sugar until smooth. Add egg, flour, pecans, vanilla and salt; mix well.

3. Drop batter, by teaspoonfuls, 4 inches apart on cookie sheet (these cookies spread while baking). Be sure to include 1 pecan half on each cookie.

4. Bake for 8-10 minutes. Remove from oven; allow to stand for ½ minute, then transfer cookies, with a spatula, to a wire rack to cool. If cookies stick to the pan, place in the oven and warm again briefly.

Analysis per serving: Calories: 78   Protein: 1g   Carbohydrate: 9g   Fat: 5g   Cholesterol: 13mg   Fiber: 0.3g   Sodium: 20mg

FORGOTTEN COOKIES

Makes 3 dozen

Amazingly, these cookies are not baked—heat from the warmed oven does the "cooking". Pop them into a preheated oven before going to bed and find the finished sweet treats in the morning.

Preparation: 15-20 minutes
Bake: overnight

2   egg whites
2/3   cup sugar
1   cup semi-sweet chocolate chips
1   cup chopped pecans or walnuts, or 1/2 cup each
1   teaspoon vanilla or peppermint extract

1.   Preheat oven to 350 degrees. Cover cookie sheet with aluminum foil.

2.   In a dry, clean, medium-sized bowl, beat egg whites lightly and gradually add sugar. Beat until very stiff. Fold in chocolate chips, nuts and vanilla.

3.   Drop cookies by teaspoonful onto prepared cookie sheet. Place in oven; turn oven off and forget! Do not open oven. Leave overnight.

Analysis per 2 cookies: Calories: 86   Protein: 1g   Carbohydrate: 10g   Fat: 5g   Cholesterol: 0   Fiber: 0.3g   Sodium: 5mg

ROSEMARY SHORTBREAD COOKIES

Makes about 20 cookies

Rosemary is a familiar herb that thrives in our San Diego climate. Its unusual use in a sweet recipe is both intriguing and delicious. This is our favorite cookie and goes particularly well with iced desserts.

Preparation: 20 minutes
Bake: 15-20 minutes

1/2   cup butter
1/3   cup sugar
1 1/4 cups sifted flour
1-2   tablespoons finely chopped fresh rosemary
       Extra sugar, for sprinkling

1.   Preheat oven to 350 degrees. Grease a cookie sheet.

2.   In a large bowl, cream butter with sugar until smooth. Work in flour and rosemary to make a soft dough, then shape into a ball.

3.   Roll out dough on a floured board until 1/4-inch thick. Cut into rounds, using a 2-inch fluted cookie cutter, and arrange on prepared cookie sheet.

4.   Bake for 15-20 minutes or just until turning brown. Cool on a wire rack and dust with the extra sugar.

Analysis per serving: Calories: 55   Protein: 1g   Carbohydrate: 6g   Fat: 3g   Cholesterol: 8mg   Fiber: 0.2g   Sodium: 31mg

CHOCOLATE PEPPERMINT CANDY SQUARES

Serves 6-8

Advance preparation is needed to chill candy squares at each stage. As this candy is deliciously rich, be sure to cut it into small squares for serving.

Preparation: 40 minutes
Chill: 3 hours
Bake: 25 minutes

FIRST LAYER

2	squares unsweetened chocolate
½	cup butter or margarine
2	large eggs
1	cup sugar
½	cup all-purpose flour
½	cup chopped nuts

SECOND LAYER

1½	cups powdered sugar
3	tablespoons butter or margarine, softened
1½	tablespoons heavy cream
1	teaspoon peppermint extract

THIRD LAYER

1½	squares unsweetened chocolate
1½	tablespoons butter or margarine
1	teaspoon vanilla extract
	Raspberries or mint leaves, for garnish (optional)

1. Preheat oven to 350 degrees. Grease an 8-inch square pan.

2. First Layer: In a double boiler over simmering water, heat chocolate and butter together until melted, stirring frequently. Remove from heat. Beat in eggs and sugar. Add flour and nuts and mix well.

3. Pour into prepared pan and bake for 25-30 minutes. Cool completely.

4. Second Layer: In a medium-sized bowl, mix powdered sugar, butter, cream and peppermint extract until smooth. Spread over first layer of baked chocolate. Refrigerate for at least 1 hour.

5. Third Layer: In a double boiler, over simmering water, melt chocolate with butter, stirring frequently; add vanilla and blend. Pour over chilled second layer. Chill for another hour.

6. Cut into 1-inch squares and serve garnished with raspberries or mint leaves.

Analysis per serving: Calories: 531 Protein: 5g Carbohydrate: 56g Fat: 36g Cholesterol: 57mg Fiber: 1.1g Sodium: 177mg

INDEX

A

Aioli
  Light Aioli 176
  Red Pepper Aioli Without
    Egg 146
Almonds
  Almond Cake with Berry
    Sauce 236
  Almond-Crusted Broccoli and
    Spinach Casserole 204
  Cornish Hens with Almond-
    Honey-Mustard Glaze 178
  Orange and Almond Flourless
    Cake 233
Appetizers (See also Dips &
    Spreads)
  Ceviche Dolsa 23
  Chicken Satay 26
  Chilled Mushrooms
    Mediterranean 15
  Marinated Dill-Seed
    Carrots 16
  No-Fry Tortilla Chips 21
  Olives in Rosemary-Scented
    Oil 22
  Pepper Wedges with Tomatoes
    and Basil 13
  Rancho del Sol Guacamole 17
  Scallop Ceviche 22
  Steamed Chicken and Shrimp
    Dim Sum 25
  Stir-fried Shrimp with Two
    Sauces 24
  Turkish Lentil Fingers 14
Apples
  Apple and Cranberry Pie with
    Nut Topping 226
  Baked Yams with Apples and
    Nuts 200
  Chicken Baked with Onions,
    Apples and Dried Fruit 174
  Deliciously Simple Apple
    Cake 235
  Puréed Celery Root with
    Apples 191
Apricots
  Apricot-Hazelnut Tart 225
  Apricot-Orange Ice 211
Artichoke Hearts, Roman Lamb
    with, 121
Arugula
  Pasta with Green Olives,
    Arugula and Escarole 88

Salad of New Potatoes,
    Arugula and Mint 71
Asparagus
  Asian Chilled Asparagus 184
  Risotto with Asparagus and
    Mushrooms 98
Avocado
  Avocado and Papaya Salad
    with Mango Dressing 67
  Avocado Bread 240
  Avocados, Note about 67
  California Avocado Tacos
    with Fresh Tomato
    Salsa 205
  Chilled Avocado Soup 35
  Rancho del Sol Guacamole 17

B

Barbecue
  Barbecue, Menu for 33
  Barbecued Flank Steak with
    Pineapple-Ginger
    Marinade 113
  Barbecued Mexican-Style Flank
    Steak 115
  Barbecued Salmon with Dill-
    Cucumber Butter 151
  Broiled Shrimp with Soy-Citrus
    Marinade 140
  Butterflied Leg of Lamb with
    Red-Wine or Herb
    Marinade 122
  Carne Asada California
    Style 114
  Chicken Satay 26
  Grilled Chicken Salad with
    Citrus Salsa 78
  Grilled Chicken with Melon
    Relish 166
  Grilled Thresher Shark with
    Tomato and Green-Onion
    Salsa 155
  Grilled Whole Red Snapper
    with Oregano 153
  Picnic Steak with Ravigote
    Sauce 112
  Rosemary-Roasted
    Onions 196
  San Diego Seafood
    Kebabs 143
  Thai Grilled Fish with
    Lemongrass and Basil 144

Beans (See also Green Beans)
  Black Beans with Cumin and
    Vegetables 185
  Chicken Chili 163
  Collage of Summer Vegetables
    with Black Beans 184
  Old Town Black Bean Soup 49
  Warm Chicken and Black Bean
    Salad with Lime
    Vinaigrette 79
  White Bean and Tomato
    Salad 68
  White Beans with Tomatoes
    and Herbs 188
Beef
  Barbecued Flank Steak with
    Pineapple-Ginger
    Marinade 113
  Barbecued Mexican-Style Flank
    Steak 115
  Carne Asada California
    Style 114
  Korean Marinated Beef 118
  Mediterranean Meatloaf 110
  Picnic Steak with Ravigote
    Sauce 112
  Roast Fillet of Beef with
    Cornichon-Tarragon
    Sauce 111
  Stir-Fried Beef with Tomato and
    Onion 116
  Vietnamese Lemongrass-
    Sautéed Beef 117
Belgian Endive Salad, Watercress
    and 58
Berries (See also individual
    names)
  Geranium Cream with Fresh
    Blackberries 215
  Sliced Bananas and Berries
    with Papaya Sauce 213
  Summer Berries in Caramelized
    Mascarpone Sauce 217
Bouquet Garni, Note about 15
Bread (See also Tea Breads)
  Braided Herb Bread 105
  Rosemary Bread 104
  Yogurt Dinner Rolls with
    Herbs 106
Broccoli
  Almond-Crusted Broccoli and
    Spinach Casserole 204
  Broccoli and Grape
    Salad 65

Ginger-Lemon Broccoli 189
Butter, clarified, Note about 119

C

Cabbage, Thai-Flavored 190
Cakes & Tortes
    Almond Cake with Berry
        Sauce 236
    Cappuccino Nut Torte 231
    Chocolate Decadence 228
    Deliciously Simple Apple
        Cake 235
    Devilish Cocoa Cake with
        Raspberry Sauce 230
    Fresh Plum Cake 238
    Guiltless Chocolate Cake with
        Orange Liqueur
        Frosting 229
    Mocha Chocolate-Pecan
        Cake 232
    Orange and Almond Flourless
        Cake 233
    Orange Cake with Raisins and
        Pecans 237
    Rich Chocolate Cherry
        Torte 234
Candy (See Desserts & Sweets)
Cantaloupe Sherbet 210
Carne Asada California
    Style 116
Carrots
    Carrot and Potato Soup with
        Chervil 46
    Chilled Carrot and Orange
        Soup 36
    Marinated Dill-Seed
        Carrots 16
    Summer Squash and Carrot
        Soup with Lemon and
        Basil 45
Cauliflower, Lemony 189
Celery Root, Puréed with
    Apples 191
Ceviche
    Ceviche Dolsa 23
    Scallop Ceviche 22
Chicken
    Asian-Flavored Chicken
        Salad 76
    Baja Chicken and Lime
        Soup 39
    Baked Chicken with Ranchero
        Sauce 173

Baked Five-Spice Chicken 175
Chicken Baked in Yogurt
    Sauce 172
Chicken Baked with Onions,
    Apples and Dried Fruit 174
Chicken Breasts Chipotle 164
Chicken Breasts in Triple
    Mustard Sauce 167
Chicken Chili 163
Chicken Couscous Salad 75
Chicken Satay 26
Chicken Stew Provençal with
    Light Aioli 176
Chicken Stuffed with Chiles and
    Cheese 171
Chicken with Raspberry
    Vinegar Sauce 170
Grilled Chicken Salad with
    Citrus Salsa 78
Grilled Chicken with Melon
    Relish 166
Kiwi Fruit Chicken 161
Light and Easy Fresh Ginger
    Chicken 162
Parchment-Baked Chicken with
    Leeks 165
Rancho Chicken with
    Oranges 168
Roasted Chicken Breast with
    Sweet Pepper Sauce 169
Spicy Shrimp with Chicken
    Cilantro 142
Steamed Chicken and Shrimp
    Dim Sum 25
Tagine of Chicken with
    Dates 177
Tangerine Peel Chicken with
    Walnuts 160
Thai Fried Rice with
    Chicken 102
Vietnamese Chicken Salad 77
Warm Chicken and Black Bean
    Salad with Lime
    Vinaigrette 79
Chile (See Peppers)
Chili, Chicken 163
Chocolate
    Cappuccino Nut Torte 231
    Chocolate Cappuccino
        Frosting 231
    Chocolate Decadence 228
    Chocolate Peppermint Candy
        Squares 244
    Devilish Cocoa Cake with
        Raspberry Sauce 230

Forgotten Cookies 243
Guiltless Chocolate Cake with
    Orange Liqueur
    Frosting 229
Mocha Chocolate-Pecan
    Cake 232
Rich Chocolate Cherry
    Torte 234
The Ultimate Chocolate
    Dessert 227
Chutney, Loquat 30
Cilantro Pesto 137
Condiments (See also Salsas)
    Loquat Chutney 30
    Melon Relish 166
Cookies
    Forgotten Cookies 243
    Light and Crisp Praline
        Cookies 242
    Rosemary Shortbread
        Cookies 243
Corn
    Bacon-Flavored Sweet Corn
        Chowder with Wild
        Rice 48
    Marinated Shrimp and Corn
        Salad 74
    Mazatlan Shrimp Chowder
        with Corn 43
    Mexican Sautéed Zucchini with
        Corn 202
    Scallops with Tomato and Corn
        Salsa 135
Cornish Hens
    Cornish Hens with Almond-
        Honey-Mustard Glaze 178
    Cornish Hens with Plum-Rice
        Stuffing 179
Couscous
    Chicken Couscous Salad 75
    Lemon Couscous 95
    Note about 95
Cranberries
    Apple and Cranberry Pie with
        Nut Topping 226
    Cranberry, Chile and Cilantro
        Salsa 27
    Turkey, Wild Rice and
        Cranberry Salad 81
Crème Fraîche, Note on
    making 218
Croutons, Herbed 57
Cucumber
    Cucumber Dressing With
        Jalapeño and Dill 83

INDEX

Cucumber, Mint and Chive
   Salad 58
Green Cucumber Salsa 27
White Gazpacho 37

D

Dates, Tagine of Chicken
   with 177
Desserts *(See also Cakes & Tortes;
   Cookies; Pies & Tarts)*
   Lime Chiffon Mousse 215
   Mexican Bread Pudding with
      Maple-Pecan Sauce 219
   Upside-Down Lemon
      Delight 222
   Candy
      Chocolate Peppermint Candy
         Squares 244
   Chocolate Desserts
      Cappuccino Nut Torte 231
      Chocolate Cappuccino
         Frosting 231
      Chocolate Decadence 228
      Devilish Cocoa Cake with
         Raspberry Sauce 230
      Forgotten Cookies 243
      Guiltless Chocolate Cake
         with Orange Liqueur
         Frosting 229
      Mocha Chocolate-Pecan
         Cake 232
      Rich Chocolate Cherry
         Torte 234
      The Ultimate Chocolate
         Dessert 227
   Frozen Desserts
      Apricot-Orange Ice 211
      Cantaloupe Sherbet 210
      Fresh Raspberry Sorbet 210
      Frozen Coffee-Pecan Dessert
         with Caramel Sauce 212
      Lemon Ice Cream 211
      Pumpkin Ice Cream Pie in
         Oatmeal-Nut Crust 223
   Fruit Desserts
      Double-Baked Caramel Pears
         with Ice Cream 216
      Geranium Cream with Fresh
         Blackberries 215
      Poached Green Figs with
         Mascarpone Cheese 214
      Red Fruit Summer
         Pudding 218

Sliced Bananas and Berries
   with Papaya Sauce 213
Strawberries with Strawberry
   Sauce 212
Summer Berries in
   Caramelized Mascarpone
   Sauce 217
Meringue Desserts
   Caramelized Meringue Ring
      with Mangos 221
   Lemon Pavlova 220
The Ultimate Chocolate Dessert
   227
Dill-Cucumber Butter 151
Dips & Spreads
   Baked Eggplant and Garlic
      Appetizer 12
   California Black Olive
      Caviar 16
   Cranberry, Chile and Cilantro
      Salsa 27
   Creamy Tomatillo Salsa 29
   Green Cucumber Salsa 27
   Light Aioli 176
   Loquat Chutney 30
   Moroccan Peppers Salsa 28
   Papaya and Tomato Salsa 29
   Rancho del Sol Guacamole 17
   Red Pepper Aioli Without
      Egg 146
   Southwest Salsa 28
   Spiced Vegetarian Pâté 20
   Wild Mushroom and Hazelnut
      Pâté 19
   Winter Squash Spread with
      Garlic and Cilantro 18
Dressings *(See Salad Dressings)*
Duck, Asian Honey 180

E

Eggplant
   Baked Eggplant and Garlic
      Appetizer 12
   Grilled Eggplant and Spinach
      Salad 62
   Penne with Eggplant and
      Vegetables 89
   Spinach, Eggplant and Red
      Pepper Lasagna 94
Escarole
   Baked Escarole with Garlic and
      Anchovies 193
   Pasta with Green Olives,
      Arugula and Escarole 88

F

Fajitas, Old Town Vegetable 206
Fennel
   Baked Sea Bass with Fennel
      and Spinach 148
   Chicken Stew Provençal with
      Light Aioli 176
   Fennel Gratin 194
   Hearty Lentil Soup with
      Winter Squash and
      Fennel 52
   Sweet Red Pepper and Fresh
      Fennel Salad 63
Figs
   Poached Green Figs with
      Mascarpone Cheese 214
Fish *(See Seafood & Fish; see also
   individual names)*
Flowers, Edible 97
Frostings
   Chocolate Cappuccino
      Frosting 231
   Lemon Glaze 239
   Nut Topping 226
   Orange Liqueur Frosting 229
Fruit *(See Desserts: Fruit. See also
   individual names)*

G

Garlic
   Baked Eggplant and Garlic
      Appetizer 12
   Herbed Roasted Potatoes with
      Garlic 197
   Light Aioli 176
   Pistou 47
   Red Pepper Aioli Without
      Egg 146
   Winter Squash Spread with
      Garlic and Cilantro 18
Garnishes
   Edible Flowers 97
   Green Vegetable Garnish 50
Gazpacho
   Gazpacho Salad with Herb
      Dressing 61
   White Gazpacho 37
Grape
   Broccoli and Grape Salad 65
Grapefruit
   Fresh Pink Grapefruit Chiffon
      Pie 224

Green Beans
  Green Beans with Red Pepper and Honey-Roasted Pecans 186
  Green Beans with Walnut-Dill Sauce 187
Green-Onion Quiche 203
Guacamole, Rancho del Sol 17

H

Halibut
  Baked Halibut with Cilantro-Citrus Sauce 147
  Halibut in Herbal Zabaglione Sauce with Red Pepper 146
Ham, Cheese and Spinach Roulade 127
Hazelnuts
  Apricot-Hazelnut Tart 225
  Hazelnuts, Note on removing skins 223
  Wild Mushroom and Hazelnut Pâté 19
Herbs de Provence, Note about 67

I

Ice Cream (See Desserts: Frozen)

J

Jícama
  Fiesta Salad with Cumin Dressing 60
  Jícama Slaw with Peanut Dressing 59
Julienne, Note about 63

K

Kasha Salad with Fruit and Nuts 70
Kiwi Fruit Chicken 161

L

Lamb
  Butterflied Leg of Lamb with Red-Wine or Herb Marinade 122

Ginger-Mustard Lamb Rib Chops 119
  Lamb Roast with Coriander Seeds 120
  Roman Lamb with Artichoke Hearts 121
Lasagna, Spinach, Eggplant and Red Pepper 94
Leeks
  Leeks and Zucchini in Wine-Cream Sauce 194
  Parchment-Baked Chicken with Leeks 165
  Sausage and Leek Pie 128
  Scallops in Leek Sauce 134
Lemon
  Ginger-Lemon Broccoli 189
  Lemon Couscous 95
  Lemon Glaze 239
  Lemon Herb Tea Bread 239
  Lemon Ice Cream 211
  Lemon Pavlova 220
  Lemony Cauliflower 189
  Lemony Sea Scallops 133
  Minted Citrus Salad 65
  Upside-Down Lemon Delight 222
Lemongrass
  Spicy Shrimp Soup with Lemongrass and Lime 40
  Lemongrass, Note about keeping 40
  Note about 144
  Thai Grilled Fish with Lemongrass and Basil 144
  Vietnamese Lemongrass-Sautéed Beef 117
Lentil
  Brown Rice and Lentil Pilaf 100
  Hearty Lentil Soup with Winter Squash and Fennel 52
  Turkish Lentil Fingers 14
Lime
  Baja Chicken and Lime Soup 39
  Lime Chiffon Mousse 215
  Lime Cilantro Dressing 73
  Lime Vinaigrette 79
Linguine with Baked Tomatoes 90
Loquat Chutney 30

M

Mahi Mahi and Vegetables, Tagine of 149

Mango
  Caramelized Meringue Ring with Mangos 221
  Mango Dressing 67
  Mango Rice with Almonds 96
Marinades
  Ginger Marinade 152
  Herb 122
  Honey Marinade 180
  Korean 118
  Oregano 115
  Papaya Seed 114
  Pineapple-Ginger 113
  Red-Wine 122
  Soy-Citrus 140
  Yogurt 172
Meatloaf, Mediterranean 110
Melon Relish 166
Menus
  Menu for a Beach or Boating Picnic 131
  Menu for a Buffet Salad Luncheon 55
  Menu for a Celebration Dinner 209
  Menu for a Mexican Buffet 109
  Menu for an Easily Portable Picnic 87
  Menu for a Patio Barbecue 33
  Menu for a Taste of Asia 159
  Menu of Mediterranean Flavors 11
  Vegetarian Menu 183
Mexican
  Achiote Salsa 206
  Baja Chicken and Lime Soup 39
  Baked Chicken with Ranchero Sauce 173
  Barbecued Mexican-Style Flank Steak 115
  California Avocado Tacos with Fresh Tomato Salsa 205
  Carne Asada California Style 114
  Ceviche Dolsa 23
  Chicken Breasts Chipotle 164
  Chicken Stuffed with Chiles and Cheese 171
  Cranberry, Chile and Cilantro Salsa 27
  Mango Rice with Almonds 96
  Mazatlan Shrimp Chowder with Corn 43

Mexican Bread Pudding with Maple-Pecan Sauce 219
Mexican Green Rice 96
Mexican Sautéed Zucchini with Corn 202
Mushroom-Stuffed Green Chiles with Goat Cheese Sauce 192
Old Town Vegetable Fajitas 206
Rancho Chicken with Oranges 168
Rancho del Sol Guacamole 17
Sautéed Pork Tenderloin in Tomatillo Salsa 126
Scallop Ceviche 22
Spicy Shrimp with Chicken Cilantro 142
Mint Vinaigrette 64
Mushrooms
Black Forest Mushrooms 195
Chilled Mushrooms Mediterranean 15
Mushroom-Stuffed Green Chiles with Goat Cheese Sauce 192
Polenta with Sun-Dried Tomatoes and Mushrooms 103
Risotto with Asparagus and Mushrooms 98
Spiced Vegetarian Pâté 20
Wild Mushroom and Hazelnut Pâté 19
Mussels in Sherry-Orange Vinaigrette with Prosciutto 132

N

Nuts (See also Almonds & Pecans)
Apricot-Hazelnut Tart 225
Forgotten Cookies 243
Nut Topping 226
Spiced Basmati Pilaf with Nuts and Dried Fruit 101

O

Olives
California Black Olive Caviar 16
Olives in Rosemary-Scented Oil 22
Pasta with Green Olives, Arugula and Escarole 88
Pasta with Spinach, Tomatoes and Greek Olive Sauce 91
Onions
Chicken Baked with Onions, Apples and Dried Fruit 174
Elegant Baked Onions 196
Green-Onion Quiche 203
Rosemary-Roasted Onions 196
Stir-Fried Beef with Tomato and Onion 116
Watermelon and Red Onion Salad with Mint 66
Orange
Apricot-Orange Ice 211
Brown Rice Salad with Mandarin Oranges 69
Chilled Carrot and Orange Soup 36
Minted Citrus Salad 65
Orange and Almond Flourless Cake 233
Orange Cake with Raisins and Pecans 237
Orange Liqueur Frosting 229
Orange Pecan Bread 241
Orange Vinaigrette 70
Rancho Chicken with Oranges 168
Sherry-Orange Vinaigrette 133
Wilted Spinach with Oranges 198
Oregano Marinade 115
Orzo, Shrimp with Orzo and Sun-Dried Tomatoes 92

P

Pacific Rim
Asian Chilled Asparagus 184
Asian Fruit Juice Dressing 84
Asian Honey Duck 180
Asian-Flavored Chicken Salad 76
Asian-Spiced Soup with Scallop and Shrimp Dumpling 42
Baked Five-Spice Chicken 175
Broiled Salmon with Ginger Marinade 152
Broiled Shrimp with Soy-Citrus Marinade 140
Chicken Satay 26
Chili-Garlic Sauce 144
Cilantro Pesto 137
Fish Sauce, Note about 123
Kiwi Fruit Chicken 161
Korean Marinated Beef 118
Light and Easy Fresh Ginger Chicken 162
Mango Rice with Almonds 96
Pork Stir-Fried with Fresh Ginger 123
Rice with Asian Spices 97
Soy and Sesame Seed Dressing 83
Spiced Basmati Pilaf with Nuts and Dried Fruit 101
Spicy Shrimp Soup with Lemongrass and Lime 40
Steamed Chicken and Shrimp Dim Sum 25
Stir-fried Shrimp with Two Sauces 24
Tangerine Peel Chicken with Walnuts 160
Thai Fried Rice with Chicken 102
Thai Garlic Shrimp 137
Thai Grilled Fish with Lemongrass and Basil 144
Thai-Flavored Cabbage 190
Vietnamese Chicken Salad 77
Vietnamese Lemongrass-Sautéed Beef 117
Papaya
Avocado and Papaya Salad with Mango Dressing 67
Chilled Papaya Soup 36
Papaya and Tomato Salsa 29
Papaya Sauce 213
Papaya Seed Marinade 114
Pasta
Chicken Couscous Salad 75
Easy Agnolotti Soup 38
Lemon Couscous 95
Linguine with Baked Tomatoes 90
Pasta with Fresh Basil and Marinated Tomatoes 90
Pasta with Green Olives, Arugula and Escarole 88

Pasta with Spinach, Tomatoes and Greek Olive Sauce 91
Pasta with Sun-Dried Tomato Pesto 93
Penne with Eggplant and Vegetables 89
Shrimp with Orzo and Sun-Dried Tomatoes 92
Pâté
  Spiced Vegetarian Pâté 20
  Wild Mushroom and Hazelnut Pâté 19
Pears
  Asian Pear and Smoked Turkey Salad 80
  Double-Baked Caramel Pears with Ice Cream 216
  Pear and Gorgonzola Salad 66
Pecans
  Cappuccino Nut Torte 231
  Frozen Coffee-Pecan Dessert with Caramel Sauce 212
  Light and Crisp Praline Cookies 242
  Mocha Chocolate-Pecan Cake 232
  Orange Cake with Raisins and Pecans 237
  Orange Pecan Bread 241
Penne with Eggplant and Vegetables 89
Peppers
  Chicken Stuffed with Chiles and Cheese 171
  Peppers, Note about charring and peeling 29
  Bell Peppers
    Moroccan Peppers Salsa 28
    Pepper Wedges with Tomatoes and Basil 13
    Red Pepper Aioli Without Egg 146
    Roasted Chicken Breast with Sweet Pepper Sauce 169
    Spinach, Eggplant and Red Pepper Lasagna 94
    Sweet Red Pepper and Fresh Fennel Salad 63
  Chile Peppers
    Baked Chicken with Ranchero Sauce 173
    Chicken Breasts Chipotle 164

Mushroom-Stuffed Green Chiles with Goat Cheese Sauce 192
Pesto
  Cilantro Pesto 137
  Pasta with Sun-Dried Tomato Pesto 93
Picnic
  Menu for Easily Portable Picnic 87
  Menu for Beach or Boating Picnic 131
Pies & Tarts
  Apple and Cranberry Pie with Nut Topping 226
  Apricot-Hazelnut Tart 225
  Fresh Pink Grapefruit Chiffon Pie 224
  Pumpkin Ice Cream Pie in Oatmeal-Nut Crust 223
  Sausage and Leek Pie 128
Pilaf
  Brown Rice and Lentil Pilaf 100
  California Wild Rice Pilaf 99
  Spiced Basmati Pilaf with Nuts and Dried Fruit 101
Pistou 47
Pita, Note on toasting 18
Plums
  Cornish Hens with Plum-Rice Stuffing 179
  Fresh Plum Cake 238
  Plum Glaze 179
Polenta with Sun-Dried Tomatoes and Mushrooms 103
Pork
  Four-Peppercorn Pork Roast with Red-Wine Sauce 125
  Pork Fillets in Mustard Sauce 124
  Pork Stir-Fried with Fresh Ginger 123
  Sausage and Leek Pie 128
  Sautéed Pork Tenderloin in Tomatillo Salsa 126
Potatoes
  Carrot and Potato Soup with Chervil 46
  Herbed Roasted Potatoes with Garlic 197
  New Potatoes in Lemon-Herb Sauce 197
  Roasted New Potato Salad with Rosemary and Shallots 72

Salad of New Potatoes, Arugula and Mint 71
Poultry (See individual names)
Pudding
  Mexican Bread Pudding with Maple-Pecan Sauce 219
  Upside-Down Lemon Delight 222
Pumpkin
  Pumpkin Ice Cream Pie in Oatmeal-Nut Crust 223
  Pumpkin Soup with Green Vegetable Garnish 50

Q

Quiche, Green-Onion 203

R

Raspberries
  Almond Cake with Berry Sauce 236
  Fresh Raspberry Sorbet 210
  Raspberry Sauce 230
Red Bell Pepper (See Peppers: Bell)
Red Snapper
  Grilled Whole Red Snapper with Oregano 153
  Red Snapper Baked with Vegetables 154
Rice
  Bacon-Flavored Sweet Corn Chowder with Wild Rice 48
  Brown Rice and Lentil Pilaf 100
  Brown Rice Salad with Mandarin Oranges 69
  California Wild Rice Pilaf 99
  Mango Rice with Almonds 96
  Mexican Green Rice 96
  Rice with Asian Spices 97
  Risotto with Asparagus and Mushrooms 98
  Spiced Basmati Pilaf with Nuts and Dried Fruit 101
  Thai Fried Rice with Chicken 102
  Turkey, Wild Rice and Cranberry Salad 81
Roquefort Cheese Dressing 84

INDEX

Rosemary
Olives in Rosemary-Scented Oil 22
Roasted New Potato Salad with Rosemary and Shallots 72
Rosemary Bread 104
Rosemary Shortbread Cookies 243

S

Salad
Avocado and Papaya Salad with Mango Dressing 67
Broccoli and Grape Salad 65
Brown Rice Salad with Mandarin Oranges 69
Chilled Spaghetti Squash Salad with Mint Vinaigrette 64
Cucumber, Mint and Chive Salad 58
Fiesta Salad with Cumin Dressing 60
Gazpacho Salad with Herb Dressing 61
Green Beans with Walnut-Dill Sauce 187
Grilled Eggplant and Spinach Salad 62
Grilled Scallop Salad with Lime Cilantro Dressing 73
Jícama Slaw with Peanut Dressing 59
Kasha Salad with Fruit and Nuts 70
Marinated Shrimp and Corn Salad 74
Menu for a Buffet Salad Luncheon 55
Minted Citrus Salad 65
Pear and Gorgonzola Salad 66
Roasted New Potato Salad with Rosemary and Shallots 72
Romaine Salad with Red Chili Dressing and Herbed Croutons 57
Salad of New Potatoes, Arugula and Mint 71
Turkey, Wild Rice and Cranberry Salad 81

Spinach and Salad Greens with Macadamia Nuts 56
Sweet Red Pepper and Fresh Fennel Salad 63
Watercress and Belgian Endive Salad 58
Watermelon and Red Onion Salad with Mint 66
White Bean and Tomato Salad 68
Poultry Salads
Asian Pear and Smoked Turkey Salad 80
Asian-Flavored Chicken Salad 76
Chicken Couscous Salad 75
Grilled Chicken Salad with Citrus Salsa 78
Turkey, Wild Rice and Cranberry Salad 81
Vietnamese Chicken Salad 77
Warm Chicken and Black Bean Salad with Lime Vinaigrette 79
Seafood Salads
Grilled Scallop Salad with Lime Cilantro Dressing 73
Marinated Shrimp and Corn Salad 74
Salad Dressings
Asian Fruit Juice Dressing 84
Balsamic Vinaigrette Dijonnaise 71
Balsamic Vinaigrette with Herbs 67
Buttermilk Herb Dressing 82
Citrus Salsa 78
Cucumber Dressing With Jalapeño and Dill 83
Cumin Dressing 60
Herb Dressing 61
Hoisin Marinade Dressing 62
Lime Cilantro Dressing 73
Lime Vinaigrette 79
Lowfat Creamy Garlic Dressing 82
Mango Dressing 67
Mint Vinaigrette 64
Orange Vinaigrette 70
Peanut Dressing 59
Red Chili Dressing 57
Roquefort Cheese Dressing 84

Sherry-Orange Vinaigrette 133
Soy and Sesame Seed Dressing 83
Tangerine Vinaigrette 139
Vinaigrette Piquante 56
Salmon
Barbecued Salmon with Dill-Cucumber Butter 151
Broiled Salmon with Ginger Marinade 152
Green Onion-Baked Salmon 153
Salmon with Dill or Tarragon Sauce 150
Salsa
Achiote Salsa 206
Citrus Salsa 78
Cranberry, Chile and Cilantro Salsa 27
Creamy Tomatillo Salsa 29
Fresh Tomato Salsa 205
Green Cucumber Salsa 27
Moroccan Peppers Salsa 28
Papaya and Tomato Salsa 29
Southwest Salsa 28
Tomatillo Salsa 126
Tomato and Green-Onion Salsa 155
Sauces (See also Salsas; also Marinades)
Chili-Garlic Sauce 145
Cornichon-Tarragon Sauce 111
Dill-Cucumber Butter 151
Herbal Zabaglione 14
Light Aioli 176
Loquat Chutney 30
Pistou 47
Ravigote Sauce 112
Red Pepper Aioli Without Egg 146
Sun-Dried Tomato Pesto 93
Tomato Sauce 171
Dessert Sauces
Maple-Pecan Sauce 219
Papaya Sauce 213
Raspberry Sauce 230
Sweetened Whipped Cream 233
Sausage and Leek Pie 128
Scallops
Asian-Spiced Soup with Scallop and Shrimp Dumplings 42

Grilled Scallop Salad with Lime
Cilantro Dressing 73
Lemony Sea Scallops 133
San Diego Cioppino 41
San Diego Seafood
Kebabs 143
Scallop Ceviche 22
Scallops in Leek Sauce 134
Scallops with Tomato and Corn
Salsa 135
Shrimp and Scallops
with Lemon-Honey
Mustard 136
Sea Bass, Baked, with Fennel and
Spinach 148
Seafood, Fish *(See also individual
names)*
Asian-Spiced Soup with
Scallop and Shrimp
Dumplings 42
Baked Halibut with Cilantro-
Citrus Sauce 147
Baked Sea Bass with Fennel
and Spinach 148
Barbecued Salmon with Dill-
Cucumber Butter 151
Broiled Salmon with Ginger
Marinade 152
Ceviche Dolsa 23
Green Onion-Baked
Salmon 153
Grilled Thresher Shark
with Tomato and Green-
Onion 155
Grilled Whole Red Snapper
with Oregano 153
Halibut in Herbal Zabaglione
Sauce with Red Pepper 146
Mussels in Sherry-Orange
Vinaigrette with
Prosciutto 132
Red Snapper Baked with
Vegetables 154
Salmon with Dill or Tarragon
Sauce 150
San Diego Cioppino 41
San Diego Seafood
Kebabs 143
Swordfish Mediterranean
Style 156
Tagine of Mahi Mahi and
Vegetables 149
Thai Grilled Fish with
Lemongrass and
Basil 144

Shark
Grilled Thresher Shark
with Tomato and Green-
Onion 155
Shrimp
Asian-Spiced Soup with Scallop
and Shrimp Dumplings 42
Broiled Shrimp with Soy-Citrus
Marinade 140
Grilled Sake Shrimp with
Tangerine Vinaigrette 138
Marinated Shrimp and Corn
Salad 74
Mazatlan Shrimp Chowder
with Corn 43
San Diego Cioppino 41
San Diego Seafood
Kebabs 143
Shrimp and Scallops with
Lemon-Honey Mustard 136
Shrimp in Lemon Curry 141
Shrimp with Orzo and Sun-
Dried Tomatoes 92
Spicy Shrimp Soup with
Lemongrass and
Lime 40
Spicy Shrimp with Chicken
Cilantro 142
Steamed Chicken and Shrimp
Dim Sum 25
Stir-fried Shrimp with Two
Sauces 24
Thai Garlic Shrimp 137
Sorbets *(See Desserts: Frozen)*
Soups
Asian-Spiced Soup with
Scallop and Shrimp
Dumpling 42
Bacon-Flavored Sweet Corn
Chowder with Wild Rice 48
Baja Chicken and Lime
Soup 39
Carrot and Potato Soup with
Chervil 46
Chilled Avocado Soup 35
Chilled Carrot and Orange
Soup 36
Chilled Papaya Soup 36
Chilled Spinach-Tarragon
Soup 34
Curried Squash Soup 51
Easy Agnolotti Soup 38
French Country Soup 47
Hearty Lentil Soup with Winter
Squash and Fennel 52

Mazatlan Shrimp Chowder
with Corn 43
Old Town Black Bean
Soup 49
Pumpkin Soup with Green
Vegetable Garnish 50
Roasted Summer Vegetable
Soup with Herbs 44
San Diego Cioppino 41
Spicy Shrimp Soup with
Lemongrass and Lime 40
Summer Squash and Carrot
Soup with Lemon and
Basil 45
White Gazpacho 37
Spinach
Almond-Crusted Broccoli and
Spinach Casserole 204
Baked Sea Bass with Fennel
and Spinach 148
Chilled Spinach-Tarragon
Soup 34
Grilled Eggplant and Spinach
Salad 62
Ham, Cheese and Spinach
Roulade 127
Mexican Green Rice 96
Pasta with Spinach, Tomatoes
and Greek Olive Sauce 91
Spinach and Salad Greens with
Macadamia Nuts 56
Spinach, Eggplant and Red
Pepper Lasagna 94
Spinach with Pine Nuts 198
Wilted Spinach with
Oranges 198
Spreads *(See Dips & Spreads)*
Squash
Chilled Spaghetti Squash Salad
with Mint Vinaigrette 64
Curried Squash Soup 51
Foil-Baked Julienne of Summer
Squash 199
Hearty Lentil Soup with Winter
Squash and Fennel 52
Summer Squash and Carrot
Soup with Lemon and
Basil 45
Winter Squash Spread with
Garlic and Cilantro 18
Stews
Chicken Stew Provençal with
Light Aioli 176
Roman Lamb with Artichoke
Hearts 121

Tagine of Chicken with
   Dates 177
Tagine of Mahi Mahi and
   Vegetables 149
Strawberries with Strawberry
   Sauce 212
Sun-Dried Tomatoes *(See*
   Tomatoes: Sun-Dried)
Sweets *(See Desserts)*
Swordfish Mediterranean
   Style 156

T

Tacos
   California Avocado Tacos with
      Fresh Tomato Salsa 205
Tagine
   Tagine of Chicken with
      Dates 177
   Tagine of Mahi Mahi and
      Vegetables 149
   Tagine, about 149
Tangerine
   Tangerine-Peel Chicken with
      Walnuts 160
   Tangerine Vinaigrette 139
Tarts *(See Pies & Tarts)*
Tea Bread
   Avocado Bread 240
   Lemon Herb Tea Bread 239
   Orange Pecan Bread 241
Tomatillo
   Creamy Tomatillo Salsa 29
   Tomatillo Salsa 126
Tomatoes
   Fresh Tomato Salsa 205
   Gazpacho Salad with Herb
      Dressing 61
   Linguine with Baked
      Tomatoes 90
   Papaya and Tomato Salsa 29
   Pasta with Fresh Basil and
      Marinated Tomatoes 90

Pasta with Spinach, Tomatoes
   and Greek Olive Sauce 91
Pepper Wedges with Tomatoes
   and Basil 13
Roasted Tomato Slices with
   Basil Crumbs 201
Scallops with Tomato and Corn
   Salsa 135
Southwest Salsa 28
Stir-Fried Beef with Tomato and
   Onion 116
Tomato and Green-Onion
   Salsa 155
Tomato Sauce 171
White Bean and Tomato
   Salad 68
White Beans with Tomatoes
   and Herbs 188
Sun-Dried Tomatoes
   Pasta with Fresh Basil and
      Marinated Tomatoes 90
   Polenta with Sun-Dried
      Tomatoes and
      Mushrooms 103
   Shrimp with Orzo and Sun-
      Dried Tomatoes 92
   Sun-Dried Tomato Pesto 93
Tortes *(See Cakes & Tortes)*
Tortilla Chips, No-Fry 21
Turkey
   Asian Pear and Smoked Turkey
      Salad 80
   Mediterranean Meatloaf 110
   Turkey, Wild Rice and
      Cranberry Salad 81

V

Vegetables *(See also individual*
   names)
   Almond-Crusted Broccoli and
      Spinach Casserole 204
   Black Forest Mushrooms 195

Chilled Mushrooms
   Mediterranean 15
Collage of Summer Vegetables
   with Black Beans 184
French Country Soup 47
Green Vegetable Garnish 50
Roasted Summer Vegetable
   Soup with Herbs 44
Old Town Vegetable
   Fajitas 206
Puréed Celery Root with
   Apples 191
Vegetarian Menu 183
Vinaigrette *(See Salad Dressings)*

W

Watercress and Belgian Endive
   Salad 58
Watermelon and Red Onion
   Salad with Mint 66

Y

Yams, Baked, with Apples and
   Nuts 200
Yogurt
   Yogurt Marinade 172
   Yogurt, Note about how to
      drain 37

Z

Zucchini
   Leeks and Zucchini in Wine-
      Cream Sauce 194
   Mexican Sautéed Zucchini with
      Corn 202
   Zucchini with Fresh
      Cilantro 201